Quick
Memory Management
Techniques

Brian Underdahl

JOHN WILEY & SONS, INC.
New York • Chichester • Brisbane • Toronto • Singapore

D1405060

Associate Publisher: Katherine Schowalter
Editor: Tim Ryan
Managing Editor: Angela Murphy
Editorial Production & Design: Electric Ink, Ltd.

Designations used by companies to distinguish their products are often claimed as trademarks. In all instances where John Wiley & Sons, Inc. is aware of a claim, the product names appear in initial capital or all capital letters. Readers, however, should contact the appropriate companies for more complete information regarding trademarks and registration.

This text is printed on acid-free paper.

Published by John Wiley & Sons, Inc.

All rights reserved. Published simultaneously in Canada.

This publication is designed to provide accurate and authoritative information in regard to the subject matter covered. It is sold with the understanding that the publisher is not engaged in rendering legal, accounting, or other professional service. If legal advice or other expert assistance is required, the services of a competent professional person should be sought.

Library of Congress Cataloging-in-Publication Data

Underdahl, Brian.
    Quick memory management techniques / by Brian Underdahl.
        p.   cm.
    Includes index.
    ISBN 0-471-05384-8 (paper)
    1. Memory management (Computer Science)   I. Title.
    QA76.9.M45U53   1994
    004.5'3—dc20   94-11329

Printed in the United States of America
10 9 8 7 6 5 4 3 2 1

Contents

Chapter 7 Managing Your Memory with Novell DOS 7 **209**

Appendix A Troubleshooting   255

Introduction

This memory of ours stores up a perfect record of the most useless facts and anecdotes and experiences.

—Mark Twain

I'll bet that memory management is one of those subjects you would just as soon ignore. After all, there are many more interesting things to do with a computer than worry about how its memory is arranged and allocated, aren't there? Just staring at flying toasters on your screen saver probably sounds more interesting. For that matter, watching wallpaper fade may even sound like more fun than spending a sunny afternoon tweaking your PC.

But there are many reasons you need this book. Perhaps you've run into one of these problems:

- Your computer is too slow.
- Your system crashes too often, especially when you run Windows programs.
- An error message like "500K conventional memory required to run this program" pops up on your screen when you try to run a program.
- You see the unforgiving "Out of memory" error.
- Your new software says "2 Meg expanded memory required."
- You want to be able to multitask more software.
- Your new CD-ROM drive uses too much memory, so you can't run the multimedia CD-ROM game you just bought.
- You'd like to use disk compression to double your disk space, but can't afford to give up so much memory.

You can solve all the problems listed above with this book. And I'm not going to make you read through tons of boring, irrelevant technical details. This book is not a course in applied computer science that gives you everything you need to write a scholarly paper about the history of computers.

In this book we're following a very different course. Think of this book as your personal, no-nonsense, memory management help desk; you'll get all the help you need to make your own PC work better with the operating system and software you use.

What Is Included in This Book?

Memory is necessary for all the operations of reason.

—Blaise Pascal, *Pensées*

What you get with this book is a complete plan for solving your memory problems and making your PC run faster. All the information in the book is arranged and clearly marked so that you don't have to read any more than you need to solve your current problems. The plan I present has three basic steps:

1. Find out what memory your PC has, and how that memory is currently being used.
2. Look at the software you run and determine what kind of memory it needs to run smoothly.
3. Fix your computer's memory using the tools that come with whatever version of DOS you have.

Why the 386, 486, and Pentium?

Most PCs today use a 386 or higher processor, so the decision to concentrate on memory management for 386, 486, and Pentium systems is an easy one. Also, older PCs don't have many sophisticated memory capabilities, so memory management on those PCs is severely limited.

Why DOS 5, DOS 6, and Novell DOS 7, and Windows?

We've settled the issue of which types of systems are covered in this book—only those with an 80386, 80486, or Pentium processor. Now let's look at *operating systems*—the software that enables the computer to actually do anything, such as run application programs or access files. MS-DOS certainly isn't the only PC operating system in current use, but it's by far the most popular computer operating system that has ever existed. In sheer numbers, there are far more computers running on some variation of MS-DOS than all other operating systems combined. This book covers three versions of DOS—each version has its own chapter complete with suggestions for making Windows run better.

Each type of operating system has its own unique characteristics. For example, the commands you use to obtain a listing of files vary according to the operating system. Even the length of filenames varies between different operating systems. Different operating systems also manage memory differently from each other. Most memory management tricks you learn for one operating system will probably be almost totally useless on a computer that uses a different operating system.

Note

Because PC-DOS is nearly identical to MS-DOS, in this book I use the term MS-DOS (or sometimes just DOS) to refer to both MS-DOS and PC-DOS. Both were developed originally by Microsoft, although development of later versions of PC-DOS was taken over by IBM. Unless I include a note telling you otherwise, techniques mentioned for one version of MS-DOS should work equally well with the same numbered version of PC-DOS.

So there you have it. This book covers memory management in PCs with an 80386, 80486, or Pentium processor and some version or variation of MS-DOS. The built-in memory management tools in MS-DOS and Novell DOS are all discussed in detail.

Can I Really Do This?

> *As they to memory may come by chance;*
> *Hold me excused, pray, of my ignorance.*
>
> —Geoffrey Chaucer, "The Monk's Prologue," *Canterbury Tales*

Memory management may still sound a little scary to you. After all, you're probably not a computer scientist, so what chance do you have of understanding what needs to be done? What if you make a mistake—won't that damage something, or at least ruin all your important files? If you follow the advice in this book, you'll do just fine. If something you try doesn't work, the cautious approach outlined here will enable you to correct the problem quickly and go on to the next step.

You can successfully manage the memory on your PC. When you finish reading this book, you'll have a system that performs better and runs the programs you want, and you'll know more about how your PC works.

How to Use This Book

Many books make you to read large amounts of general information, and then make you decide for yourself what applies to your particular problem. In other words, you're expected to be an expert on a subject before you can learn about it! Not a good plan. I've arranged the chapters in this book so you can simply read and apply the information you need. For example, you don't have to read about the MS-DOS 6 memory management options if you're using Novell DOS 7. You can simply skip any chapters that don't apply to your situation.

If you're new to memory management, I suggest that you read through each chapter, beginning with Chapter 1. More advanced users are encouraged to read the safety precautions described in Chapter 4 before diving right in to the chapter that covers your version of DOS. If you need a quick solution, check Appendix A: Troubleshooting to find out where your problem is discussed in this book. Here is a quick description of each chapter:

- **Chapter 1** tells you all about the types of memory in your PC, and what each one is for. It will also familiarize you with many of the terms that used to describe memory. (This is especially important if you're in the store looking at some new software, and the box says something cryptic like "This software needs 2M EMS to run.")

- **Chapter 2** contains information that you will need only on the rarest occasions, including how to convert hexadecimal numbers into binary, and more technical descriptions of how a PC keeps track of data. You might want to glance over the headings in this chapter so that you'll know what's in there in case you ever need it.

- **Chapter 3** helps you create a plan for managing your memory. By following the advice in this chapter, you will be able to define exactly what steps you need to take to make your PC and software run better. Knowing what kind of memory your software needs to run will help you make that memory available.

- **Chapter 4** shows you how to find all the memory in your PC, so you know where you're starting from. It also shows you how to take important precautions (like making a boot disk) before proceeding with the memory management techniques described later in the book.

- **Chapter 5** covers MS-DOS 5 memory management.

- **Chapter 6** covers MS-DOS 6.x memory management.

- **Chapter 7** covers Novell DOS 7 memory management.

Finally, the appendices provide more detailed information on the historical reasons that PC memory management is as difficult as it is, troubleshooting information, and how to buy and install more memory.

Summary

Many people, especially highly paid consultants and some authors, would like you to think that PC memory management is still a black art, and too complicated for most PC users. In this book, I've set out to prove them wrong. By applying what you'll learn in this book, you'll prove them wrong, too.

The time you spend with this book will pay off, and afterward you may want to break into a few verses of "Thanks for the Memory!"

Chapter 1

A Few Things You Should Know about Memory before Starting

Memory is a faculty of wonderful use, and without which the judgment can very hardly perform its office.

—Michel De Montaigne, *Essays*

Without memory, a computer would be worthless. The first computer I ever programmed had only enough memory to hold a very small program that flashed a couple of lights on the front panel to communicate its results. Today's PCs contain literally thousands of times as much memory as those earliest small computers, and yet some things never change. There never seems to be quite enough memory for everything we'd like our computers to do for us.

In this chapter you'll learn about the basics types of memory that you'll be dealing with in your PC.

How Did We Get into Such a Mess?

You would think that a computer could be designed to manage its own memory. After all, haven't computer hardware and software made great strides since 1981? Yes—through the years, Microsoft and IBM have developed better and better versions of DOS. DOS 2, for example, added the support for hard disks necessary for the IBM-XT. DOS 3 added some networking support, new disk sizes, and more new commands to support the IBM-AT and its 80286 PC. DOS 4 added support for hard disks larger than 32M (also a feature of Compaq's special 3.31 version of DOS) and a shell program. DOS 5 added advanced memory management, and DOS 6 added disk compression.

The problem is that if you buy a new computer, you want it to be able to run your *new* software and all your *old* software. This means that your new PC must maintain *backward compatibility*.

> *"it always makes one a little giddy at first—"*
> *"Living backwards!" Alice repeated in great astonishment. "I never heard of such a thing!"*
> *"—but there's one great advantage in it, that one's memory works both ways."*
> *"I'm sure MINE only works one way." Alice remarked. "I can't remember things before they happen."*
> *"It's a poor sort of memory that only works backwards," the Queen remarked.*
>
> —Lewis Carroll, *Through the Looking Glass*

Without backward compatibility, new versions of DOS would sacrifice their ability to run thousands of existing programs, and they would also sacrifice the ability to run on millions of existing PCs. When these abilities are maintained, there are many more potential customers for DOS, for application programs, and for PC hardware itself. Clearly, backward compatibility has been one of the major factors in ensuring the success of both new versions of DOS and the PC in general.

As important as the development of backward compatibility was, it also had one unfortunate result: DOS remained an operating system hampered by the limits of 1981-era technology. Backward compatibility requires that each new version of DOS continue to support a very old memory model—one that assumes that PCs won't have more than 1M of total memory, and also that no more than 640K will be available for programs.

In this chapter you'll learn everything you need to know about PC memory types so you can grasp the basics of PC memory management. You'll learn about each type of memory that may be made available on your PC, or that a program may demand for proper operation. Once you understand how these different types of memory are related, you'll be able to better understand how to provide the memory your programs need. Study carefully and learn the subtleties that make certain memory types the ones you really need to provide if you want the best possible performance from your system.

Special Programs Your PC Uses

There are several different types of software running on your PC. You may be most familiar with applications—things like WordPerfect, Lotus 1-2-3, or Quicken. In order to make your applications work, the operating system (DOS) uses a collection of special programs to tell your PC how to act. These programs are TSRs, device drivers, and two special files called AUTOEXEC.BAT and CONFIG.SYS.

AUTOEXEC.BAT and CONFIG.SYS Files

DOS uses the CONFIG.SYS and AUTOEXEC.BAT files to tell your PC how to configure itself every time you start it. These two files contain special directions for your PC, many of which pertain to how memory is to be set up. These two files are stored in the root directory of your hard drive—usually C:\.

In order to manage your PC's memory, you will have to view these files and change them. You can look at the contents of your AUTOEXEC.BAT file now by going to the DOS prompt, switching to your root directory by typing **CD C:**, then typing **EDIT AUTOEXEC.BAT**. Viewing and editing this file is a lot like using a simple word processor program, but don't change anything right now. When you're done looking, you can press **Alt-F** and then press X to exit the file.

Warning
If you delete your AUTOEXEC.BAT or CONFIG.SYS files, your PC may not start. See the directions in Chapter 4 for creating a boot disk before you modify either of these files.

Terminate-and-Stay-Resident (TSR) Programs

Terminate-and-stay-resident (TSR) software gets its peculiar name because even when it isn't running, part of it stays in your PC's memory. TSR programs are useful because you can usually start them (using a special key combination) while you are in the middle of another program. One of the ways you will manage your PC's memory is by deciding how many of the TSRs you really need, and then deciding where in your PC's memory they should reside. For a TSR program to work on your PC, it must be loaded into memory—the most common way to load it is to type its name (and other important information) into your CONFIG.SYS or AUTOEXEC.BAT file. This process is discussed later.

Device Drivers

Device drivers are special programs that communicate between DOS and a piece of hardware. When you buy a mouse, sound card, CD-ROM drive, fax/modem, or other piece of hardware, it will usually come with a diskette containing a device driver. For instance, if you buy a mouse, you will also get a diskette that contains a device driver called MOUSE.COM.

For a device driver to work on your PC, it must be loaded into memory—the most common way to load it is to type its name (and other important information) into your CONFIG.SYS or AUTOEXEC.BAT file. This process is discussed later in the book.

Measuring Memory

> *But at my age, memory has gone and the mind is slow to grasp things.*
> *How can all these fine distinctions, these subtleties be learned?*
>
> —Aristophanes, *The Clouds*

There are three measurements of memory that you will need to work with as you solve your computer's memory management problems. The smallest unit is bytes, then kilobytes (usually called K), and megabytes (usually called M or Meg). Computers use a binary numbering system, so the fact that 1K equals 1024 bytes makes about as much sense as four quarts equal a gallon, or three feet equal a yard. You only need to memorize the following two measurements:

1 megabyte (M) = 1024 K

1 kilobyte (K) = 1024 bytes

Tip

To see how much memory your computer has right now, turn it on and watch the numbers that roll by like a car's odometer in the top left-hand corner of the screen. This number is your total memory in bytes. If your computer is already on, see the section in Chapter 4 called "Using MEM."

The smallest unit of measurement that we'll deal with is one byte. One byte is essentially enough space to store a single character (for instance, the letter "a"). In Chapter 2 we'll look at another numbering system used in dealing with your computer, *hexadecimal* (base 16) numbers. Even though yet another number system adds another layer of complication, you'll soon see why hexadecimal numbers are so important, and you'll learn how to manipulate them easily.

Now that we've had our short review of numbering systems and have seen how memory is measured, let's examine the myriad of memory types that add so much confusion to PC memory management.

The Different Types of Memory in Your PC

This section discusses the different types of memory you'll be working with. All software requires a certain amount of conventional memory (making this the most valuable type of memory). Some software also requires a specific amount of extended or expanded memory. There are two main methods you'll use in memory management. The first is finding out how much of each type of memory your software needs, and then making that memory available. Keep your precious conventional memory free by loading TSRs and device drivers into other types of memory.

Conventional Memory

The customs of the world are so many conventional follies.

—Edgar Allen Poe, "The Spectacles"

The original IBM PC was designed to use up to 1M of memory (that's 1024K). IBM decided to divide that 1024K into two primary sections (see Figure 1.1).

How Binary Numbers Work, for Anyone Who's Interested

A binary number system is particularly suited to digital computers, because every number can be represented by one of two symbols. These symbols are usually written as 1 and 0, but they can also be thought of as representing true and false or on and off. Since a computer is constructed of millions of tiny switches, it's quite easy to see why on and off (or 1 and 0) are so easy for the computer.

Unfortunately, binary numbers aren't all that familiar to most humans, so understanding the computer's numbers can be quite a task. Can you imagine seeing a price tag written in binary numbers? Would you be willing to pay 11110 dollars for a book? It's certainly easier when the tag says 30 dollars, isn't it?

Part of this awkwardness of the binary system stems from the number of digits required to represent useful numbers. It took two digits to represent the 30-dollar book's price in the decimal system, but five digits to represent its price in binary numbers. Larger values are even more extreme. The value 255, for example, requires three decimal digits and eight binary digits. Keeping track of all those digits and translating their values into our more familiar decimal system quickly becomes a major burden.

Let's quickly review the methods used to create numbering systems. This review will help you understand why computers don't use the more convenient (for humans) decimal system.

Number systems use a simple method of indicating the value of each digit—they are position-dependent. In the decimal (base ten) system, each succeeding number to the left of the first number represents a higher power of ten. Since the second digit (such as the 3 in 30) is in the first position offset to the left, it represents a value you can determine by multiplying the digit times ten to the first power. The next digit to the left represents a value determined by multiplying the digit times ten to the second power. Binary systems, like all other modern numbering systems, function in a similar manner, except that the digits are multiplied by powers of two.

For example, in the binary numbering system, the first digit represents ones. The second digit represents twos, the third represents fours, and so on. Thus, the

The first 640K is called *conventional* memory, which is where your programs are loaded when you run them. The remaining 384K is called *upper* memory (you may see it referred to as *reserved* memory in older books and manuals). Later in this chapter, you'll see how we can use some of this "reserved" memory for our own purposes.

binary number 0001 equals the decimal number 1. The binary number 0010 equals the decimal number 2. 0011 equals 3, 0100 equals 4, and 1111 equals 15.

Why not try a few yourself? Can you figure out your age in binary numbers? I'll give you a hint: 100111 is 39.

Regardless of the base of the numbering system, an additional rule holds true. There is never a single digit that represents the base number. In the base ten (decimal) number system, you must use two digits (10) to represent the base value of ten. In the base two (binary) number system, you must also use two digits (10) to represent the base value of two. To increment values in any numbering system, you add the increment to the existing number, and if any digit would exceed the highest possible value in its position, an overflow occurs and the next digit to the left is incremented. Thus, if you add one and nine in the decimal system, no higher digit is available in the ones position, so the tens position is incremented.

In a PC, one byte contains eight *bits*, or individual digital switches. Thus, one byte can store up to two hundred and fifty-six different values (0 through 255), because of the binary number system used by the computer.

Since computers use binary numbers and humans prefer decimal numbers, a compromise of sorts was agreed upon early in the evolution of computing. Two to the tenth power is 1024, a value close enough to 1000 for many purposes. Thus, the value 1024 became known as 1K (K is short for "kilo," a prefix meaning "one thousand"). 1K times 1K (1024 times 1024, or 1,048,576) became known as 1M (M is short for "mega," a prefix meaning "one million").

This compromise allowed computers and humans to use common terms to represent (if somewhat imprecisely) values easily understood by humans. This compromise also became the basis upon which computer memory was measured. A computer with 640K of memory actually has 640 times 1024 (or 655,360) *bytes* of memory. A system with 16M of memory has 16 times 1,048,576 (or 16,777,216) bytes of memory.

Conventional memory is sometimes called *lower* memory because it is the "bottom" portion—it takes up the space from 0 to 640K (see Figure 1.1). Conventional memory is a precious resource because any type of program will work in it: applications (WordPerfect, 1-2-3, etc.), TSRs, device drivers, and DOS itself. But of all these types of software, your applications absolutely

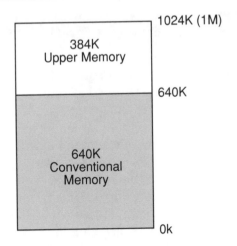

Figure 1.1 Your PC's conventional and upper memory.

must run in conventional memory—your applications may be able to use other memory *in addition to* conventional, but they all must use some amount of your conventional memory. So one of your strategies will be to keep your conventional memory free for your applications by loading TSRs and device drivers into other types of memory.

Upper Memory

One of the most important areas of memory, at least in terms of advanced memory management techniques, is *upper* memory, which consists of the 384K memory address range between 640K and 1M (see Figure 1.1). Upper memory is reserved for telling your PC how to run certain devices (like video cards), but not all of your upper memory is currently being used—we can grab those empty spaces and put them to use.

Upper memory comes in the form of *upper memory blocks*, or *UMBs*, which are the free spaces not already in use by adapters or ROMs. Depending on how your PC is configured, there may be only one usable block, or there may be several. For reasons you'll learn in later chapters, a single large upper memory block is nearly always better than a series of smaller blocks.

UMBs provide additional memory that can be used almost like conventional memory. Usually, you'll use UMBs to load special device drivers and memory-resident programs (or TSRs), such as a mouse driver, that provide your system with extra capabilities not provided by DOS. By loading these device drivers and TSRs into UMBs, you free up conventional memory for your application programs, or for additional device drivers and TSRs. Most—but not all—device drivers and TSRs can be loaded and run in UMBs if the UMBs are large enough to hold the program.

The ability to use UMBs comes from a piece of software called a *UMB provider*. The UMB provider supplied with DOS is called EMM386.EXE, and requires a 386 or higher processor to work.

Expanded Memory (EMS)

> *Achievement of any kind would be impossible for him unless he was free from those who would be for ever dragging him back into the conventional. The conventional had been tried already and had been found wanting.*
>
> —Samuel Butler, *Way of All Flesh*

Lotus (the maker of the Lotus 1-2-3 spreadsheet) was largely responsible for the early success of the PC; it was also largely responsible for the development of the first method of bypassing the 640K conventional memory limit. This method even bears the name of 1-2-3's developer, along with those of the developers of the PC's processor and the PC's operating system. It was

A Technical Note about Upper Memory

Although it is possible to use upper memory on some 80286 systems, doing so requires special third-party memory managers. The 80386, 80486, and Pentium processors can use upper memory easily, because they have the ability to address RAM at a different address than its physical location. This ability is important, because only part of the 384K of upper memory address space is actually available for use as UMBs. Space already used by adapters or ROMs cannot be used, because this would cause conflicts between those adapters or ROMs and the UMB.

Upper memory is also important because memory addresses in the first 1M of memory can be accessed in the processor's real mode. Since there's no need to switch into protected mode, using memory blocks in upper memory can be quite simple.

called the Lotus-Intel-Microsoft Expanded-Memory-Specification, or LIM-EMS. Today the method's name is usually shortened to EMS.

Originally, expanded memory came as circuit boards that had to be snapped into your computer. But starting with the 80386 PC, it was possible to *emulate* EMS memory by using special memory manager software. This memory management software can fool your computer into thinking it has some special expanded memory boards installed, when in fact it has only its regular memory chips. This ability has obviously made special EMS memory boards unnecessary in PCs that have at least an 80386 processor. Starting with MS-DOS 5, EMM386.EXE, an EMS memory manager for 80386, 80486, and Pentium processors, became a standard item that was supplied with DOS.

Note

With the version of EMM386.EXE that comes with DOS, you can make any of your PC's built-in memory chips act like expanded memory.

EMS memory also has several disadvantages, the main one of which is that EMS is an inefficient system. It's generally not possible to use EMS memory for programs, only for data. Because not all of EMS memory is available at one time, application programs can't see more than 64K of data that is in expanded memory without first asking the EMS memory manager to swap at least some of the expanded memory pages. Of course, this means that the more you need expanded memory, the more likely it will be that the data you need to access is currently paged out of the page frame and must be swapped with a current page before you can access the data. This constant page swapping really slows down your system's performance (although, of course, not as much as swapping data to and from a disk would).

Another disadvantage of EMS memory is that the 64K page frame must be located somewhere in the first 1M of memory address space, even on an 80386, 80486, or Pentium system. When the standard was developed, there weren't very many uses for the unused spaces in the 384K reserved memory space, so this wasn't a problem. Today, however, PCs often contain quite a few more adapters that may need some of that memory space. Also, there are other ways to use any unused space than by providing for a 64K EMS page frame.

A Technical Look at Expanded Memory (EMS)

When EMS was first released, it was not a new idea. Several of the manufacturers of earlier microcomputers had used a similar scheme to enable their systems to access additional memory beyond what their processor could normally address. This scheme involved a trick called *paging*. In paged memory access, a portion of the processor's memory address space is set aside for a special type of access. More than one block of memory can be addressed at the same physical location by effectively isolating several blocks of memory and then using a special circuit to activate them one at a time as needed. In the early paged memory systems, the processor activated the desired memory block by sending a command to one of the system's *i/o ports*—circuits that were used to connect the processor to the outside world.

In the EMS standard, expanded memory support was provided by special memory boards that contained all the necessary circuitry to switch the memory pages in and out of the processor's physical memory space. One of the first expanded memory boards was the Intel Aboveboard.

The EMS memory standard uses four memory pages that are each 16K in length. These four memory pages are paged in and out of a 64K *page frame*—a contiguous 64K area of memory that is reserved for swapping the expanded memory pages.

Note that although the most recent version of the EMS memory standard allows for expanded memory support without using a 64K page frame, programs that use EMS memory must be specially designed to use this feature. Unfortunately, it appears that no popular program can use EMS memory if there is no page frame.

EMS memory support is not built into DOS. Since the earliest implementations of the EMS standard were special memory boards, using EMS memory required a separate EMS memory manager specific to each type of board. If you installed an Intel Aboveboard, you couldn't use AST's EMS memory manager. Fortunately, every EMS memory board came with its own EMS memory manager.

One big advantage of EMS memory was that no new processor capabilities were required to use expanded memory. Every PC, regardless of its processor, could use EMS memory if the correct EMS memory board and EMS memory manager were installed.

EMS memory no longer has the popularity it once obtained, but it's by no means dead. You may still use programs whose only way to expand their memory horizons is to use EMS memory. Some popular software packages that require EMS:

Note

The current version of the EMS memory standard is 4.0. The first version was not 1.0, as you might expect, but 3.0. Soon after version 3.0 came version 3.2, the version actually supported by most software that requires expanded memory. Very few programs that use expanded memory actually use the more advanced features in version 4.0. In fact, unless you use a very old PC with one of the earliest expanded memory boards, you'll probably find that programs that use expanded memory won't really care which version of the EMS standard you're using.

- Microsoft Flight Simulator
- Lotus 1-2-3 for DOS
- Many games like Space Hulk, Wing Commander, and chess games
- 3D Studio
- Quattro Pro for DOS
- MSCDEX uses only EMS or conventional memory
- Intel's SatisFAXtion

The following sections will show you some alternatives that were developed after the EMS memory standard, and that are generally better suited to the future of the PC.

Extended Memory (XMS)

To many eyes the characters seem so mixed in confusion that the words cannot be distinguished.

—Hans Christian Andersen, *The Philosopher's Stone*

The terms "expanded memory" and "extended memory" may be very confusing at first. It's unfortunate that such similar terms were used to describe such different types of memory. Even so, understanding the difference between these two types of memory is very important, especially if you want to be successful in managing your PC's memory resources.

As I mentioned in the previous section, there are some real drawbacks to expanded memory—that's why extended memory was developed. The *eXtended Memory Specification*, or *XMS*, was developed and implemented to provide a standard method of accessing all extended memory. Through this standard, programs can cooperate in their use of extended memory.

Note

With the version of HIMEM.SYS that comes with MS-DOS, you can make any of your PC's memory chips act like extended memory. In Novell DOS 7, EMM386.EXE provides this service.

XMS memory is accessed with the help of an XMS memory manager, such as HIMEM.SYS. The XMS memory manager arbitrates all requests for XMS memory, allocating memory when it is requested, and preventing multiple programs from competing for the same extended memory. If one program is already using a block of XMS memory, that memory block is protected from being corrupted by another program.

XMS memory is of special interest to Windows users, because access to XMS memory allows Windows programs to use as much memory as they need. Graphical interfaces, context-sensitive on-line help, and ease of use are just some of the benefits modern Windows programs can offer, in part because of their ability to use more memory than is available to most DOS-based programs.

Note

Some older programs that use DOS extenders to enable them to access extended memory cannot substitute XMS memory for the plain extended memory they need. For these types of programs, the XMS memory manager must be configured to allow a certain amount of extended memory to be accessed directly by the DOS extender. This older method of accessing extended memory is called the *interrupt 15h interface*. This method will be discussed in detail in later chapters that deal with memory management specifics.

To help you keep these two types of memory straight, here are some of the important differences between expanded and extended memory:

- Extended memory is available only on PCs with at least an 80286 processor and over 1M of memory. Extended memory can be used for any purpose.

- Expanded memory can be made available on any PC regardless of the type of processor. For 386s, 486s, and Pentiums, you need to use the EMM386.EXE that comes with DOS; for older computers, you need a special expanded memory board and expanded memory manager.

- Some programs can use extended memory through their own built-in extended memory managers. Most programs that use extended memory, however, require extended memory to be managed by the operating system (usually DOS) or a third-party memory management tool.

High Memory (HMA)

If the terms "expanded memory" and "extended memory" aren't enough to confuse you, how about "upper memory" and "high memory"? Yes, it's true, there's another confusing memory term that sounds much like the one discussed in the previous section. *High memory*, also known as the *high memory area* or *HMA*, is a small but important area of memory address space. It is a 65,520-byte region starting at the 1M address and extending almost 64K into extended memory address space. Figure 1.2 shows how conventional, upper, and high memory are related.

Note

At 65,520 bytes, the HMA is 16 bytes less than a full 64K (65,536 bytes). This very small difference can generally be ignored, and you can safely consider the HMA to be 64K.

Because of a quirk in the way Intel processors address memory, the HMA can be accessed just like conventional memory and upper memory—in the processor's real mode. This means that using the HMA is also quite simple, but there is a catch. Generally, only one program can use the HMA. Any part of the HMA not used by the program that is loaded into the HMA is usually wasted.

The most common use for the HMA is loading a portion of the DOS *kernel*, or the primary core of DOS. Some DOS system structures, such as disk

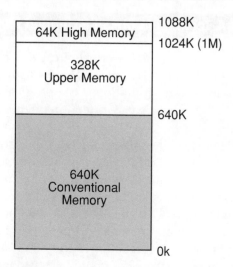

Figure 1.2   High memory.

buffers, may also load into the HMA if there is enough space available. Network software may also make use of the HMA if it is available. The HMA is made available through the services of an XMS memory manager, such as HIMEM.SYS. Only PC systems with an 80286 or higher processor and extended memory can provide the HMA.

Although you've had a brief look at the most important memory types, there are a few additional memory terms you may encounter. In most cases, these terms won't really affect your PC memory management strategies, but you should be aware of them. Let's take a short look at these final memory types.

VCPI Memory

VCPI, or *Virtual Control Program Interface,* is a memory standard designed to allow DOS extended programs to run on systems that are emulating EMS memory using extended memory. This standard applies to PCs that have an 80386 or higher processor and an expanded memory manager such as EMM386.EXE.

The VCPI standard was not designed with multitasking environments in mind, and so does not work too well if you want to run more than one

A Technical Look at Extended Memory (XMS)

Although the 8086 and 8088 were very capable processors in their time, they had many limitations that make them unsuitable for many applications today. One very important limitation was a physical limitation—these processors had only 20 of their electrical connections dedicated to generating memory addresses.

Having 20 memory address lines allows a processor to generate 1,048,576 (two to the 20th power) distinct addresses. If you want to use even one additional *linear* memory address, you must have additional memory address lines. That's why the expanded memory discussed in the previous section was the only option for using additional memory with the 8086 and 8088 processors.

Note that Intel designates memory address lines in its processors using a notation scheme starting with A0. Because the 8086 and 8088 processors have 20 memory address lines, they are designated A0 through A19.

EMS (expanded) memory has a very big disadvantage for a programmer who's developing large, powerful programs. Since the PC can only "see" a small portion of EMS memory at one time, portions of a program that attempted to execute in EMS memory could be unavailable when needed by another part of the program. If a program is executing in conventional memory, this problem can be solved by using *program overlays*, or portions of program code that are swapped in and out of memory as needed. Although this process sounds similar to the EMS page-swapping process, it is extremely difficult to use EMS page-swapping for program overlays. Unless a program is small enough to fit in a single 16K EMS memory page, the complexities of executing programs in EMS memory aren't worth the effort.

Contrast the complexities of executing a program in EMS memory with the simplicity of executing a program in linear, conventional memory. In conventional memory, a programmer can be certain what will happen when an executing program branches to another part of the program at a specified distance from the current program instruction. In EMS memory, the branch location might be in an accessible memory page, but then it might not. Before allowing the program to branch to a different part of the program, the programmer would have to perform tests to determine whether the destination was available, and if it was not, perform the necessary actions to make it available. This type of test and response would be necessary hundreds, if not thousands, of times whenever a program executed in EMS memory. This extra work, or *overhead*, would result in much slower program performance, and would severely limit a program's popularity.

One of the major improvements made in the 80286 processor that was used in the IBM-AT was the addition of 4 more memory address lines, for a total of 24.

This change enabled the 80286 to directly address 16 times as much memory as was possible with the 8086 or 8088. Since this new capacity was for memory that could be addressed in a linear manner rather than in a paged manner, this new *extended* memory shared none of expanded memory's shortcomings.

A curious trait of the 8086 and 8088 processors makes using extended memory more difficult than you might think. In these processors, because they could only address 1M of memory, any memory accesses that specify a memory address larger than 1M simply roll over and begin again at memory address 0. In order to emulate these processors exactly, the 80286, 80386, 80486, and Pentium processors must also exhibit this same, somewhat strange behavior. Even though these more advanced processors have the capability to continue right on up past the 1M memory address, in order to be fully compatible with DOS (which was, after all, designed for the 8086 and 8088), they must also act as though memory accesses beyond 1M were actually intended to be low memory address accesses.

If these advanced processors treat memory accesses above 1M as if they were for low memory addresses, how can they ever use more than 1M of memory? How can they use extended memory?

The answer is found in their ability to change operating modes. When emulating an 8086 or 8088, the 80286 or higher processor uses *real mode*. To access additional linear memory, the processor shifts into *protected mode*.

One way to understand processor operating modes is to think about bicycles. You might want to think of the 8086 and 8088 processors as being old-fashioned, balloon-tired, single-speed bicycles. The 80286 processor would be a slightly sleeker bicycle with an extra gear so you could go a little faster. The 80386, 80486, and Pentium processors would be multispeed mountain bicycles, able to handle many more tasks with ease. You can still ride any one of the newer bikes without changing gears, and it would act much like the old-fashioned bike. To get all the performance possible, though, you have to shift gears (operating modes).

As with many hardware features and options, the extended memory addressing capabilities of the 80286 and higher processors were available long before there were standards specifying how to use extended memory. With no standards and no DOS support for extended memory, conflict and confusion were the natural result. Several different companies rushed to fill the gap, producing *DOS extenders*—memory management modules that allowed programs to use extended memory. Unfortunately, DOS extenders typically followed a simple rule: "do it my way."

A Technical Look at Extended Memory (XMS) *(continued)*

The "do it my way" approach resulted in many problems. If you wanted to use two different programs that used different DOS extenders, you usually needed two completely separate system configurations. The likelihood that two DOS extended programs would cooperate was pretty remote. Trying such experiments was quite a bit like playing Russian Roulette with your data. Clearly a standard was necessary, and that standard was XMS.

application at a time. In particular, VCPI is not well suited to supporting Windows applications.

DPMI Memory

DPMI, or *DOS Protected Mode Interface*, is a memory standard designed to replace VCPI. Although DPMI provides similar services to VCPI, it is a much stronger standard, and was designed to support multiple applications.

Windows 3.x provides DPMI support, providing protected access to extended memory to a large number of programs simultaneously. Although MS-DOS does not provide DPMI support outside of Windows, Novell DOS 7 does provide DPMI support at the DOS level. Novell's support of DPMI enables the Novell DOS 7 task manager to provide DOS-level multitasking, a feature not available in MS-DOS.

You generally do not have to concern yourself too much about whether your system provides VCPI or DPMI memory. Unless you use an older DOS extended program, you'll find that most modern memory managers provide the correct types of services automatically.

DPMS Memory

DPMS, or *DOS Protected Mode Services*, sounds quite similar to DPMI, but the two standards are not related. DPMS is a method of enabling certain specially designed device drivers, TSR programs, or even application programs to run in extended memory. DPMS is a feature of Novell DOS 7, but the standard is DOS version independent, so DPMS can be used with any version of DOS.

DPMS was designed primarily to provide another possible memory location for device drivers and TSRs in addition to conventional or upper memory. In modern PCs, it is common to load so many device drivers and TSRs that some won't fit into the available UMBs, and conventional memory must be sacrificed. Using DPMS, however, enables you to load some of the device drivers or TSRs into extended memory.

For example, consider a disk caching program. By speeding up one of the slowest components of your PC, a disk cache greatly improves the system's overall performance. In fact, a disk cache may improve disk performance by a factor of ten. Unfortunately, a typical disk caching program may use over 30K of memory to store its program code. (This is in addition to the extended or expanded memory used for the cached data.) This 30K may be upper memory or conventional memory, depending on what is available. In some cases you may not be able to spare 30K, especially if the 30K is conventional memory.

If the disk caching program is designed to use DPMS memory and your system provides DPMS support, you could enjoy the benefits of the disk cache without giving up conventional or upper memory. Programs that required too much memory in the past to allow you to install disk caching would now run much faster due to your new ability to access more memory.

Novell DOS 7 is currently the only operating system including DPMS support, but it includes several device drivers and TSRs that are DPMS-aware. These include the disk cache, the Stacker disk compression, the CD-ROM driver, the deleted files tracker, and the network server. Since DPMS is not dependent on one brand or version of DOS, it's possible that other manufacturers will provide DPMS support once they understand its value.

Summary

Understanding the terms used to describe the different types of PC memory is very important. Some of these terms are so similar that it's quite easy to confuse them. In this chapter you've learned how these memory terms are used, so you will be able to better understand the options when you begin applying advanced memory management techniques on your system.

The next chapter discusses how your PC keeps track of data. You might want to skim the headings so you know what the chapter covers in case you ever need it. Then go right on to Chapter 3, where you will learn how to make a plan for managing your PC's memory.

Chapter 2

How Your PC Remembers Where It Puts Stuff

In this chapter you'll find out about the memory addressing scheme used in the PC. This information is a little more technical in nature, and with any luck you'll never need it. You may want to skip reading this chapter right now, and just skim the headings so you have an idea of what's here in case you ever need it.

A place for everything, and everything in its place.

—Victorian proverb

Understanding PC memory addressing schemes is important, because when you install a new adapter card (like a sound card or modem), try to understand the cryptic addresses shown when a program crashes, or try to configure upper memory, you need to understand segmented addressing. Often, a hardware or software product manual may include an address you must convert to a more standardized form in order for it to be of any use in memory management. In some cases, even the tools included with DOS show addresses in a form you must convert before they are useful for your purposes.

As I mentioned earlier, a PC stores information in distinct areas of memory. Each of these areas of memory has a unique address called a *memory address*. The most difficult thing about this is that a PC's memory addresses are represented in the hexadecimal numbering system. Instead of learning how to do hexadecimal math in your head, it's usually easier just to translate hexadecimal values into our more familiar decimal numbering system.

In this chapter I'll also show you how you can use QBasic (a programming language that comes with DOS) to create your own, handy conversion tool that quickly shows you decimal equivalents of hexadecimal numbers, and hexadecimal equivalents of decimal numbers. When you're working with PC memory addressing, these conversions provide the reality check necessary to ensure the accuracy of your work.

You don't have to be a math wizard to understand segmented addressing and hexadecimal numbers. All you need is to follow along carefully with this short chapter. In no time at all, you'll know all you need to about these subjects.

Understanding Hexadecimal Math

> *These are the numbers by which the metaphysic arithmeticians compute.*
>
> —Edmund Burke, *Reflections on the Revolution in France*

To understand hexadecimal numbers, let's review our our regular decimal system works. Each digit of a number represents a power of the number 10: we have the 1s column, the 10s column, the 100s column, the 1,000s column, and so on. In other words, the number 9,482 really means 9 1,000s + 4 100s + 8 10s + 2 1s.

In hexadecimal, each digit in a hexadecimal number represents a power of the number 16. Remember that the numerals we use are just symbols that represent values. In our familiar decimal numbering system, the symbols 0, 1, 2, 3, 4, 5, 6, 7, 8, and 9 represent each possible value a digit may have. Everyone agrees on the use of these symbols; otherwise, it would be impossible to determine the values of numbers.

Hexadecimal numbers (base 16) add the letters A, B, C, D, E, and F to represent the additional six values each digit may have. The letter A, for exam-

Table 2.1	Hexadecimal Numbers and Their Decimal Equivalents
Hexadecimal	**Decimal**
1	1
2	2
3	3
4	4
5	5
6	6
7	7
8	8
9	9
A	10
B	11
C	12
D	13
E	14
F	15

ple, represents ten, a value that cannot be represented by a single digit in the decimal numbering system (see Table 2.1).

Since hexadecimal is base 16, a hexadecimal number looks like this: We have the 1s column, the 16s column, the 256s column, the 4,096s column, and so on. In other words, the hexadecimal number 250A is really 2 4,096s + 5 256s + 0 16s + 10 1s. Add them all up, and they equal 9,482.

Creating Your Own Hex Converter in QBasic

Converting numbers between different numbering systems can be the key to helping you understand those numbers. You can use QBasic, a program that comes with MS-DOS 5 and MS-DOS 6, to quickly create a simple program to convert numbers between the hexadecimal and decimal numbering systems.

(Unfortunately, if you use Novell DOS 7, you won't have QBasic, so you may have to borrow someone else's system if you want to try this.)

To create your number converter, first start QBasic by typing the following command at the DOS prompt:

```
QBASIC
```

Enter the following lines to create the program:

```
INPUT "Number? (add &H before hexadecimal values)"; yourval$
PRINT yourval$; " equals "
PRINT VAL(yourval$); " in decimal, and "
PRINT HEX$(VAL(yourval$)); " in hexadecimal."
```

Next, save the program by pressing **Alt-F**, and then pressing **S** to display the Save As dialog box. Enter a name, such as **HCONVERT** in the File **N**ame text box. Press **Enter**. Your screen should now look like Figure 2.1. To run your program from the DOS prompt, type **QBASIC HCONVERT.BAS**.

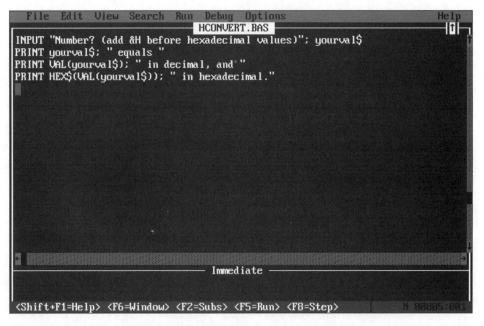

Figure 2.1   **The completed QBasic hex converter program.**

This program takes any legal decimal or hexadecimal number and displays its value in both decimal and hexadecimal numbers. As long as the number you input is in the correct format, the program will provide the proper conversions. The proper format for decimal numbers contains only the digits 0–9. Hexadecimal numbers can contain the digits 0–9 and the letters A–F, and must start with "&H" to tell the program that the number is a hexadecimal number.

Test the program by pressing **F5**, and then entering a decimal or hexadecimal value at the prompt. Figure 2.2 shows the result of entering the hexadecimal value &H13A60. The decimal equivalent value is 80,480.

Press **Enter** to return to QBasic. To convert additional values, press **F5** again.

You may want to modify this program to make it more convenient. For example, you could print the values on your printer instead of displaying them on-screen, or you may decide to add additional program logic that repeats the conversion until you press the Break key. Regardless of any modi-

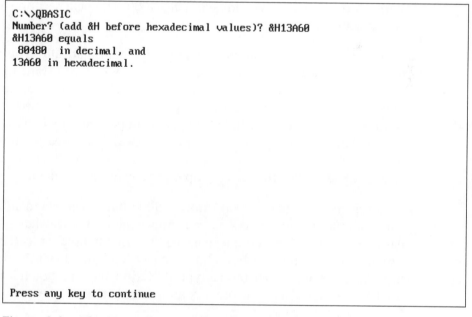

```
C:\>QBASIC
Number? (add &H before hexadecimal values)? &H13A60
&H13A60 equals
 80480  in decimal, and
13A60 in hexadecimal.



















Press any key to continue
```

Figure 2.2   The HCONVERT.BAS program converts values to their
decimal and hexadecimal equivalents.

fications, the HCONVERT.BAS program provides a simple, no-cost way to convert between decimal and hexadecimal numbers.

Memory Pages

Programmers wanted a common way to indentify blocks of memory, so *memory pages* were created. The PC's conventional memory and upper memory space was divided into 16 non-overlapping 64K memory pages.

The first ten memory pages—0000, 1000, 2000, 3000, 4000, 5000, 6000, 7000, 8000, and 9000—are also conveniently known as *conventional memory*. Pages A000 through F000 are *upper memory*. For the purposes of memory management, all addresses are treated as though they were part of one of these memory pages. Instead of dealing with thousands of segment/offset combinations, a simplified method is used. In this method, the segment is always one of the memory pages, and the leftmost three digits of the offset are added to the rightmost three digits of the segment.

For example, an address like 13A6 would be in page 1000. A segmented address like 4500:38A0 would be in page 4000. The next section shows more on segmented addressing.

DOS manages conventional memory pages automatically. You only have to become involved in memory management when you want to use other types of memory, such as upper memory. In fact, your most common use of memory addresses will likely be to specify a range of upper memory addresses to include or exclude from use as upper memory blocks. For example, you might specify the 32K range B000–B7FF as areas to use as upper memory blocks; this would mean that you could load TSRs and device drivers into B000–B7FF, thus freeing up more conventional memory.

Just as memory pages 0000 through 9000 have been standardized as the conventional memory pages, certain upper memory pages have fairly standard uses, as well. For example, page F000 is usually used (at least in part) for system ROMs. Figure 2.3 shows how the DOS command DEBUG displays the first 128 bytes of page F000 on a typical PC. In Chapter 4 you'll learn how to use DEBUG as well as some other common tools to examine memory searching for available space.

```
C:\>DEBUG
-D F000:0000
F000:0000   30 31 32 33 43 6F 70 79-72 69 67 68 74 20 4D 79   0123Copyright My
F000:0010   6C 65 78 20 43 6F 72 70-6F 72 61 74 69 6F 6E 20   lex Corporation
F000:0020   31 39 38 39 23 FE FF 00-01 02 03 80 05 00 00 08   1989#..........
F000:0030   09 0A 0B 00 6E 01 8B 17-6E 1A 6E 01 B9 2E 75 01   ....n...n.n...u.
F000:0040   6E 01 6E 01 6E 01 A0 71-7B 01 21 FF A1 FF 21 55   n.n.n..q{.!...!U
F000:0050   A1 55 21 AA A1 AA 21 FF-A1 FF 20 11 21 08 21 04   .U!...!... .!.!.
F000:0060   21 01 21 FF A0 11 A1 70-A1 02 A1 01 A1 FF FA 2E   !.!....p........
F000:0070   8E 16 D0 66 2E 8E 1E C4-66 E4 64 A8 04 75 3B 80   ...f....f.d..u;.
-Q

C:\>
```

Figure 2.3   DEBUG displays the first 128 bytes of memory page F000.

In most cases, you will only need to know the page number of the memory you want to deal with, which means that you can skip the rest of the material in this chapter. Occasionally, you may need to deal with a more complicated memory numbering system called *segments* and *offsets*. For instance, if you are using DOS 5, or if you get a memory error that lists a strange memory location like 173D:3A60, you may need to read the next section on segmented addressing.

What Is Segmented Addressing?

> *I have used loose and round numbers (the exact unit being yet undetermined) merely to give a general idea of the measures and weights proposed, when compared with those we now use.*
>
> —Thomas Jefferson, *Letters*

Although memory pages are quite straightforward and simple to understand, memory addressing is often more complicated. In fact, the memory-page numbering system that we've already discussed is actually a simplification of the real memory addresses (called segment/offset) that look like this: 0000:0000, 1000:0000, 2000:0000, and so on. The *segment* is the number before the colon that specifies a region of memory. The *offset* is the number after the colon that specifies a distance from the beginning of the segment number. When we speak of memory pages, we're usually talking about the 16 very special segments mentioned in the preceding section. These 16 special segments are each exactly 64K in length, and don't overlap because each successive one starts immediately following the previous one.

Unfortunately, memory addressing isn't always quite so simple. There's no rule that says memory segments have to start at those nice, convenient addresses, and there's no rule that says memory segments can't overlap. In fact, memory segments often do overlap, and you may well encounter specific memory addresses represented in segment/offset numbers that don't seem to bear much resemblance to the memory page numbers you need for memory management purposes. For example, if your system crashes repeatedly after you've instructed your memory manager to use a range of memory addresses for upper memory, you may see an error message telling you there's a conflict at an address like E4F0:33A0. You know you'll have to correct the error, but what does the message mean in memory management terms?

Since memory management uses a simplified version of segment/offset addressing, the key to understanding the address shown in the error message is to convert the address to the simplified version. This simplified address will then indicate where your system is encountering the conflict, and will show you how to correct the problem. Let's see how this works in practical terms by converting the address E4F0:33A0 into the simplified memory page address scheme.

Start by breaking the address into its segment and offset pieces, E4F0 and 33A0. To convert this to a memory page address, you drop the right digit of the offset number and add the result to the segment number (don't forget to add the values as hexadecimal numbers):

$$
\begin{array}{r}
E4F0 \\
+\,33A \\
\hline
E82A
\end{array}
$$

So now we can see that the memory conflict is at E82A, an address in the E000 memory page. Later, when you read the chapter on managing memory with your DOS version's memory managers, you'll see how knowing that this address is causing a conflict enables you to exclude the address from use as upper memory. Regardless of the segment/offset address you encounter, you can use this same technique to find the simplified memory page address you'll need for memory management purposes.

Understanding Multiple Addressing

As if segmented addressing and hexadecimal numbers weren't confusing enough on their own, there's another complication that can make PC memory addressing difficult to understand. *Multiple addressing* describes the way several quite different segment and offset combinations can specify the same physical memory address. It's almost as if someone could dial several different combinations of numbers and still reach your telephone.

How Did We Get into This Mess?

Segmented addressing is another of DOS's concessions to backward compatibility. As I noted earlier, the 8088 processor used in the first IBM-PC has 20 memory address lines, allowing access to 1M of memory. Internally, however, the 8088 is a 16-bit processor. The processor's address *registers*—internal memory structures used in nearly all operations—can handle only 16, not 20 bits of address data. Since each address line must be controlled by one data bit, two registers are necessary to generate the 20 bits of each memory address. These two registers are called the *segment register* and the *offset register.*

The newer 80x86 processors have larger address registers, and can therefore address larger amounts of memory in a single register. In fact, programs running on the 80386, 80486, or Pentium can actually specify the size of a memory segment. These more advanced processors aren't physically limited to 64K segments, but must use them for compatibility when running DOS and DOS programs.

Since both the segment and offset registers in the 8086 and 8088 processors are 16-bit registers, they can each hold 65,536 different values (two to the 16th power). Thus each segment is exactly 65,536 bytes (64K) in length. Because the segment register contains only the top 16 bits of each 20-bit address, this also means each segment starts 16 bytes after the beginning of the previous segment. Later we'll examine the implications of this fact.

How Can Different Addresses Be the Same?

A rose by any other name would smell as sweet.

—Shakespeare, *Romeo and Juliet*

Multiple addressing results from segmented addressing. Since each segment is 65,536 bytes in length, and each new segment begins 16 bytes after the previous segment, there are literally thousands of segment/offset combinations for any memory address (see Figure 2.4).

Let's look at an example to see how this works in the real world. If we pick a decimal physical address such as 80,480 and convert it to hexadecimal, it is 13A60h. One way to represent this address in segment/offset notation is 13A6:0000, or segment 13A6, offset 0h. Another simple way to describe the same memory address is 1396:0100, or segment 1396, offset 100h. Both segment/offset combinations describe the same physical address. You can prove

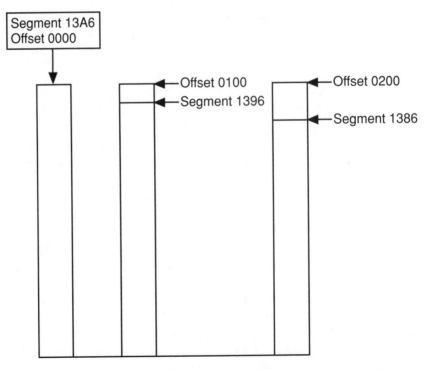

Figure 2.4   How different addresses can refer to the same area in memory.

this by using the trick you learned earlier. Simply take the segment, append a 0 to the end, and add the offset.

Of course, these two aren't the only segment/offset combinations you can use, either. The combinations 03A8:FFE0, 06F9:CAD0, and 1386:0200 are all valid, as well. With a little effort you'll be able to find many more. Just use the trick of converting the segment to a five-digit hexadecimal number and then add your four-digit offset number. The four leftmost digits of the remainder are the new segment number. (Don't forget to pad the remainder with zeros on the left so you have a five-digit remainder.)

As you can easily see, multiple addressing can disguise a physical address so well even an expert (or a computer nerd complete with pocket protector and leaky ball-point pens) has trouble determining the actual physical address. Fortunately, for the purposes of advanced memory management, certain conventions (no, not the Shriners) help make sense of this confusion.

Summary

Segmented memory addressing can seem like a very complex, unintelligible subject. As you've learned in this chapter, though, it's not that bad once you understand a few tricks. Understanding how segmented memory addresses relate to physical memory addresses makes it much simpler to convert from one segment/offset combination to another. This knowledge helps you understand how you specify memory addresses using memory page notation—a vital subject as you attempt to apply advanced memory management techniques on your system.

Now that you've learned the basics of PC memory, it's time to define your goals. In the next chapter you'll learn how to determine what your programs really need, and how to devise a compromise that suits your needs.

Chapter 3

Making a Plan: Deciding What Types of Memory You Need and How Much

Look before you leap.

—Proverb

This chapter is about defining goals. To make the most out of your PC's memory, you'll need to deal with two main issues:

- Making sure that your software has enough of the right kind of memory to work properly.
- Managing the trade-off between making your PC run faster and making it able to run more software.

The first thing you need to do is look at all your software to see what types of memory it needs (and how much). If you use only a single program, it's pretty easy to determine the best way to set up your PC's memory for that program. If you're more typical, though, you probably use a number of different programs, each with its own requirements. Once you've defined your goals, you can proceed to the chapter that addresses the software you use (DOS 5, DOS 6, or Novell DOS 7) and find out how to maximize your computer's use of memory.

Determining What Memory Your Software Needs

Chances are that you use a variety of software, so the first thing you need to do is write down the names of everything you use. The following sections will help you determine how much of each kind of memory your programs need. This is very important, because memory management is like a juggling act. All programs need a certain amount of conventional memory in order to run. Some programs also need a set amount of expanded (EMS) memory or extended (XMS) memory. Some programs can use either EMS or XMS. And some device drivers (programs that come with DOS and do things like make your mouse or CD-ROM work) can use conventional or upper memory. Learning what part of memory to load all your programs into is at the heart of memory management.

To help determine your requirements, you'll need to list the programs you use along with the types and amounts of memory they need. You may want to make up a list similar to the following:

Program or Device Driver	Conventional Memory	EMS Memory	XMS Memory	Uses Upper Memory?

Make your list large enough to include all the device drivers and TSR programs you load in CONFIG.SYS and AUTOEXEC.BAT, as well as the application programs you generally use. In the following sections you'll learn how to complete this form and then use the information for memory management.

Tip

To view your CONFIG.SYS and AUTOEXEC.BAT files, go to the DOS prompt and type **EDIT CONFIG.SYS**. Type **EDIT AUTOEXEC.BAT** to view that file. For more information, see Chapter 1.

Conventional Memory

All PC programs require conventional memory, and since you're using DOS as your operating system, you automatically have conventional memory available. Conventional memory is a precious resource because all software is designed to use it—anything will work in conventional memory. The trick is freeing up as much of your 640K of conventional memory as possible for software that needs it the most. If one of your programs requires 500K of conventional memory, and you have only 490K available, that program won't run at all.

Determining How Much Conventional Memory You Need

Conventional memory is usually in short supply. Even though your PC has 640K of conventional memory, much of that conventional memory is used up before you ever get a chance to run an application. Device drivers, TSRs, and DOS itself compete for conventional memory resources, sometimes reducing memory available for application programs from 640K to 440K or less.

One of the main reasons that device drivers, TSR programs, and DOS itself use so much conventional memory is that any PC program knows how to use this most universal of memory types. All PCs have conventional memory, so this is the one type of memory any program can count on finding.

Sometimes the best question to ask isn't how much conventional memory a program needs, but how much it can use. You'll usually find it best to provide the maximum conventional memory possible. There are two ways to do this. You can simply decide to skip certain device drivers and TSRs and forego the services they provide, or you can load as much as possible into other types of memory (like upper memory) instead of conventional memory.

A Technical Look at How Some Software Uses Conventional Memory

To cope with differing memory configurations, programs may use *overlays*, or sections of the program that are read into memory as they are needed. When another section of the program is needed, it may overwrite in memory a portion of the program that is not currently in use—or, if enough memory is available, both sections of the program may be loaded into different areas of memory. If enough memory is available for many different overlays to be loaded at the same time, the program will run much faster than it can if the same memory must constantly be swapped between overlays. While such a program may be able to run in 256K of memory, it may be many times faster if it can use 512K.

In many cases, the first approach is appropriate. Many PC users load quite a few device drivers and TSRs by habit, without really considering whether they're needed. ANSI.SYS is one such example. Almost no modern PC programs require the services of ANSI.SYS, yet a very large percentage of PC users automatically load this memory waster every time they start their systems. If you don't need ANSI.SYS, why throw away about 9K of conventional memory? Another common memory waster is SETVER.EXE. You may not even realize this program is being loaded on your system, because it is automatically added by the DOS setup program. While SETVER doesn't typically waste as much memory as ANSI.SYS, any memory it does use is usually just wasted.

There's another common program you may be loading (as either a device driver or as a TSR) that may simply be wasting memory. Do you load a mouse driver in CONFIG.SYS or AUTOEXEC.BAT? Did you know that Windows uses its own mouse driver and ignores any a mouse driver loaded in CONFIG.SYS or AUTOEXEC.BAT? Unless you use a mouse with DOS programs, you can probably skip the mouse driver in CONFIG.SYS or AUTOEXEC.BAT and save the memory it used for more productive purposes.

Tip

To test whether a device driver or TSR is really needed, add the word REM and a space to the beginning of the line in CONFIG.SYS or AUTOEXEC.BAT that loads the device driver or TSR. Restart your system and make certain everything still works as expected. If there are no problems, you can probably get along fine without the device driver or TSR.

It's pretty safe to assume that you'll need some of the device drivers or TSRs that are loaded when you start your system. Certain types of disk drives, sound boards, and fax boards often require their own memory-resident software. Unless you load their device drivers or TSRs, you won't be able to use these types of PC enhancements. In addition, you probably load software enhancements like DOSKEY that extend DOS's capabilities and make your system easier to use. Next we'll consider a better alternative than simply skipping these types of system enhancements: loading them into upper memory.

Note

All modern DOS versions allow you to load the DOS *kernel*—the basic part of DOS itself—into the HMA (High Memory Area). Loading the DOS kernel high should be the first step you take toward increasing available conventional memory. The later chapters on DOS-version-specific memory management will show you how to load DOS high in your DOS version.

Upper Memory

Most device drivers and TSR programs can use upper memory just as easily as they can use conventional memory. No special program code needs to be developed, and you usually don't even need to worry about whether your device drivers and TSR programs can use upper memory.

How Much Upper Memory Do You Need?

Because upper memory is treated as a direct extension of conventional memory, using upper memory frees conventional memory for other purposes. For example, loading a 17K mouse driver into upper memory instead of conventional memory provides 17K more conventional memory for your application programs. Each additional device driver or TSR you load into upper memory releases more conventional memory.

Let's look at an example of what this can mean in the real world. My system is loaded with a large variety of adapter boards and other hardware, most requiring their own device drivers or TSR programs. In addition, I appreciate the utility, performance enhancements, and convenience provided by several other device drivers and TSRs (such as a mouse driver, the SmartDrive disk cache, and DOSKEY). Table 3.1 shows the conventional and upper memory used by the device drivers and TSR programs that are normally loaded on my system.

As Table 3.1 shows, the six device drivers and TSR programs that are loaded into upper memory use a total of 93,792 bytes. If these programs were loaded into conventional memory, application programs would find only 503K of conventional memory, rather than the 595K that is currently available.

Even though Table 3.1 shows that many of the device drivers and TSRs are using upper memory, you can also see that a number of the programs are loaded into conventional memory. Why aren't they all in upper memory? Wouldn't applications benefit from even more free conventional memory?

Table 3.1 Some Typical Memory Use Statistics		
Name	Conventional Memory Used (Bytes)	Upper Memory Used (Bytes)
MSDOS	18,333	0
ASPI4DOS	6,672	0
HIMEM	1,168	0
EMM386	3,120	0
SATISFAX	3,968	0
IFSHLP	3,872	0
COMMAND	3,248	0
CASMGR	5,520	0
MVSOUND	0	10,832
ASWCDTSH	0	14,640
MOUSE	0	17,120
MSCDEX	0	16,176
SMARTDRV	0	30,368
DOSKEY	0	4,656
Total	45,901	93,792

Actually, there are several different situations that prevent some device drivers or TSRs from loading into upper memory. In the next two sections we'll see how you can determine which programs cannot use upper memory.

Can Your Device Drivers Go into Upper Memory?

Device drivers are special programs you load using the DEVICE or DEVICE-HIGH directive in CONFIG.SYS. Device drivers enable your system to access special system hardware or software services. These may include SCSI disk drives, CD-ROMs, scanners, fax boards, sound cards, and so on.

Because upper memory is outside the range of memory addresses managed automatically by DOS, upper memory is not immediately available when your system is started. To make upper memory available, your system must first load a memory manager that provides upper memory access. Any device drivers that must be loaded before this upper memory access is available cannot, therefore, be loaded into upper memory.

In MS-DOS, EMM386.EXE provides upper memory block access. But since HIMEM.SYS must be loaded before EMM386.EXE, neither program has access to upper memory while it is initially being loaded. This fact precludes both of these device drivers from being loaded into upper memory.

Note

The device driver for DoubleSpace, the MS-DOS disk-compression software, must also be loaded before upper memory is available. Initially, DBLSPACE.BIN loads into conventional memory, but can later be moved to upper memory using a special CONFIG.SYS command:

```
DEVICEHIGH=C:\DOS\DBLSPACE.SYS /MOVE
```

HIMEM.SYS and EMM386.EXE are usually, but not always, the only device drivers you must load prior to upper memory block availability. The ASPI4DOS device driver shown in Table 3.1 is an example of another type of device driver that often must be loaded before upper memory blocks are available. In this case, ASPI4DOS is a device driver that enables the system to access a SCSI disk drive. Device drivers for disk drives usually must be loaded before any type of memory manager, and thus must use conventional memory.

While it's pretty clear that DEVICE drivers that are loaded before upper memory blocks are available can't be loaded into upper memory, it may not be immediately clear why some others that are loaded later end up in conventional memory. Unfortunately, some device drivers, especially older ones, simply won't function correctly in upper memory. Fortunately, such device drivers are pretty rare, but they do exist. For example, some SCSI hard drives require the SmartDrive disk cache to use *double buffering*—a memory management technique designed to prevent the loss of data. SmartDrive's double buffering is installed by loading SmartDrive as a device driver with the following command:

```
DEVICE=C:\DOS\SMARTDRV.EXE /DOUBLE_BUFFER
```

Double buffering cannot be loaded into upper memory, because upper memory blocks can be remapped (as discussed in Chapter 2). Double buffering overcomes problems caused by some SCSI adapters that cannot correctly deal with memory remapping, so allowing double buffering to be placed in memory that might be moved won't solve the problem.

Sometimes a device driver could function correctly in upper memory, but no matter how hard you try, all attempts to load the device driver correctly in upper memory fail. In most instances, this failure is caused by a simple problem: The device driver is too large to fit into any of the upper memory blocks. Device drivers can be loaded into upper memory only if a single upper memory block is large enough to hold the complete device driver as it is being loaded. The size of a device driver during loading isn't always the same as it is after the device driver is loaded.

Some device drivers expand during loading, or shrink after they're loaded. The SATISFAX driver shown in Table 3.1, for example, uses slightly less than 4K of memory once it has been loaded, but requires a contiguous memory block of nearly 30K during loading. Unfortunately, when device drivers require larger memory blocks to load than to execute, it can be very difficult to provide upper memory blocks large enough for loading the device driver high, and conventional memory is used instead.

Sometimes you can accomplish the goal of loading more device drivers into upper memory blocks by simply changing the order of the CONFIG.SYS directives that load device drivers. Load the largest device drivers first, and the available upper memory blocks may be large enough to fit more into upper memory. In later chapters we'll examine some sophisticated techniques you can use with your specific DOS version memory manager.

Can Your TSRs Go into Upper Memory?

TSR programs are similar to device drivers in purpose: They provide services that extend and enhance DOS. TSRs generally have fewer upper memory compatibility problems than do device drivers, in part because TSRs seldom address the low-level system issues common to many device drivers. TSRs are more likely to provide additional software functions, such as the command recall and editing functions provided by DOSKEY.

TSRs share one problem with device drivers: They can only be loaded into upper memory blocks if large enough upper memory blocks are available. TSRs have an extreme disadvantage compared to device drivers in this area, though. All device drivers are loaded before any TSR gets its chance to load. This is true even if you use the INSTALL or INSTALLHIGH directives in CONFIG.SYS.

Some TSRs differ from device drivers in an important way. When their services are no longer needed, some TSRs can be removed from memory, freeing the memory for other purposes.

Nearly all TSRs create a connection with the DOS services that look for keystrokes. Usually, a TSR simply sits in memory, waiting for its specific "hotkey" to be pressed to activate the program. If you load several TSRs, each TSR makes its own addition to the chain of command, leaving previous changes intact. This succession of modifications, however, usually requires TSRs to be removed in the reverse of their load order. That is, you must unload the last loaded TSR first, then you can unload the next previous TSR. This fact makes it very important to consider when and where TSRs are loaded. For example, there's really very little reason to unload a TSR from upper memory; only those loaded into conventional memory take away from application software memory. Therefore, it's usually better to load as many "permanent" TSRs into upper memory as possible, and later load in conventional memory any TSRs you might eventually want to unload. That way you'll be able to unload TSRs from conventional memory without first unloading TSRs that were loaded into upper memory.

Expanded Memory (EMS)

Some programs absolutely require expanded memory (EMS) to run. If you have one of these programs, then you obviously need to configure at least part of your PC's memory as EMS. Look on the box that your software came in, or look through its documentation to find out if it needs expanded memory. On the chart shown earlier, write down the name of your software and how much EMS memory it requires.

Other programs don't absolutely require EMS to run, but they can use EMS to run faster. Lotus 1-2-3 Release 2.x is probably the most popular example. You *can* run 1-2-3 without EMS memory, but you can use tin cans and a string for a telephone, too. If your software runs better with EMS, make a note of that on the chart in Figure 3.1. You might want to create some EMS memory for that program, depending on what your other software requires.

Other programs can use either EMS or XMS memory to supplement conventional memory. In fact, many more modern programs can use either EMS or XMS memory, but they'll often automatically select their preferred type if it's available. The version of the SmartDrive disk cache program supplied with DOS 5, for example, uses XMS memory by default, but can use EMS memory if you prefer. Many other programs absolutely require EMS memory to run.

Tip
EMS memory is an inefficient type of memory—you probably want to set up your PC to use EMS memory only if you have a program that absolutely requires it.

Check all the device drivers and TSR programs you load in CONFIG.SYS or AUTOEXEC.BAT to see whether they require EMS memory. Consult the program's documentation. Be sure you have the most recent documentation for the program, because an older version of the program may not use memory in the same way as a newer version. The SmartDrive disk cache that comes with DOS is a good example of how different program versions use different options. The MS-DOS 5 SmartDrive program, SMARTDRV.SYS, can use either XMS or EMS memory. The newer versions of SmartDrive supplied with MS-DOS 6 and Windows 3.1, SMARTDRV.EXE, no longer use EMS memory.

Other typical device drivers and TSR programs that may use EMS memory include Microsoft's MSCDEX.EXE CD-ROM extensions program and Intel's CASMGR.EXE fax board software. You may be surprised to learn that both of these programs can use EMS memory to reduce the amount of conventional memory they use, but neither can use XMS memory. If Microsoft and Intel can't make the switch in major programs they supply, is it any wonder that smaller manufacturers have a problem?

The Disadvantages of Using EMS Memory

For EMS memory to work, you must devote a solid, contiguous 64K block of upper memory to it. This 64K block is called the *EMS page frame*. Of course, if a 64K block of memory is allocated as the EMS page frame, that memory is no longer available for other uses (such as loading device drivers and TSR programs into upper memory). As a result, those device drivers and TSRs take up precious space in your conventional memory area.

Because 64K is a lot of memory to give up for a EMS page frame, you may want to avoid using EMS memory if none of your software absolutely needs it. As I mentioned above, check to see whether your device drivers and TSRs can use either EMS or XMS memory. Also EMS memory is much slower than XMS memory, so if you have the choice, XMS is better.

Unfortunately, some device drivers and TSRs don't give you any options. Microsoft's MSCDEX.EXE CD-ROM extensions program and Intel's CAS-MGR.EXE fax board software, as mentioned earlier, can use conventional memory or EMS memory, but not XMS memory. If you really must use such software, you'll have to consider your options carefully. For example, you may find that by not providing EMS memory, you're able to load additional device drivers and TSRs into upper memory. If so, you may free more conventional memory than MSCDEX.EXE or CASMGR.EXE wastes when loaded totally into conventional memory. Other programs that use EMS memory may present similar complex choices. We'll discuss how to make these difficult decisions a little later.

> **Note**
>
> There's no inherent reason that programs such as MSCDEX.EXE and CASMGR.EXE must use EMS memory. Novell's NWCDEX.EXE CD-ROM extensions program, for example, is quite happy using DPMS memory. NWCDEX.EXE and DPMS.EXE are included in Novell DOS 7.

EMS Memory and Windows

If you don't use Windows, you don't need to read this section. Although Windows and Windows programs don't use EMS memory, Windows can provide EMS memory to DOS programs while they are running under Windows. Unfortunately, Windows can provide EMS memory only if your DOS memory manager has reserved the 64K EMS page frame.

If you use only Windows programs, or if none of your DOS programs requires EMS memory, don't specify that your memory manager supply EMS memory. You'll save the 64K block of upper memory that would be used for the EMS page frame, have more space for device drivers and TSRs in upper memory, and have more conventional memory available.

How Much EMS Memory Do You Need?

If you've determined that you really do need EMS memory, it's important to decide exactly how much EMS memory is enough. This can be difficult, because EMS memory requirements don't often specify exact, accurate numbers. More often, program documentation simply states something on the order of "uses EMS memory, if available."

Understanding how a program uses EMS memory can provide the key that allows you to unlock the mystery of how much EMS memory you really need to provide. There are three main classes of programs that use EMS memory:

- Device drivers or TSR programs can sometimes use a small amount of EMS memory for program *buffers*—memory areas that hold temporary data. Usually, these types of programs would store their buffers in conventional memory if EMS memory were not available. It's generally safe to assume that these programs need very little EMS memory, probably less than 64K each.

- Business programs, such as older DOS spreadsheet programs, often can use EMS memory to store some data. Lotus 1-2-3 Release 2.x, for example, can use larger spreadsheets if EMS memory is available. Unless you work with gigantic spreadsheet models, however, you probably don't need more than 256K or possibly 512K of EMS memory to load and use even the largest spreadsheet you'll ever create.

- Game programs, especially those with extensive graphics and sound, sometimes use EMS memory to store program data when the program is first loaded into memory. This allows much faster access than would be possible if the same information had to be read from disk when needed. In effect, these programs create their own "virtual disk drive" in EMS memory to greatly improve program performance. If you use these types of programs, you'll need to allocate as much EMS memory as possible.

Use these program classifications to determine how much EMS memory you need to provide. Remember, though, that if you enable EMS memory on your system, available upper memory will be reduced by 64K, the size of the EMS page frame. If you only need EMS memory for device driver or TSR buffers, you may be better off without the EMS page frame, because you'll be able to load more device drivers and TSRs into upper memory blocks instead of loading them into conventional memory. In fact, unless you need EMS memory for another type of program, providing EMS memory simply to provide device driver or TSR buffer space usually doesn't provide the best use of your system's memory resources.

Extended Memory (XMS)

Technically, any memory chips you have above 1M are extended memory. (You have to set up DOS to use these memory chips properly.) Some programs absolutely require extended memory (XMS) to run. Check your documentation, and record the name of the program along with the amount of XMS it needs on the chart shown earlier.

Some programs can use either XMS or EMS memory. If the same memory chips in your PC can be set up as either XMS or EMS memory, should you care which type of memory is made available? Is there any advantage to using XMS instead of EMS?

- With EMS memory, you have to devote 64K to a page frame in upper memory. XMS memory does not require a page frame, so using XMS memory in place of EMS memory saves 64K of upper memory space that can be used by other programs.

- XMS memory is often faster than EMS, because EMS memory is emulated by converting some XMS memory to EMS memory. This extra step requires additional processing, so using EMS memory may be slower than using XMS memory.

Many newer versions of programs that formerly used EMS memory have been updated to use XMS memory instead. This is especially true if the older program version is a DOS program and the newer version is a Windows program. If you're using an old program that requires EMS memory, you may want to upgrade to one of the newer, more powerful equivalents. Not only will you gain the new features of the of the modern program, but your memory management task will be greatly simplified. If your software can use either EMS or XMS memory, choose XMS.

How Much XMS Memory Do You Need?

XMS memory is really the rising star of PC memory management, because unlike EMS memory, XMS memory is often used for running programs, not just storing data. Windows programs use XMS memory to provide a linear address space, which enables them to use as much memory as they need without the limitations of conventional memory. Disk caching programs, such as SmartDrive, use XMS memory to improve overall system performance, benefiting every application you use.

Usually, it's best to provide as much XMS memory as possible. There are, however, some cases when this may not be true:

- If you use programs that require large amounts of EMS memory and you are using MS-DOS 5, you'll have to choose between allocating XMS and EMS memory.

- If you use old programs that include their own DOS-extenders, you'll probably find that such programs cannot use XMS extended memory.

Their method of accessing extended memory is incompatible with the XMS standard.

Both of these cases provide substantial arguments for upgrading. In the first case, upgrading to a newer DOS version enables your system to share a memory pool between XMS and EMS memory (see "Creating a Shared Memory Pool" later in this chapter). In the second case, you'll want to upgrade to a newer, XMS-aware version of your application software. If the application software manufacturer doesn't have a newer version that is XMS-aware, you may want to consider stepping up to a competing product that has kept up with the times.

Choosing between Extended (XMS) and Expanded (EMS) Memory

One of the most difficult memory management questions you may face is how to choose between XMS and EMS memory. Is EMS memory ever a better alternative than XMS memory? The answer depends on several factors. Let's see why.

Because you'll probably use upper memory whether or not you need EMS memory, choosing between XMS and EMS memory probably won't be decided by your choice of memory managers. You must use a memory manager to provide either EMS and XMS memory. In MS-DOS, XMS memory is managed by HIMEM.SYS. EMS memory is provided by EMM386.EXE, which also provides access to upper memory, whether or not EMS memory is activated. If you use the memory management tools provided by MS-DOS, you'll probably use both memory managers even if you don't have any need for EMS memory. If you use Novell DOS 7, you only need one memory manager, EMM386.EXE.

So how do you choose between providing EMS and XMS memory? Ultimately, it comes down to this:

1. If your software requires EMS, you need to configure enough EMS memory for the program to work.

2. If your software doesn't need EMS, then don't worry about it.

3. If your software can use either EMS or XMS, use XMS.

Tip

If you have DOS 6, you don't need to worry about dividing up your existing memory into EMS and XMS. The version of EMM386.EXE that comes in DOS 6 will do this automatically for you.

Before you decide to configure all of your extended memory as XMS memory, however, consider that there are several classes of programs that are unable to use XMS memory. If you use these types of programs, you'll want to give careful consideration to your various memory management options.

- Programs that use only conventional memory won't benefit directly from XMS memory. Older DOS programs (such as DOS-based word processors or database managers) are often in this category, but even some newer programs are limited to using conventional memory. These types of programs may, however, benefit from an increase in available conventional memory resulting from loading device drivers or TSRs into upper, EMS, or XMS memory.

- Programs that can only use EMS memory in addition to conventional memory also won't gain a direct benefit from XMS memory. These may include DOS-based spreadsheet programs like Lotus 1-2-3 Release 2.x. Like the first category of programs, however, the loading of device drivers and TSRs into upper, EMS, or XMS memory may provide additional conventional memory for these types of programs.

- Programs that use DOS extenders, such as early versions of Paradox or Lotus 1-2-3 Release 3.0, may not recognize XMS memory. Even though these programs use extended memory, they require a special method of accessing extended memory, and won't be able to use XMS memory.

Creating a Compromise

A compromise is the art of dividing a cake in such a way that everyone believes that he has got the biggest piece.

—Dr. Ludwig Erhard

PC memory management usually involves compromise. As you know, different programs require different types and amounts of memory. What may be best for one application program may not work at all for another. A configuration that provides the best overall system performance may make some programs run so poorly that they're barely usable.

Compromise is an art. Done well, it can be a beautiful balance between competing interests. Done poorly, it can be an ugly mess.

Balancing Memory and Performance

Mountain tall and ocean deep
Trembling balance duly keep.

—Ralph Waldo Emerson, *Essays*

Memory management compromises often require a delicate balancing act, with program memory requirements on one side of the balance and system performance considerations on the other. Trying to create the proper balance may make you feel as though you're trying to walk a tightrope with someone on each side actively attempting to make you fall off.

The real trick is determining exactly the correct balance which will give you the performance you want while allowing you to use effectively the programs you need. Let's consider the two sides to see how you can create that balance.

When Is It Better to Opt for Performance?

Several factors contribute to PC performance. As you plan your balancing act, keep the following points in mind:

- Disk caching is one of the most important of system performance enhancements. No matter how fast your disk drives may be, they're at least an order of magnitude or more slower than the system processor and memory. If your PC can find information in memory instead of reading data from a disk, overall performance will be greatly improved. Programs that are disk-intensive, such as database programs, will realize a greater benefit from disk caching than will programs that do relatively little disk access.

- Memory used for disk caching usually will not be available for application program use. A few disk-caching programs, such as SmartDrive, are able to share XMS memory with Windows (and in some cases, with other programs that use XMS memory), but the performance benefits are reduced when the memory is shared.

- High-speed modems and communications software sometimes have a difficult time sharing processor time with disk caching. If you experience data loss, you may have to disable disk caching while you're using a communications program.

When Is It Better to Maximize Memory?

If you use programs that simply won't run unless they're able to use all system memory, your choice is easy—you must maximize memory even if overall performance suffers. But there are other instances that may make you decide in favor of slightly reduced performance, as well.

Actually, although it may seem like a contradiction, some of your software may run faster if your PC runs slower overall. Programmers sometimes use a technique of developing modular programs that allow only the core of the program to be loaded into memory initially. As you use the program, the separate program modules, or *overlays*, are loaded into available memory. If a different module is required, it may either be loaded in unused memory, or—if all memory is in use—the module may replace a module not currently in use. This scheme allows you to run programs much larger than your system's physical memory would otherwise allow, but it requires considerable processing and disk access to load and unload program modules. If you can give the program more memory, less memory swapping may be necessary, and the program may run faster. Where do you get this extra memory? It may come from not loading such items as your disk caching software.

Another instance where maximizing memory instead of performance may make good sense is if you use software applications that do very little disk access, but you want to use special memory-resident tools such as background communications programs or pop-up appointment reminders. In some cases, the instant availability of such tools may boost your personal productivity far more than faster system performance would. If you use a task swapping environment, such as Novell DOS 7, you may find that the ability to jump instantly between your favorite applications makes allocating more memory for programs a better choice than allocating that same memory to performance improvements.

As you can see, creating a balance between program memory and system performance may require you to do some serious thinking about how you intend to use your system. Sometimes, though, it's just not possible to create a compromise that works well enough to suit all your needs. Next we'll look at what you can do if a compromise doesn't seem possible.

What to Do about Conflicting Interests

Sometimes it's impossible to avoid the issue of conflicting interests. You just may not be able to find a single system configuration that works with all of your applications. One program, a game perhaps, may require you to load an absolute minimum of device drivers and TSRs, and to allocate every possible byte as EMS memory. Your word processor, however, may be a Windows program, and not be able to use EMS memory at all. Finally, an important communications application may experience severe data loss unless it has its own preferred configuration in place.

There are two primary solutions to the problem of such conflicting interests. The first, creating multiple configurations, requires more work to set up and use, but has the advantage of working with any DOS version, or even with multiple DOS versions. The second, creating a shared memory pool, is more limited because it addresses only a specific type of conflict, and is available only with certain DOS versions (or with some third-party memory managers).

Let's first have a look at the more general solution, creating multiple configurations, and then at the shared memory pool option.

Creating Multiple Configurations

Each specific set of CONFIG.SYS directives and AUTOEXEC.BAT commands creates a unique system configuration. Different configurations may vary in how memory is allocated, which device drivers and TSRs are loaded, or even in the order in which device drivers and TSRs are loaded. Sometimes a small change in CONFIG.SYS or AUTOEXEC.BAT makes a major difference in how your PC operates. For example, changing the line in CONFIG.SYS that loads EMM386.EXE from

```
DEVICE=C:\DOS\EMM386.EXE NOEMS
```

to

```
DEVICE=C:\DOS\EMM386.EXE RAM
```

creates two major changes. By replacing NOEMS with RAM, you direct EMM386.EXE to make EMS memory available. In addition, 64K less upper memory will be available, possibly causing some device drivers or TSRs to use conventional memory instead of upper memory.

To see how much difference a small change can make, consider the following change to the first example:

```
DEVICE=C:\DOS\EMM386.EXE NOEMS I=A000-AFFF
```

Everyone knows that PCs only have 640K of conventional memory, right? On most systems, the above line extends conventional memory to 704K! Before you try this for yourself, be aware that if you use this directive, your computer will lock up as soon as you try to use any program that uses graphics.

Tip

To see how much memory your computer has right now, turn it on and watch the numbers that roll by like a car's odometer in the top left-hand corner of the screen. This number is your total memory in bytes. If your computer is already on, see the section in Chapter 4 called "Using MEM."

If you've decided that you need multiple configurations for different purposes, start by filling out the memory requirement form you found early in this chapter (see, it really is there for a good reason). You may want to make several copies so you can have one for each proposed configuration. Once you know what you need, you can plan your different configurations. Next you can decide how you'll implement the alternates.

Creating a Boot Diskette   Many PC users don't realize that the first PCs didn't have hard disks. Booting from a diskette wasn't an option with those early systems, it was the only way to accomplish anything. But even after hard disks became common, the first place the PC looked for its basic operating instructions was drive A:. Only if drive A: was empty would the system look to the hard disk, drive C:. That's the same method used by today's PCs, too. First check for a boot diskette in drive A:, and then go to drive C: if there's nothing in drive A:.

Note

Some PCs can be configured to always boot from drive C: even if drive A: contains a diskette. Usually, this is accomplished through a special setup program. Unless there's a way to bypass this special setup and boot from drive A: in an emergency, you're playing a dangerous game if you configure your system this way, because even a minor problem with your hard disk could render your PC totally useless.

Because PCs still look for a boot diskette in drive A: before attempting to boot from drive C:, it's quite easy to create alternate system configurations using boot diskettes. You can set up the configuration files on your hard disk so they create your normal system configuration, and use boot diskettes when you need to use a different configuration. That way, your PC will start up using your standard configuration unless there's a diskette in drive A: at boot time. When you want to use an application program that needs its own special setup, simply insert the proper boot diskette and restart the system.

There are two primary kinds of boot diskettes. I classify them as *standard* boot diskettes and *intelligent* ones. What's the difference between the two? It's simple: The intelligent boot diskette doesn't force you to use the diskette except for the initial system startup. A standard boot diskette, the kind you've probably created in the past, contains more files than necessary, and doesn't transfer total system control to your hard disk. Let's see what I mean.

When you boot your system, DOS looks for CONFIG.SYS and AUTO-EXEC.BAT in the root directory of the boot disk, either drive A: or drive C:. If these files are found, the commands and directives they contain are processed, first those in CONFIG.SYS and then those in AUTOEXEC.BAT. It doesn't matter whether you're booting from drive A: or drive C:, the process is the same. The commands and directives must specify what you want the system to do in terms your PC can understand.

The following example shows a typical CONFIG.SYS file that might be contained on a standard boot disk. Don't worry if you don't understand what all the commands mean—several are specific to the device drivers needed on one individual PC. Your PC will probably have other commands not shown here.

A typical CONFIG.SYS file on a standard boot disk:

```
DEVICE=\UTILITY\ASPI4DOS.SYS
DEVICE=\DOS\HIMEM.SYS
DEVICE=\DOS\EMM386.EXE RAM 512 I=E000-EFFF I=B000-B7FF
DOS=HIGH,UMB
FILES=50
FCBS=1
STACKS=9,256
DEVICE=\FAX\SATISFAX.SYS IOADDR=0350
DEVICEHIGH=\PROAUDIO\MVSOUND.SYS D:3 Q:15
DEVICEHIGH=\UTILITY\ASWCDTSH.SYS /D:CDROM1
DEVICEHIGH=\WINDOWS\MOUSE.SYS /S100 /Y
DEVICE=\WINDOWS\IFSHLP.SYS
BUFFERS=10,0
```

Pay special attention to the DEVICE= and DEVICEHIGH= lines. Notice that each line contains a complete path so the system knows where to find each device driver. In the first line, DEVICE=\UTILITY\ASPI4DOS.SYS, the driver named ASPI4DOS.SYS is located in a subdirectory called UTILITY, which is located directly below the root directory on the boot disk. (The \ before UTILITY tells your system to consider UTILITY as a subdirectory located directly below the root directory.) As each DEVICE= or DEVICE-HIGH= directive is processed, the system knows exactly where to look.

Although this set of directives will process correctly and all the device drivers will load as they should, there are major deficiencies in this CONFIG.SYS file. The first problem is quite simple. If you want to create boot diskettes, you probably don't want to start completely from scratch. In fact, you probably only need one or two minor changes in CONFIG.SYS or AUTOEXEC.BAT, not completely different versions of these files. It's sensible, therefore, to simply make copies of your existing CONFIG.SYS and AUTOEXEC.BAT files onto your boot diskette, and just modify those copies as necessary.

If you try using modified versions of your existing CONFIG.SYS and AUTOEXEC.BAT files, however, you'll probably be greeted with quite a few error messages when you try to restart your PC using your boot diskette. Why would the same lines that work correctly in your normal CONFIG.SYS and AUTOEXEC.BAT files fail when you attempt to boot from a diskette? What's wrong here?

Look at the following modified version of the same CONFIG.SYS file and see if you can spot the difference:

```
DEVICE=C:\UTILITY\ASPI4DOS.SYS
DEVICE=C:\DOS\HIMEM.SYS
DEVICE=C:\DOS\EMM386.EXE RAM 512 I=E000-EFFF I=B000-B7FF
DOS=HIGH,UMB
FILES=50
FCBS=1
STACKS=9,256
DEVICE=C:\FAX\SATISFAX.SYS IOADDR=0350
DEVICEHIGH=C:\PROAUDIO\MVSOUND.SYS D:3 Q:15
DEVICEHIGH=C:\UTILITY\ASWCDTSH.SYS /D:CDROM1
DEVICEHIGH=C:\WINDOWS\MOUSE.SYS /S100 /Y
DEVICE=C:\WINDOWS\IFSHLP.SYS
BUFFERS=10,0
```

Did you notice that each DEVICE= and DEVICEHIGH= line now includes the drive letter, C:? That simple change tells the system to look for these files in the proper place, their directories on drive C:, even if the PC is booting from drive A:. Of course, you could just create all those subdirectories on drive A: and copy each device driver to the proper location on drive A:, but why bother? Not only would that be a lot more work, but your system would take longer to boot, too, because reading the device driver files from the diskette would be much slower than reading them from the hard disk. In addition, by keeping the device drivers in one place, it's easier to make certain you're always using the latest version after you upgrade your hardware or software drivers.

You should modify your CONFIG.SYS and AUTOEXEC.BAT files to include the drive letters before you copy those files from your hard disk to your boot diskettes. After all, there's no penalty to having the drive letters in your main copies of these two files, and your boot diskette copies will then automatically include this information.

You should have one boot diskette, your emergency boot diskette, that contains copies of all the drivers you need and all the standard system files to start your system. You'll use this diskette in the event that it's impossible to access the hard disk, so you must have everything you need on the emergency boot diskette.

Adding the drive letters to the commands and directives in CONFIG.SYS and AUTOEXEC.BAT is the first, but not the most important step in creating an intelligent boot diskette. The second step is just as easy, but has a major impact on system operation.

Have you ever booted your PC from a diskette and then run a program on another disk? When you exited the program, you were probably greeted with a message telling you to insert the diskette containing COMMAND.COM in drive A:. If the program you were running was on a diskette in drive A:, you probably had to swap diskettes several times as you loaded and quit the program, and maybe when you tried to perform some of the program's functions, as well. The reason for this annoying behavior is simple: By default, your system looks for the DOS command interpreter, COMMAND.COM, in the root directory of the boot disk (the same place it looks for CONFIG.SYS and AUTOEXEC.BAT). If you boot from drive A:, your PC assumes that COMMAND.COM can be found in the root directory of drive A:.

Fortunately, there's a simple way to tell your PC to look for COMMAND.COM on drive C: even if you boot from a diskette. In fact, you can even tell your system to look someplace other than the root directory, too. To do so, use the CONFIG.SYS SHELL= directive, as in the following example:

```
SHELL=C:\DOS\COMMAND.COM C:\DOS\ /E:512 /P
```

This directive tells your system to load COMMAND.COM from the \DOS directory on drive C:, to look in that same directory when the transient portion of COMMAND.COM must be reloaded as you exit from a program, to increase the environment size to 512 bytes, and to make that copy of COMMAND.COM permanent for the session.

If you include a similar line in CONFIG.SYS on your boot diskette, you'll eliminate those messages telling you to place the diskette with COM-

MAND.COM in drive A:. In fact, once you boot from your intelligent diskette, you'll be able to use your system exactly as though you booted from the hard disk, except with your alternate system configuration.

Although we haven't considered any of the actual commands you'll use in your alternate configurations yet, you may want to try the techniques presented in this section to create your own intelligent boot diskettes. Later, when we cover your specific DOS version's memory managers, you'll be able to use those same diskettes as the basis for your customized setups.

Now we'll have a short look at another alternative: multiple configurations on the same disk.

Using the MS-DOS 6 Multiconfig Options   Although an intelligent boot diskette offers a good method of reconfiguring your system for different purposes, it's not the most convenient way to change system configurations. This is especially true if you must use several different configurations, or if you must change configurations quite often. Diskettes are easy to lose, and can be damaged fairly easily, too.

MS-DOS 6 introduced a set of new CONFIG.SYS commands designed to allow you to create multiple configurations within a single CONFIG.SYS file. Table 3.2 provides a brief description of these commands.

The MS-DOS 6.x multiple configuration commands are covered in detail in Chapter 6, so for now we'll just have a quick look at what you can do with these commands. Suppose you normally use Windows programs on your PC, but you have one old program that uses a DOS extender to access extended (non-XMS) memory. You could use a boot diskette before running the old program, but MS-DOS 6.x gives you a better choice. You might also have a laptop computer in addition to your desktop system, and might sometimes want to use Interlink to share files.

Within CONFIG.SYS, you can create a menu displaying the two choices—your normal configuration, and the special configuration that loads the Interlink drivers. Because you want the normal configuration to load most of the time, you'll use the MENUDEFAULT command to specify that the normal configuration will load automatically if you don't press a key within five seconds after the menu displays. Most of the configuration statements will be common to both configurations, so you'll place those statements in com-

Table 3.2	MS-DOS 6.x Multiple Configuration Commands
Command	**Description**
?	Causes DOS to ask for confirmation before carrying out the command.
INCLUDE	Executes the commands in another configuration block.
MENUCOLOR	Sets the text and background colors for the startup menu.
MENUDEFAULT	Specifies the default menu item on the startup menu and sets a timeout value.
MENUITEM	Defines up to nine menu items on the startup menu.
SUBMENU	Defines an item on a startup menu and displays another set of choices.

mon blocks. In fact, you'll probably have only one or two statements that differ between the two configurations. These statements will go in the labeled configuration blocks called by the MENUITEM statements. You might even use the MENUCOLOR command to display the menu in colors other than DOS's normal white on black. The following sample CONFIG.SYS shows one example of how you might organize all of this:

```
[MENU]
MENUCOLOR=14,1
MENUITEM=INTERLINK,   Load Interlink driver
MENUITEM=NO_DRIVERS,  Don't load drivers
MENUDEFAULT=NO_DRIVERS,5

[NORMAL]
DEVICE=C:\UTILITY\ASPI4DOS.SYS
DEVICE=C:\DOS\HIMEM.SYS
DEVICE=C:\DOS\EMM386.EXE RAM 512 I=E000-EFFF I=B000-B7FF M9
DOS=HIGH,UMB
FILES=50
FCBS=1
STACKS=9,256
LASTDRIVE=Z
DEVICE=C:\FAX\SATISFAX.SYS IOADDR=0350
DEVICEHIGH=/L:1 C:\PROAUDIO\MVSOUND.SYS D:3 Q:15
DEVICEHIGH=/L:1 C:\UTILITY\ASWCDTSH.SYS /D:CDROM1
```

```
DEVICEHIGH=/L:2 C:\WINDOWS\MOUSE.SYS /S100 /Y
SHELL=C:\DOS\COMMAND.COM C:\DOS\ /E:512 /p

[INTERLINK]
INCLUDE NORMAL
DEVICE=C:\DOS\INTERLNK.EXE /DRIVES:10 /AUTO /COM

[NO_DRIVERS]
INCLUDE NORMAL

[COMMON]
DEVICE=C:\WINDOWS\IFSHLP.SYS
BUFFERS=10,0
```

The menu selection you make can be used to direct the execution of AUTOEXEC.BAT commands, too. When you make a selection, the name of the configuration block you select is stored in a DOS environment variable called CONFIG. In the above example, if you don't make a selection, the configuration block called NO_DRIVERS is automatically selected after five seconds. The CONFIG environment variable is then assigned the value NO_DRIVERS, and you can test the value of the variable in AUTOEXEC.BAT.

You aren't limited to only two configurations, either. The main menu can include up to nine choices, and each of them can display additional menus with up to nine choices. Frankly, though, it's difficult to imagine anyone who needs so many different configuration options.

Using the Novell DOS 7 Multiconfig Options   If you use Novell DOS 7, you also have the option of creating multiple configurations within a single CONFIG.SYS file. Although Novell DOS 7 doesn't recognize the MS-DOS 6.x multiple configuration commands, it has its own set of special commands you can use to display a menu and allow the user to make a selection. Table 3.3 briefly lists the Novell DOS 7 multiple configuration commands.

You can use the Novell DOS 7 multiple configuration commands to create a menu of configuration options in much the same manner as shown in the above example of the MS-DOS 6 multiple configuration commands. You cannot control the screen colors as you can in MS-DOS 6.x, but all of the other basic options exist. See Chapter 7 for more detailed information on the the Novell DOS 7 multiple configuration commands.

Table 3.3	Novell DOS 7 Multiple Configuration Commands
Command	Description
?	Causes DOS to ask for confirmation before carrying out the command.
ECHO	Displays a message (such as a menu option).
EXIT	Prevents any further CONFIG.SYS commands from being executed.
GOSUB	Calls a configuration block as a subroutine. Control returns to the next line.
GOTO	Branches execution to the specified configuration block.
SWITCH	Selects a configuration block based on user response.
TIMEOUT	Specifies the length of time to wait before making an automatic selection.

Creating a Shared Memory Pool

Sometimes it's hard to understand why you should have to worry about how your computer's memory is configured, isn't it? After all, if you install 16M of memory in your PC, shouldn't programs be able to use what they need without requiring you to determine whether they need EMS or XMS memory? Unfortunately, while both types of memory may be allocated from the same physical memory, the two memory specifications aren't really compatible. If a program needs EMS memory, it probably can't use XMS memory instead, and vice-versa. If your favorite game program insists that all system memory be allocated as EMS memory, you'll probably have to have separate configurations for the game program and Windows, which uses XMS but not EMS memory.

It's really complications like this one that make PCs so difficult for many people. Most people just don't care about what type of memory their PC has, as long as they can run their programs.

Fortunately, the version of EMM386.EXE included with MS-DOS 6.x has changed the way EMS and XMS memory are created from the system's physical memory. Unless you specifically prevent EMM386.EXE from doing so, it now allocates both EMS and XMS memory from a shared pool. When a program requests either type of memory, EMM386.EXE provides the correct type and amount from the common memory pool. You no longer have to specify how much XMS memory should be converted to EMS memory. In fact, you probably would be better off not specifying an amount, and simply allowing EMM386.EXE to control memory allocation itself. If you're still using MS-DOS 5, this new version of EMM386.EXE is probably worth the upgrade cost all by itself!

Summary

In this chapter you've learned how to define your memory management goals and how to determine what your programs need. You've learned that in memory management it isn't always possible to provide every program with all the resources it could use, while at the same time achieving maximum system performance. As you learned, though, it is possible to create a good compromise that works well for your specific needs.

In the next chapter we'll begin looking at some of the tools you can use to find all the memory that's available on your system. You'll use the tools that come with DOS to find even more memory than you thought you had.

Chapter 4

Finding All Your Memory

Eureka!

—Archimedes

In the first part of this book, you've learned the basics of memory management. You've learned about the often confusing array of terms used to describe the different types of PC memory, and how to understand the methods used to address memory in your system. You also learned how to define your memory management goals. These essentials provide a solid foundation for the remainder of this book, which deals with actually using the memory management tools that are available to you.

Before going any farther, though, I'd like to say a few words about memory management tools and how I'll be presenting them. I hope you agree that my approach makes using these tools much easier than they have ever seemed before. One of the most difficult aspects of learning about different memory management tools is that the tools themselves often change, depending on which DOS version you're using. As you wade through often dry, boring text, keeping track of which commands and options apply to your version can be overwhelming. Why does it have to be so difficult? Why should you have to keep track of details that should be presented simply and clearly?

I search and search in vain.

—Sophocles, *Oedipus Rex*

Believe me, you're not alone in asking these questions. That's why I've decided to use a different approach. Instead of lumping all of the different versions of memory management tools together and making you sort out the details, I'll be using separate sections for the different versions. You can simply skip over the material that doesn't apply to your DOS version.

For example, the MEM command appears in each of the three major DOS versions in common use today. But each of these versions, MS-DOS 5, MS-DOS 6.x, and Novell DOS 7, has different options for the MEM command. All you need to do is to read the appropriate section that applies to the version of DOS you use.

A Memory Management Plan

Regardless of the DOS version you prefer, you'll follow many of the same steps in managing your PC's memory. Basically, these steps are as follows:

1. Define your goals (see Chapter 3).

2. Create a boot disk in case of emergencies (see Chapter 3).

3. Examine your current memory status. This chapter shows you how to see what's happening with memory using the tools provided with your version of DOS (such as MEM and DEBUG).

4. Alter your CONFIG.SYS and AUTOEXEC.BAT files using EDIT (see Chapter 1). The following chapters on specific DOS versions provide guidelines on the changes you'll need to make including using REM to disable commands temporarily, changing the order in which you load TSRs and device drivers in order to squeeze them perfectly into open memory slots, and placing device drivers and TSRs into upper memory.

5. Reboot your system to make your changes active (a quick way to reboot is to press the **Ctrl-Alt-Del** keys simultaneously). If you weren't successful, return to step 3 and repeat the process until your memory is configured the way you want it.

As you work through these steps, you'll probably return to steps 3–5 several times to test new variations of system configurations. Don't forget to save your changes following step 4, and to reboot as indicated in step 5.

So now let's move onward, and begin learning to use DOS's memory management tools.

Using MEM

The MEM command supplies you with detailed information showing how your system's memory is being used, and what areas of memory are still available for use. It tells you what device drivers, TSRs, and other programs are currently loaded into memory, as well as how much memory each is currently using. It also shows you the addresses of unused, and therefore available, memory blocks.

> *If we do not find anything pleasant, at least we shall find something new.*
>
> —Voltaire

Knowing how memory is already being used is basic to being able to make better use of available memory resources. If you know, for example, that a device driver or TSR is loaded into conventional memory, but would fit into an upper memory block, you could probably free some conventional memory by loading the device driver or TSR into upper memory. If you can see that a device driver or TSR you're trying to load into upper memory is still being placed in conventional memory, you can probably use one of the memory detail reports to determine why. Finally, if upper memory is in short supply, you can use the memory detail report to help plan the most efficient use of memory.

Tip

As you juggle different system configurations, you'll probably create several different MEM report printouts. Label each with the current date and time so you can keep track of your progress.

Since the MEM command differs somewhat in each of the major DOS versions, each has its own section. You can save yourself some time by simply skipping those that do not apply to your DOS version.

Note

Don't worry if your MEM reports display different numbers than those shown in the following sections. Your reports will show the information specific to your system, and it's very unlikely you'll have numbers that match those in the examples.

Using the MS-DOS 5 MEM Command

The MS-DOS 5 MEM command is a basic memory management tool that tells you how your system's memory is being used. In this section, we'll examine the options available with this version of the MEM command.

Tip

The MS-DOS 5 MEM command lacks the ability to display a single screenful of information at a time. If you are viewing MEM reports on-screen, you can add | **MORE** after any MEM switches (such as **MEM /DEBUG | MORE**) to display one page at a time. You may also find it convenient to redirect the report to your printer using the > **PRN** redirection operator.

If you use the MEM command without any switches, you'll see a basic memory report similar to the following:

```
   655360 bytes total conventional memory
   655360 bytes available to MS-DOS
   608832 largest executable program size

   917504 bytes total EMS memory
   425984 bytes free EMS memory

 15728640 bytes total contiguous extended memory
        0 bytes available contiguous extended memory
 12910592 bytes available XMS memory
          MS-DOS resident in High Memory Area
```

As a memory management tool, the basic MEM memory report doesn't really provide you very much useful information. While memory totals are displayed, there's really no information displayed that you can use to help you plan your memory management strategy. For that information, you'll need to use one of the optional reports.

Using the /CLASSIFY Option

The first MS-DOS 5 MEM report option is the /CLASSIFY option (which you can abbreviate as /C). This report displays information on each device driver, TSR, or program loaded into conventional or upper memory. It also shows the memory size of each of these, as well as the size of any unused available memory. The /CLASSIFY report does not show memory addresses, but as you'll learn in Chapter 5, memory address information isn't too useful in MS-DOS 5, anyway.

Tip

Use the /CLASSIFY option whenever you check the status of your memory. Type **MEM /C** at the DOS prompt. Also, you may want to use |MORE to display one page at a time. You can combine these commands by typing **MEM /C |MORE**.

The following example shows a typical MS-DOS 5 MEM /CLASSIFY report— to get this report, type **MEM /C** at the DOS prompt:

```
Conventional Memory :

    Name              Size in Decimal        Size in Hex
  ------------      ----------------------   ------------

    MSDOS             18160    ( 17.7K)         46F0
    ASPI4DOS           6656    (  6.5K)         1A00
    HIMEM              1152    (  1.1K)          480
    EMM386             3104    (  3.0K)          C20
    SATISFAX           3952    (  3.9K)          F70
    IFSHLP             3856    (  3.8K)          F10
    COMMAND            3200    (  3.1K)          C80
    CASMGR             5504    (  5.4K)         1580
    FREE                 64    (  0.1K)           40
    FREE                272    (  0.3K)          110
    FREE             609136    (594.9K)         94B70
```

```
Total  FREE :        609472      (595.2K)

Upper Memory :

    Name             Size in Decimal        Size in Hex
  -------------    ---------------------    -------------
    SYSTEM           250912   (245.0K)        3D420
    MVSOUND           10784   ( 10.5K)        2A20
    ASWCDTSH          14592   ( 14.3K)        3900
    MOUSE             17072   ( 16.7K)        42B0
    MSCDEX            16160   ( 15.8K)        3F20
    SMARTDRV          30352   ( 29.6K)        7690
    DOSKEY             4640   (  4.5K)        1220
    FREE               2000   (  2.0K)        7D0
    FREE                 96   (  0.1K)        60
    FREE              13440   ( 13.1K)        3480
    FREE               6896   (  6.7K)        1AF0
    FREE              17792   ( 17.4K)        4580

Total  FREE :         40224      ( 39.3K)

Total bytes available to programs (Conventional+Upper) : 649696 (634.5K)
Largest executable program size :                        608832 (594.6K)
Largest available upper memory block :                    17792 ( 17.4K)

     917504 bytes total EMS memory
     425984 bytes free EMS memory

   15728640 bytes total contiguous extended memory
          0 bytes available contiguous extended memory
   12910592 bytes available XMS memory
              MS-DOS resident in High Memory Area
```

As you examine the MEM /CLASSIFY report, you can learn several pieces of quite useful information. First, you can tell whether a device driver or TSR is loaded into conventional memory or into upper memory. You may find that one or more device drivers or TSRs that you intended to load into upper memory are actually being loaded into conventional memory. As you apply the memory management techniques you'll learn in Chapter 5, you'll rely heavily upon the MEM /CLASSIFY report to determine the success of your efforts.

The next useful piece of information provided by this report is the *memory image size* of each device driver, TSR, and program currently loaded. The memory image size is the amount of memory actually used by a device driver, TSR, or program once it has been loaded into memory. Usually, this size will be similar to the file size of the device driver, TSR, or program, but you'll encounter some surprises here, too.

For example, the memory image size of the mouse driver shown in the above report is 17,072 bytes. The file size for that same driver is 55,160. This discrepancy between memory image size and file size produces one of the most perplexing problems in memory management—device drivers or TSRs that seem like they should fit into upper memory but load into conventional memory, instead. Even though the device driver or TSR shrinks to its memory image size once it's loaded into memory, free memory at least as large as the file size must be available during loading. In Chapter 5 you'll learn how to deal with this problem.

Using the /DEBUG Option

The next MS-DOS 5 MEM report option is the /DEBUG report. This report is considerably more technically oriented than the /CLASSIFY report, showing DOS's internal device drivers in addition to the items you load in CONFIG.SYS and AUTOEXEC.BAT. The /DEBUG report also shows the memory address where each device driver, TSR, or program is loaded.

Unfortunately for the non-nerd PC user, the /DEBUG report shows all of its information using hexadecimal (base 16) notation rather than the more familiar decimal numbers. I guess Microsoft felt that anyone brave enough to try to understand such a detailed report would be able to convert mentally between number systems with ease. For those of you who can't make such an easy conversion, you can use the following QBasic program to convert between decimal and hexadecimal numbers:

```
INPUT "Number? (add &H before hexadecimal values)"; yourval$
PRINT yourval$; " equals "
PRINT VAL(yourval$); " in decimal, and "
PRINT HEX$(VAL(yourval$)); " in hexadecimal."
```

See Chapter 2 for more information on entering and using this program.

The MS-DOS 5 MEM /DEBUG report includes quite a bit of information, most of which you'll never use. The following is an example of a typical /DEBUG report:

```
Address     Name          Size      Type
-------     --------      ------    ------
000000                    000400    Interrupt Vector
000400                    000100    ROM Communication Area
000500                    000200    DOS Communication Area

000700      IO            000A60    System Data
                CON                     System Device Driver
                AUX                     System Device Driver
                PRN                     System Device Driver
                CLOCK$                  System Device Driver
                A: - C:                 System Device Driver
                COM1                    System Device Driver
                LPT1                    System Device Driver
                LPT2                    System Device Driver
                LPT3                    System Device Driver
                COM2                    System Device Driver
                COM3                    System Device Driver
                COM4                    System Device Driver

001160      MSDOS         0013D0    System Data

002530      IO            006B30    System Data
                ASPI4DOS  001A00      DEVICE=
                  SCSIMGR$             Installed Device Driver
                HIMEM     000480      DEVICE=
                  XMSXXXX0             Installed Device Driver
                EMM386    000C20      DEVICE=
                  EMMXXXX0             Installed Device Driver
                SATISFAX  000F70      DEVICE=
                  $INTELFX             Installed Device Driver
                IFSHLP    000F10      DEVICE=
                  IFS$HLP$             Installed Device Driver
                          000A70      FILES=
                          000050      FCBS=
                          000200      BUFFERS=
                          0008F0      LASTDRIVE=
                          000BC0      STACKS=
```

```
009070       MSDOS        000040     System Program

0090C0       COMMAND      000030     Data
009100       COMMAND      000A50     Program
009B60       MSDOS        000040     -- Free --
009BB0       COMMAND      000200     Environment
009DC0       MSDOS        000110     -- Free --
009EE0       CASMGR       001580     Program
00B470       MEM          000120     Environment
00B5A0       MEM          0176F0     Program
022CA0       MSDOS        07D340     -- Free --
09FFF0       SYSTEM       0114A0     System Program

0B14A0       IO           002A30     System Data
             MVSOUND      002A20       DEVICE=
             MVPROAS                   Installed Device Driver
0B3EE0       IO           003910     System Data
             ASWCDTSH     003900       DEVICE=
             CDROM1                    Installed Device Driver
0B7800       MSDOS        0007D0     -- Free --
0B7FE0       SYSTEM       010020     System Program

0C8010       IO           0042C0     System Data
             MOUSE        0042B0       DEVICE=
             MS$MOUSE                  Installed Device Driver
0CC2E0       MSDOS        000060     -- Free --
0CC350       MSCDEX       003F20     Program
0D0280       SMARTDRV     007690     Program
0D7920       DOSKEY       001220     Program
0D8B50       MSDOS        003480     -- Free --
0DBFE0       SYSTEM       0024F0     System Program

0DE4E0       MSDOS        001AF0     -- Free --
0DFFE0       SYSTEM       019A80     System Program

0F9A70       MSDOS        004580     -- Free --


     655360 bytes total conventional memory
     655360 bytes available to MS-DOS
     608832 largest executable program size
```

```
    Handle      EMS Name       Size
    - - - - - - -   - - - - - - - -   - - - - - -
         0                     060000
         1                     008000
         2                     010000

    917504 bytes total EMS memory
    425984 bytes free EMS memory

  15728640 bytes total contiguous extended memory
         0 bytes available contiguous extended memory
  12910592 bytes available XMS memory
             MS-DOS resident in High Memory Area
```

As you examine the MEM /DEBUG report, keep in mind that the first address is zero, not one. Although you probably start counting items using the number one to designate the first item, computers often use zero to designate the first location.

The /DEBUG report begins by identifying quite a few internal system structures, such as the interrupt vectors, ROM and DOS communications areas, and standard system device drivers. These items provide no information that is useful from a memory management standpoint, because you cannot modify any of these.

The first items of importance to memory management are the installed device drivers, which are identified by DEVICE=. Depending on the particular device driver, some of these items may be candidates for loading into upper memory. Chapter 3 provided information on determining whether device drivers could be loaded into upper memory.

Program items listed after the installed device drivers but before address 09FFF0 (see the left column of the report) are TSRs and programs that are loaded into conventional memory. You can identify program items by the name shown in the second column of information. Any program items that are TSRs (as opposed to application programs or MEM itself) may also be candidates for loading into upper memory. Address 09FFF0 signals the end of conventional memory.

Device drivers and TSRs that are currently loaded into upper memory are listed following address 09FFF0. Available upper memory blocks are the items following address 09FFF0 that are marked "-- Free --." To maximize available conventional memory, you'll want to place as many device drivers and TSRs into these free upper memory blocks as possible.

The final information in the /DEBUG report details available conventional, EMS, extended, and XMS memory. Don't worry if you see "0 bytes available contiguous extended memory," as shown above. This simply means that all extended memory is being managed as XMS memory, which is exactly what you want in most cases. (The only exception to this is if you use programs that include their own DOS extenders—see Chapter 3 for more information on DOS extenders.)

The /DEBUG report seems to include quite a bit of information, but in reality you'll probably find that the /CLASSIFY report provides all the information you'll need for memory management purposes. Also, because the /DEBUG report reports information only in hexadecimal numbers, you'll probably find that the /DEBUG report is a little harder to understand.

Using the /PROGRAM Option

The final MS-DOS 5 MEM report option, the /PROGRAM report, is very similar to the /DEBUG report. In fact, you may even have difficulty noticing the differences between these two reports. The /DEBUG report shows more detail on internal DOS structures than the /PROGRAM report, but otherwise the two reports are identical. Here's a typical /PROGRAM report:

```
Address     Name        Size      Type
-------     --------    ------    ------
000000                  000400    Interrupt Vector
000400                  000100    ROM Communication Area
000500                  000200    DOS Communication Area

000700      IO          000A60    System Data

001160      MSDOS       0013D0    System Data

002530      IO          006B30    System Data
            ASPI4DOS    001A00      DEVICE=
            HIMEM       000480      DEVICE=
            EMM386      000C20      DEVICE=
```

	SATISFAX	000F70	DEVICE=
	IFSHLP	000F10	DEVICE=
		000A70	FILES=
		000050	FCBS=
		000200	BUFFERS=
		0008F0	LASTDRIVE=
		000BC0	STACKS=
009070	MSDOS	000040	System Program
0090C0	COMMAND	000030	Data
009100	COMMAND	000A50	Program
009B60	MSDOS	000040	-- Free --
009BB0	COMMAND	000200	Environment
009DC0	MSDOS	000110	-- Free --
009EE0	CASMGR	001580	Program
00B470	MEM5	000120	Environment
00B5A0	MEM5	0176F0	Program
022CA0	MSDOS	07D340	-- Free --
09FFF0	SYSTEM	0114A0	System Program
0B14A0	IO	002A30	System Data
	MVSOUND	002A20	DEVICE=
0B3EE0	IO	003910	System Data
	ASWCDTSH	003900	DEVICE=
0B7800	MSDOS	0007D0	-- Free --
0B7FE0	SYSTEM	010020	System Program
0C8010	IO	0042C0	System Data
	MOUSE	0042B0	DEVICE=
0CC2E0	MSDOS	000060	-- Free --
0CC350	MSCDEX	003F20	Program
0D0280	SMARTDRV	007690	Program
0D7920	DOSKEY	001220	Program
0D8B50	MSDOS	003480	-- Free --
0DBFE0	SYSTEM	0024F0	System Program
0DE4E0	MSDOS	001AF0	-- Free --
0DFFE0	SYSTEM	019A80	System Program
0F9A70	MSDOS	004580	-- Free --

```
 655360 bytes total conventional memory
 655360 bytes available to MS-DOS
 608832 largest executable program size

 917504 bytes total EMS memory
 425984 bytes free EMS memory

15728640 bytes total contiguous extended memory
       0 bytes available contiguous extended memory
12910592 bytes available XMS memory
         MS-DOS resident in High Memory Area
```

Because the /PROGRAM report is just a simplified version of the /DEBUG report, there's really no point in using the /PROGRAM report for memory management purposes.

Of the three MS-DOS 5 MEM report options, the /CLASSIFY option should serve all of your memory management needs at least as well as either of the other two reports.

If you are using MS-DOS 5, you can now skip the next two sections on the MS-DOS 6.x and Novell DOS 7 MEM commands and go directly to the section on using MSD.

Using the MS-DOS 6.x MEM Command

If you use MS-DOS 6.x, you'll find the MEM command is even more useful as a basic memory management than it was in version 5. In this section, we'll examine the options available with this version of the MEM command.

Note

MS-DOS 6.x, the term used in this book, refers to both MS-DOS 6.0 and MS-DOS 6.2.

The basic MEM report in MS-DOS 6.x is a greatly enhanced version of the version 5 report. For the first time, the basic report now includes information on upper memory, as well as statistics showing how much of each type of memory has been used and how much is still available. The following is a typical MS-DOS 6.x basic MEM report—to get this report, type **MEM** at the DOS prompt.

```
Memory Type        Total  =  Used   +   Free
----------------   -------   -------    -------
Conventional        640K       45K       595K
Upper               131K       92K        39K
Reserved            384K      384K         0K
Extended (XMS)*   15,229K    2,621K    12,608K
----------------   -------   -------    -------
Total memory      16,384K    3,142K    13,242K

Total under 1 MB    771K      137K       634K

Total Expanded (EMS)                896K (917,504 bytes)
Free Expanded (EMS)*                416K (425,984 bytes)

 * EMM386 is using XMS memory to simulate EMS memory as needed.
   Free EMS memory may change as free XMS memory changes.

Largest executable program size     595K (609,136 bytes)
Largest free upper memory block      17K  (17,808 bytes)
MS-DOS is resident in the high memory area.
```

This basic report points out one of the major memory management improvements in MS-DOS 6.x—a shared XMS/EMS memory pool. The note

```
 * EMM386 is using XMS memory to simulate EMS memory as needed.
   Free EMS memory may change as free XMS memory changes.
```

tells you that both types of memory are being allocated from the same physical memory. This shared memory pool greatly simplifies your memory management task in MS-DOS 6.x, because you don't have to decide between allocating memory as EMS or XMS memory.

Using the /PAGE Option

The first MS-DOS 6.x MEM option isn't a report, but rather a usability enhancement. The /PAGE option, which you can specify as /P, causes long MEM reports to be displayed one page at a time.

Using the /CLASSIFY Option

The first MS-DOS 6.x MEM optional report is the /CLASSIFY option (which
you can abbreviate as /C). This report builds on the basic MEM report by
showing how much conventional and upper memory is being used by each
loaded device driver, TSR, and program. The following is a typical MEM
/CLASSIFY report—to get this report, type **MEM /C** at the DOS prompt.

```
Modules using memory below 1 MB:

  Name        Total      =  Conventional  +  Upper Memory
  --------   ----------    --------------    ------------
  MSDOS       18,333  (18K)   18,333  (18K)        0   (0K)
  ASPI4DOS     6,672   (7K)    6,672   (7K)        0   (0K)
  HIMEM        1,168   (1K)    1,168   (1K)        0   (0K)
  EMM386       3,120   (3K)    3,120   (3K)        0   (0K)
  SATISFAX     3,968   (4K)    3,968   (4K)        0   (0K)
  IFSHLP       3,872   (4K)    3,872   (4K)        0   (0K)
  COMMAND      3,248   (3K)    3,248   (3K)        0   (0K)
  CASMGR       5,520   (5K)    5,520   (5K)        0   (0K)
  MVSOUND     10,832  (11K)        0   (0K)   10,832  (11K)
  ASWCDTSH    14,640  (14K)        0   (0K)   14,640  (14K)
  MOUSE       17,120  (17K)        0   (0K)   17,120  (17K)
  MSCDEX      16,176  (16K)        0   (0K)   16,176  (16K)
  SMARTDRV    30,368  (30K)        0   (0K)   30,368  (30K)
  DOSKEY       4,656   (5K)        0   (0K)    4,656   (5K)
  Free       649,536 (634K)  609,232 (595K)   40,304  (39K)
```

```
Memory Summary:

Type of Memory        Total    =    Used    +    Free
----------------   ----------   ----------   ----------
Conventional          655,360       46,128      609,232
Upper                 134,096       93,792       40,304
Reserved              393,216      393,216            0
Extended (XMS)*    15,594,544    2,683,952   12,910,592
----------------   ----------   ----------   ----------
Total memory       16,777,216    3,217,088   13,560,128

Total under 1 MB      789,456      139,920      649,536

Total Expanded (EMS)               917,504    (896K)
Free Expanded (EMS)*               425,984    (416K)

* EMM386 is using XMS memory to simulate EMS memory as needed.
  Free EMS memory may change as free XMS memory changes.

Largest executable program size    609,136    (595K)
Largest free upper memory block     17,808     (17K)
MS-DOS is resident in the high memory area.
```

The MEM /CLASSIFY report contains several pieces of quite useful information. First, you can tell whether a device driver or TSR is loaded into conventional memory, upper memory, or both. You may find that one or more device drivers or TSRs that you intended to load into upper memory are actually being loaded into conventional memory, or into a combination of conventional and upper memory. For example, the SMARTDRV disk cache may be split into two pieces if it cannot be totally loaded into upper memory. As you apply the memory management techniques you'll learn in Chapter 6, you'll rely heavily upon the MEM /CLASSIFY report to determine the success of your efforts.

The next useful piece of information provided by this report is the *memory image size* of each device driver, TSR, and program currently loaded. The memory image size is the amount of memory actually used by a device driver, TSR, or program once it has been loaded into memory. Usually, this size will be similar to the file size of the a device driver, TSR, or program, but you'll encounter some surprises here, too.

For example, the memory image size of the mouse driver shown in the above report is 17,120 bytes. The file size for that same driver is 55,160. This discrepancy between memory image size and file size produces one of the most perplexing problems in memory management—device drivers or TSRs that seem like they should fit into upper memory but load into conventional memory, instead. Even though the device driver or TSR shrinks to its memory image size once it's loaded into memory, free memory at least as large as the file size must be available during loading. In Chapter 6 you'll learn how to deal with this problem.

Using the /DEBUG Option

The next MS-DOS 6 MEM report option is the /DEBUG report (which you can abbreviate as /D). This report is considerably more technically oriented than the /CLASSIFY report, showing DOS's internal device drivers in addition to the items you load in CONFIG.SYS and AUTOEXEC.BAT. The /DEBUG report also shows the memory address where each device driver, TSR, or program is loaded.

The MS-DOS 6 MEM /DEBUG report includes quite a bit of information, some of which you'll never use, but some which will be very useful as you fine-tune your memory management scheme. The following is an example of a typical /DEBUG report:

```
Conventional Memory Detail:

    Segment          Total        Name      Type
    -------       ----------------  ----------  --------
     00000        1,039   (1K)                Interrupt Vector
     00040          271   (0K)                ROM Communication Area
     00050          527   (1K)                DOS Communication Area
     00070        2,656   (3K)    IO          System Data
                                   CON         System Device Driver
                                   AUX         System Device Driver
                                   PRN         System Device Driver
                                   CLOCK$      System Device Driver
                                   A: - C:     System Device Driver
                                   COM1        System Device Driver
                                   LPT1        System Device Driver
                                   LPT2        System Device Driver
                                   LPT3        System Device Driver
                                   COM2        System Device Driver
```

```
                                    COM3        System Device Driver
                                    COM4        System Device Driver
        00116         5,072   (5K)  MSDOS       System Data
        00253        27,456  (27K)  IO          System Data
                      6,656   (7K)    SCSIMGR$  Installed Device=ASPI4DOS
                      1,152   (1K)    XMSXXXX0  Installed Device=HIMEM
                      3,104   (3K)    EMMXXXX0  Installed Device=EMM386
                      3,952   (4K)    $INTELFX  Installed Device=SATISFAX
                      3,856   (4K)    IFS$HLP$  Installed Device=IFSHLP
                      2,672   (3K)              FILES=50
                         80   (0K)              FCBS=1
                        512   (1K)              BUFFERS=10
                      2,288   (2K)              LASTDRIVE=Z
                      3,008   (3K)              STACKS=9,256
        00907            80   (0K)  MSDOS       System Program
        0090C            64   (0K)  COMMAND     Data
        00910         2,656   (3K)  COMMAND     Program
        009B6            80   (0K)  MSDOS       -- Free --
        009BB           528   (1K)  COMMAND     Environment
        009DC           288   (0K)  MEM         Environment
        009EE         5,520   (5K)  CASMGR      Program
        00B47        88,992  (87K)  MEM         Program
        02101       520,160 (508K)  MSDOS       -- Free --
```

Upper Memory Detail:

Segment	Region	Total		Name	Type
0B14A	1	10,816	(11K)	IO	System Data
		10,784	(11K)	MVPROAS	Installed Device=MVSOUND
0B3EE	1	14,624	(14K)	IO	System Data
		14,592	(14K)	CDROM1	Installed Device=ASWCDTSH
0B780	1	2,016	(2K)	MSDOS	-- Free --
0C801	2	17,104	(17K)	IO	System Data
		17,072	(17K)	MS$MOUSE	Installed Device=MOUSE
0CC2E	2	112	(0K)	MSDOS	-- Free --
0CC35	2	16,176	(16K)	MSCDEX	Program
0D028	2	30,368	(30K)	SMARTDRV	Program
0D792	2	4,656	(5K)	DOSKEY	Program
0D8B5	2	13,456	(13K)	MSDOS	-- Free --
0DE4E	3	6,912	(7K)	MSDOS	-- Free --

```
0F9A7      4     17,808   (17K)  MSDOS        -- Free --
```

Memory Summary:

Type of Memory	Total	=	Used	+	Free
Conventional	655,360		46,128		609,232
Upper	134,096		93,792		40,304
Reserved	393,216		393,216		0
Extended (XMS)*	15,594,544		2,683,952		12,910,592
Total memory	16,777,216		3,217,088		13,560,128
Total under 1 MB	789,456		139,920		649,536

Handle	EMS Name	Size
0		060000
1		008000
2		010000

```
Total Expanded (EMS)              917,504   (896K)
Free Expanded (EMS)*              425,984   (416K)
```

```
* EMM386 is using XMS memory to simulate EMS memory as needed.
  Free EMS memory may change as free XMS memory changes.
```

```
Memory accessible using Int 15h        0   (0K)
Largest executable program size  609,136   (595K)
Largest free upper memory block   17,808   (17K)
MS-DOS is resident in the high memory area.
```

```
XMS version  3.00; driver version  3.16
EMS version  4.00
```

Don't be confused by the addresses displayed by the MEM /DEBUG report. Computers use zero to designate the first memory location.

The /DEBUG report begins by showing the details of how conventional memory is allocated. This section of the report identifies quite a few internal system structures, such as the interrupt vectors, ROM and DOS communications areas, and standard system device drivers. These items provide no information that is useful from a memory management standpoint, because you cannot modify any of them.

The first items of importance to memory management are the installed device drivers, which are identified by DEVICE=. Depending on the particular device driver, some of these items may be candidates for loading into upper memory. Chapter 3 provided information on determining whether device drivers could be loaded into upper memory.

Program items listed in the conventional memory detail section after the installed device drivers are TSRs and programs that are loaded into conventional memory. You can identify program items by the name shown in the Name column. Any program items that are TSRs (as opposed to application programs or MEM itself) may also be candidates for loading into upper memory.

Next the report shows the details of upper memory usage. This section of the report may show one or more *regions*—each of which represents a single, contiguous upper memory block. Device drivers and TSRs that are currently loaded into upper memory are listed in this section of the report. Available upper memory blocks are the items which are marked "-- Free --." To maximize available conventional memory, you'll want to place as many device drivers and TSRs into these free upper memory blocks as possible.

The final information in the /DEBUG report details available conventional, EMS, extended, and XMS memory. Don't worry if you see "Memory accessible using Int 15h 0 (0K)," as shown above. This simply means that all extended memory is being managed as XMS memory, which is exactly what you want in most cases. (The only exception to this is if you use programs that include their own DOS extenders—see Chapter 3 for more information on DOS extenders.)

One very important memory management enhancement in MS-DOS 6.x, compared to MS-DOS 5, is that you now have the ability to specify which upper memory region should be used to load specific device drivers and TSRs. The MS-DOS 6.x MEM /DEBUG report is very useful in determining exactly where each device driver or TSR is being loaded. By default, when you simply use DEVICEHIGH, INSTALLHIGH, LOADHIGH, or LH without specifying which upper memory region to use, each device driver or TSR loads into the largest available upper memory block. As you'll learn in Chapter 6, you can often make much more efficient use of memory by using the smallest possible upper memory region to load each device driver or TSR.

Using the /FREE Option

The next MEM report option is the /FREE option (which you can abbreviate as /F). This report shows the total size and the available size of conventional memory and the upper memory regions. Although the /FREE report does not show nearly the level of detail that is included in the /DEBUG report, you'll find this report especially useful when you're working on system configurations, because the information on free memory blocks won't scroll off the screen. The following is a typical MEM /FREE report:

```
Free Conventional Memory:

    Segment          Total
    -------     ----------------
     009B6              80     (0K)
     009DC             288     (0K)
     00B47          88,992     (87K)
     02101         520,160    (508K)

    Total Free:  609,520    (595K)

Free Upper Memory:

    Region   Largest Free       Total Free        Total Size
    ------   --------------    --------------    --------------
       1      2,016    (2K)      2,016    (2K)     27,488    (27K)
       2     13,456   (13K)     13,568   (13K)     81,888    (80K)
       3      6,912    (7K)      6,912    (7K)      6,912     (7K)
       4     17,808   (17K)     17,808   (17K)     17,808    (17K)
```

The Free Upper Memory section of the MEM /FREE report is particularly useful, because it shows the total size of each upper memory region. If you're having difficulties loading device drivers or TSRs into upper memory because the device driver or TSR takes more memory to load than its memory image size, compare the total size of each upper memory region with the disk file size of the device driver or TSR. You won't be able to load a device driver or TSR into an upper memory region unless the total size of the region exceeds the disk file size of the device driver or TSR.

Using the /MODULE Option

The final MS-DOS 6.x MEM report option is the /MODULE option (which you can abbreviate as /M). This report shows where a device driver or TSR is loaded into memory, and how much memory it is currently using. To use this option, you must specify which device driver or TSR you want to examine. For example, the following report shows the result of using the command MEM /M:MOUSE:

```
MOUSE is using the following memory:

 Segment  Region      Total       Type
 -------  ------   ---------------  --------
  0C801      2      17072  (17K)   Installed Device=MOUSE
                   ---------------
 Total Size:       17,072  (17K)
```

The /MODULE report is most useful when you're trying to locate a single device driver or TSR, but don't want to wade through the entire /DEBUG report. For those few device drivers or TSRs that can use more than one memory region, using the /MODULE report can also ensure that you don't miss one of the memory areas.

As you work through your memory management options in Chapter 6, you'll find the MS-DOS 6.x MEM command to be one of your most useful tools. You can now skip forward in this chapter to the section on MSD to see another valuable tool.

Using the Novell DOS 7 MEM Command

Many of Novell DOS 7's commands are similar to the commands in MS-DOS, but there are significant differences, especially in command options. The Novell DOS 7 MEM command, for example, has ten optional reports, a much larger variety than the MS-DOS 5 or MS-DOS 6.x MEM commands offer. Still, the Novell DOS 7 MEM command is a basic memory management tool, because it provides the detailed information you need to optimize your system's memory usage.

If you use the Novell DOS 7 MEM command without any optional switches, you'll see a basic report similar to the following:

```
+ Memory Type --------- Total Bytes ( Kbytes  ) ----- Available For Programs -+
|                      |                          |                           |
|  Conventional        |      655,360 (     640K )|        609,136 (     594K )|
|  Upper               |      314,208 (     306K )|         40,304 (      39K )|
|  Extended            |   15,728,640 (  15,360K )|              0 (       0K )|
|  Extended via XMS    |      --------            |     12,910,592 (  12,608K )|
|  EMS                 |      917,504 (     896K )|        425,984 (     416K )|
+---------------------------------------------------------------------------
|  Largest executable program:  609,136 ( 594K )                             |
+---------------------------------------------------------------------------+
```

While the basic Novell DOS 7 MEM command provides general information on memory usage, it does not provide the kind of detailed information you'll need for memory management purposes. In the following sections, we'll examine the optional reports to see how you can use them to assist you as you apply the techniques covered in Chapter 7.

Using the /P Option

The first Novell DOS 7 MEM option isn't a report, but rather a usability enhancement. The /P causes long MEM reports to be displayed one page at a time.

Tip

You may find it useful to redirect MEM reports to your printer using the > PRN redirection operator, as in **MEM /C > PRN**.

Using the /A Option

The Novell DOS 7 MEM /A option is really just the equivalent of adding together all of the other report options. The /A option displays all memory information in a single, large report. Because this same information is shown in the individual reports, I won't include an example of the /A report here.

In most cases, you'll find it's better to concentrate on the one report that details the memory information you really need, rather than trying to wade through the complete /A report.

Using the /B Option

The Novell DOS 7 MEM /B option displays information on how conventional memory is being used. This report shows the same information as the first section of the /A report. The following is a typical MEM /B report:

```
+-- Address --- Name ----- Size ------------- Type ---------------------------+
|    0:0000 | -------- |    400h,   1,024 | Interrupt vectors                |
|   40:0000 | -------- |    100h,     256 | ROM BIOS data area               |
|   50:0000 |     DOS  |    200h,     512 | DOS data area                    |
|   70:0000 |     BIOS |    A60h,   2,656 | Device drivers                   |
|  116:0000 |     DOS  |   13D0h,   5,072 | System                           |
|  253:0000 |     DOS  |   6B40h,  27,456 | System                           |
|  255:0000 | SCSIMGR$ |   1A00h,   6,656 | DEVICE = installed device driver |
|  3F6:0000 | XMSXXXX0 |    480h,   1,152 | DEVICE = installed device driver |
|  43F:0000 | EMMXXXX0 |    C20h,   3,104 | DEVICE = installed device driver |
|  502:0000 | $INTELFX |    F70h,   3,952 | DEVICE = installed device driver |
|  5FA:0000 | IFS$HLP$ |    F10h,   3,856 | DEVICE = installed device driver |
|  907:0000 |     DOS  |     50h,      80 | System                           |
|  90C:0000 | COMMAND  |     40h,      64 | Data                             |
|  910:0000 | COMMAND  |    A60h,   2,656 | Program                          |
|  9B6:0000 | -------- |     50h,      80 | FREE                             |
|  9BB:0000 | COMMAND  |    210h,     528 | Environment                      |
|  9DC:0000 |     MEM  |    120h,     288 | Environment                      |
|  9EE:0000 | CASMGR   |   1590h,   5,520 | Program                          |
|  B47:0000 |     MEM  |  15810h,  88,080 | Program                          |
| 20C8:0000 | -------- |  7F370h, 521,072 | FREE                             |
| 9FFF:0000 |     DOS  |  114B0h,  70,832 | System                           |
+-----------------------------------------------------------------------------+
```

The first part of the MEM /B report shows system information, such as the interrupt vectors, ROM and DOS data areas, and standard system device drivers. These items provide no information that is useful from a memory management standpoint, because you cannot modify any of them.

The first items of importance to memory management are the installed device drivers, which are identified by DEVICE=. Depending on the particular device driver, some of these items may be candidates for loading into upper memory. Chapter 3 provided information on determining whether device drivers could be loaded into upper memory.

Program items listed in the conventional memory detail section after the installed device drivers are TSRs and programs that are loaded into conventional memory. You can identify program items by the name shown in the Name column. Any program items that are TSRs (as opposed to application programs or MEM itself) may also be candidates for loading into upper memory.

Using the /CLASSIFY Option

The MEM /CLASSIFY option displays a summary version of the /B report. Only those device drivers and TSRs you load into conventional memory are listed in the /CLASSIFY report. The following is a typical /CLASSIFY report:

```
Conventional memory:

+- Name ------------- Size in Decimal ------ Size in Hex -+
|      DOS |    89,169 (      87K )  |          15C51      |
|  SCSIMGR$ |     6,656 (       6K )  |           1A00      |
|  XMSXXXX0 |     1,152 (       1K )  |            480      |
|  EMMXXXX0 |     3,104 (       3K )  |            C20      |
|  $INTELFX |     3,952 (       3K )  |            F70      |
|  IFS$HLP$ |     3,856 (       3K )  |            F10      |
|   COMMAND |     2,720 (       2K )  |            AA0      |
|   COMMAND |       528 (       0K )  |            210      |
|    CASMGR |     5,520 (       5K )  |           1590      |
+----------+-------------------------+--------------------
|    FREE  |   609,520 (     595K )  |          94CF0      |
+-----------------------------------------------------------+


+ Memory Type --------- Total Bytes ( Kbytes  ) ----- Available For Programs -+
|                       |                           |                         |
| Extended              |  15,728,640 ( 15,360K )   |          0 (      0K )   |
| Extended via XMS      |  --------                 | 12,910,592 ( 12,608K )   |
| EMS                   |     917,504 (    896K )   |    425,984 (    416K )   |
+----------------------------------------------------------------------------
| Largest executable program:  609,136 ( 594K )                              |
+----------------------------------------------------------------------------+
```

You probably won't find much use for the /CLASSIFY report as a memory management tool. The /DEBUG and /PROGRAM reports are more useful, because they show both conventional and upper memory usage. The /CLASSIFY report usually will fit on a single screen, however, so you can use it to make a quick check on your progress as you juggle system configurations.

Using the /DEBUG Option

The MEM /DEBUG report is quite similar to the /PROGRAM report I'll discuss shortly. This report shows all loaded programs, as well as both system and loaded device drivers. The primary difference between the /DEBUG and /PROGRAM reports is in the level of detail presented on system (or internal) device drivers. Because you cannot modify system device driver settings, this extra detail simply makes the /DEBUG report more complicated without adding any useful memory management information. Therefore, I won't bother including a copy of the /DEBUG report here.

Using the /F Option

The MEM /F option reports on memory segment FFFF only. This memory segment is the high memory area (HMA), which is most often used to load part of the DOS kernel. The following is a typical MEM /F report:

```
+- Address --- Name ----- Size ------------- Type --------------------------+
| FFFF:A120 |     DOS |   14C8h,   5,320 | BUFFERS=  10 disk buffers        |
+---------------------------------------------------------------------------+
```

The MEM /F report displays information that is also included in the /DEBUG and /PROGRAM reports. As a memory management tool, the MEM /F report isn't too useful unless you simply want to see whether the DOS kernel is in the HMA.

Using the /I Option

The MEM /I option displays a summary of the internal and loaded device drivers without showing loaded programs or TSRs. The following is a typical MEM /I report:

```
+- Address --- Name ----- Size ------------- Type --------------------------+
|     70:0023 | CON       |                 | System device driver         |
|     70:0035 | AUX       |                 | System device driver         |
|     70:0047 | PRN       |                 | System device driver         |
|     70:0059 | CLOCK$    |                 | System device driver         |
|     70:006B |     A:-C: |                 | System device driver         |
|     70:007B | COM1      |                 | System device driver         |
|     70:008D | LPT1      |                 | System device driver         |
|     70:009F | LPT2      |                 | System device driver         |
|     70:00B8 | LPT3      |                 | System device driver         |
```

```
|  70:00CA | COM2     |       |        | System device driver              |
|  70:00DC | COM3     |       |        | System device driver              |
|  70:00EE | COM4     |       |        | System device driver              |
| 116:0048 | NUL      |       |        | System device driver              |
| 255:0000 | SCSIMGR$ | 1A00h,|  6,656 | DEVICE = installed device driver  |
| 3F6:0000 | XMSXXXX0 |  480h,|  1,152 | DEVICE = installed device driver  |
| 43F:0000 | EMMXXXX0 |  C20h,|  3,104 | DEVICE = installed device driver  |
| 502:0000 | $INTELFX |  F70h,|  3,952 | DEVICE = installed device driver  |
| 5FA:0000 | IFS$HLP$ |  F10h,|  3,856 | DEVICE = installed device driver  |
+----------+----------+-------+--------+-----------------------------------+
| B14C:0000| MVPROAS  | 2A20h,| 10,784 | DEVICE = installed device driver  |
| B3F0:0000| CDROM1   | 3900h,| 14,592 | DEVICE = installed device driver  |
| C803:0000| MS$MOUSE | 42B0h,| 17,072 | DEVICE = installed device driver  |
| D039:2192|  D:-F:   |       |        | DEVICE = installed device driver  |
+----------+----------+-------+--------+-----------------------------------+
```

The MEM /I report is divided into a conventional memory section (above the divider bar) and an upper memory section. This report shows a quick summary of where device drivers are loaded, but otherwise isn't too useful for memory management purposes.

Using the /M Option

The MEM /M option displays a map that displays graphically how the first 1M of system memory is being used. Figure 4.1 shows a typical MEM /M report.

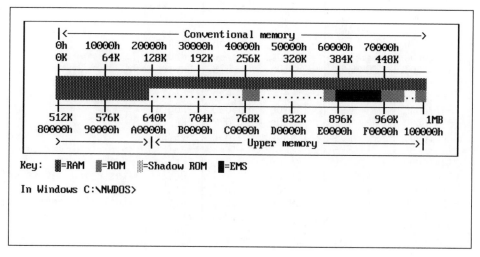

Figure 4.1   The MEM /M report shows memory usage graphically.

Sometimes a picture really is worth a thousand words. The MEM /M report doesn't display any information you won't also see in the MEM /DEBUG or MEM /PROGRAM reports, but because it shows you graphically how memory is being used, you may find areas of upper memory that aren't currently in use but that might be available.

Using the /PROGRAM Option

The MEM /PROGRAM option displays information on all loaded device drivers, TSRs, and programs. The MEM /PROGRAM report is quite similar to the MEM /DEBUG report, but with less information on internal device drivers. The following is a typical MEM /PROGRAM report:

```
+- Address --- Name ----- Size ------------- Type ----------------------------+
|   0:0000   | -------- |   400h,   1,024 | Interrupt vectors
|  40:0000   | -------- |   100h,     256 | ROM BIOS data area
|  50:0000   |    DOS   |   200h,     512 | DOS data area
|  70:0000   |   BIOS   |   A60h,   2,656 | Device drivers
| 116:0000   |    DOS   |  13D0h,   5,072 | System
| 116:00CC   |    DOS   |   10Fh,     271 |   HANDLES=, FCBS=   5 total blocks
| 253:0000   |    DOS   |  6B40h,  27,456 | System
| 255:0000   | SCSIMGR$ |  1A00h,   6,656 |   DEVICE = installed device driver
| 3F6:0000   | XMSXXXX0 |   480h,   1,152 |   DEVICE = installed device driver
| 43F:0000   | EMMXXXX0 |   C20h,   3,104 |   DEVICE = installed device driver
| 502:0000   | $INTELFX |   F70h,   3,952 |   DEVICE = installed device driver
| 5FA:0000   | IFS$HLP$ |   F10h,   3,856 |   DEVICE = installed device driver
| 6EC:0000   |    DOS   |   957h,   2,391 |   HANDLES=, FCBS=  45 total blocks
| 907:0000   |    DOS   |    50h,      80 | System
| 90C:0000   | COMMAND  |    40h,      64 | Data
| 910:0000   | COMMAND  |   A60h,   2,656 | Program
| 9B6:0000   | -------- |    50h,      80 | FREE
| 9BB:0000   | COMMAND  |   210h,     528 | Environment
| 9DC:0000   |   MEM    |   120h,     288 | Environment
| 9EE:0000   | CASMGR   |  1590h,   5,520 | Program
| B47:0000   |   MEM    | 15810h,  88,080 | Program
| 20C8:0000  | -------- | 7F370h, 521,072 | FREE
| 9FFF:0000  |    DOS   | 114B0h,  70,832 | System
+----------+---------+-----------------+---------------------------------------
| B14A:0000  |    DOS   |  2A40h,  10,816 | System
| B14C:0000  | MVPROAS  |  2A20h,  10,784 |   DEVICE = installed device driver
| B3EE:0000  |    DOS   |  3920h,  14,624 | System
| B3F0:0000  | CDROM1   |  3900h,  14,592 |   DEVICE = installed device driver
| B780:0000  | -------- |   7E0h,   2,016 | FREE
| B7FE:0000  |    DOS   | 10030h,  65,584 | System
| C801:0000  |    DOS   |  42D0h,  17,104 | System
```

```
  C803:0000 | MS$MOUSE |  42B0h,  17,072 | DEVICE = installed device driver
  CC2E:0000 | -------- |    70h,     112 | FREE
  CC35:0000 |   MSCDEX |  3F30h,  16,176 | Program
  D028:0000 | SMARTDRV |  76A0h,  30,368 | Program
  D039:2192 |    D:-F: |                  | DEVICE = installed device driver
  D792:0000 |   DOSKEY |  1230h,   4,656 | Program
  D8B5:0000 | -------- |  3490h,  13,456 | FREE
  DBFE:0000 |      DOS |  2500h,   9,472 | System
  DE4E:0000 | -------- |  1B00h,   6,912 | FREE
  DFFE:0000 |      DOS | 19A90h, 105,104 | System
  F9A7:0000 | -------- |  4590h,  17,808 | FREE
+-----------+----------+------------------+----------------------------------
| FFFF:A120 |      DOS |  14C8h,   5,320 | BUFFERS=  10 disk buffers         |
+-----------------------------------------------------------------------------+


+ Memory Type --------- Total Bytes ( Kbytes  ) ----- Available For Programs -+
|
| Conventional              655,360 (    640K )        609,136 (    594K )    |
| Upper                     314,208 (    306K )         40,304 (     39K )    |
| Extended               15,728,640 ( 15,360K )              0 (      0K )    |
| Extended via XMS          --------             12,910,592 ( 12,608K )       |
| EMS                       917,504 (    896K )        425,984 (    416K )    |
+-----------------------------------------------------------------------------
| Largest executable program:  609,136 ( 594K )                              |
+-----------------------------------------------------------------------------+
```

The MEM /PROGRAM report is the most useful MEM report option for memory management purposes. This report shows all of the information you need to know where device drivers and TSRs are loaded, as well as their *memory image size*—the amount of memory a device driver or TSR uses once it has been loaded into memory. Usually, this size will be similar to the file size of the device driver, TSR, or program, but you'll encounter some surprises here, too.

For example, the memory image size of the mouse driver shown in the above report is 17,072 bytes. The file size for that same driver is 55,160. This discrepancy between memory image size and file size produces one of the most perplexing problems in memory management—device drivers or TSRs that seem like they should fit into upper memory but load into conventional memory, instead. Even though the device driver or TSR shrinks to its memory image size once it's loaded into memory, free memory at least as large as the file size must be available during loading. In Chapter 7 you'll learn how to deal with this problem.

Using the /S Option

The MEM /S option displays a summary of system structure information (such as the amount of memory used for file handles, file control blocks, and disk buffers). The following is a typical MEM /S report:

```
+- Address --- Name ----- Size ------------ Type ---------------------------+
|   116:00CC |      DOS |   10Fh,     271 | HANDLES=, FCBS=  5 total blocks |
|   6EC:0000 |      DOS |   957h,   2,391 | HANDLES=, FCBS= 45 total blocks |
+------------+----------+-----------------+---------------------------------
| FFFF:A120  |      DOS |  14C8h,   5,320 | BUFFERS=  10 disk buffers       |
+-------------------------------------------------------------------------+
```

The MEM /DEBUG and MEM /PROGRAM reports include the information displayed by the MEM /S report, but the MEM /S report provides a summary that is easy to understand. Whenever possible, you'll want to adjust your system configuration settings to place as much of the system structure into the high memory area (segment FFFF) as possible. Chapter 7 provides more information on adjusting the settings that affect system structures.

Using the /U Option

The MEM /U option displays a detailed listing of upper memory. Although similar to the upper memory sections of the MEM /DEBUG and MEM /PRO-GRAM reports, the MEM /U report includes additional information not shown in either of those two reports. The following is a typical MEM /U report:

```
+- Address --- Name ----- Size ------------ Type ---------------------------+
|  B14A:0000 |      DOS |  2A40h,  10,816 | System                          |
|  B14C:0000 |  MVPROAS |  2A20h,  10,784 |  DEVICE = installed device driver
|  B3EE:0000 |      DOS |  3920h,  14,624 | System                          |
|  B3F0:0000 |   CDROM1 |  3900h,  14,592 |  DEVICE = installed device driver
|  B780:0000 | -------- |   7E0h,   2,016 | FREE                            |
|  B7FE:0000 |      DOS | 10030h,  65,584 | System                          |
+------------+----------+-----------------+---------------------------------
| C000:0000  | -------- |  6000h,  24,576 | ------------ ROM --------------
+------------+----------+-----------------+---------------------------------
|  C801:0000 |      DOS |  42D0h,  17,104 | System                          |
|  C803:0000 | MS$MOUSE |  42B0h,  17,072 |  DEVICE = installed device driver
|  CC2E:0000 | -------- |    70h,     112 | FREE                            |
|  CC35:0000 |   MSCDEX |  3F30h,  16,176 | Program                         |
|  D028:0000 | SMARTDRV |  76A0h,  30,368 | Program                         |
|  D039:2192 |    D:-F: |                 |  DEVICE = installed device driver
|  D792:0000 |   DOSKEY |  1230h,   4,656 | Program                         |
|  D8B5:0000 | -------- |  3490h,  13,456 | FREE                            |
```

```
| DBFE:0000 |    DOS |   2500h,   9,472 | System
+-----------+--------+------------------+------------------------------------
| DC00:0000 | ------ |   4000h,  16,384 | ------------ ROM --------------
+-----------+--------+------------------+------------------------------------
| DE4E:0000 | ------ |   1B00h,   6,912 | FREE
| DFFE:0000 |    DOS |  19A90h, 105,104 | System
+-----------+--------+------------------+------------------------------------
| E000:0000 |    EMS |  10000h,  65,536 | ---------- EMS memory -----------
| F000:0000 | ------ |   9000h,  36,864 | ------------ ROM --------------
+-----------+--------+------------------+------------------------------------
| F9A7:0000 | ------ |   4590h,  17,808 | FREE
+-----------+--------+------------------+------------------------------------
| FE00:0000 | ------ |   2000h,   8,192 | ------------ ROM --------------
+-----------+--------+------------------+------------------------------------+
```

The MEM /U report shows areas in upper memory it has identified as being ROMs (Read Only Memory), and it shows where the EMS page frame is located (if any exists). Because device drivers and TSRs can generally use only upper memory blocks that are large enough to hold the entire device driver or TSR in one block, it's important to create the largest possible contiguous upper memory blocks. The MEM /U report can be quite useful in helping you determine which areas are available for the creation of upper memory blocks. You may find this report especially useful in helping to determine the best location for an EMS page frame.

Chapter 7 provides more information on configuring your system using Novell DOS 7. The next section covers another tool that can provide quite useful information on your system's memory, MSD. This tool is provided not only with MS-DOS, but also with most versions of Windows. If you don't have MSD available on your system, you can jump forward to the section on using DEBUG to really dig deep into your PC's memory.

Using MSD to Examine How Your PC Is Configured

And while the strangest things assembled here I find,
I'll search this labyrinth of flames with serious mind.

—Johann Wolfgang Von Goethe, *Faust*

MSD, the Microsoft System Diagnostics, is another very useful tool you can apply as you work on optimizing your system's memory management configuration. Like MEM, MSD will provide quite a bit of interesting information, along with a lot of very strange details that will be of absolutely no use to you.

Note

MSD was originally designed as a diagnostic tool for Microsoft's customer support engineers. It has been quietly supplied with several versions of MS-DOS and several versions of Windows. If MSD.EXE is not located in your DOS directory, you'll probably find it in your Windows directory.

You can use MSD to display information on who really built your computer, on system memory, and on many aspects of your hardware and software. To load MSD, enter the command **MSD** at the DOS prompt. Although MSD can be run in a DOS session under Windows, you can't trust the answers you'll see if you do so. Once MSD is loaded, you'll see a screen similar to Figure 4.2.

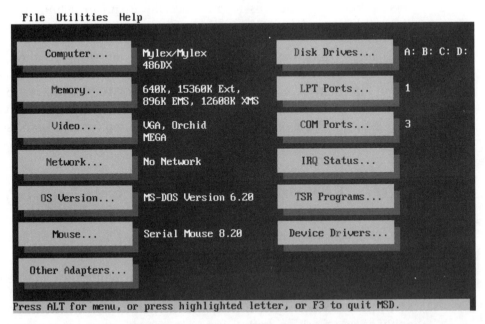

Figure 4.2   The MSD main screen enables you to select the information you wish to see.

Examining the Memory Report

For the purposes of memory management, the MSD memory report provides the most useful information. This report (see Figures 4.3 and 4.4) shows how all upper memory is allocated. In addition, it shows information on the version number of any EMS, XMS, and VCPI memory currently available.

Make special note of any memory blocks marked as available or possibly available on the MSD memory report. These are upper memory areas that are not currently in use. Those marked as available can be used as upper memory blocks, and those marked as possibly available can probably be used as upper memory blocks.

Each row on the MSD memory display represents 16K of memory. Each individual column in a row represents 1K. In Figure 4.3, the addresses between E000 and EFFF are marked with a P, which means that this area is the EMS page frame. Since there are four rows completely filled with the letter P, you can see that the 64K block of memory between E000 and EFFF is being used for the EMS page frame—exactly the amount of space always used by the EMS page frame.

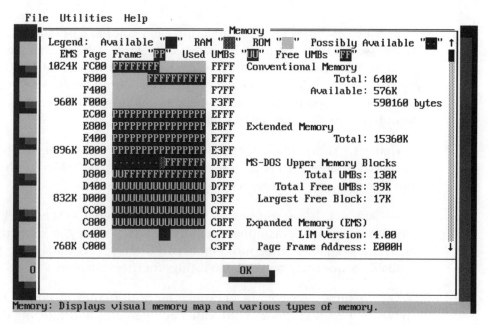

Figure 4.3   The MSD memory report shows upper memory usage.

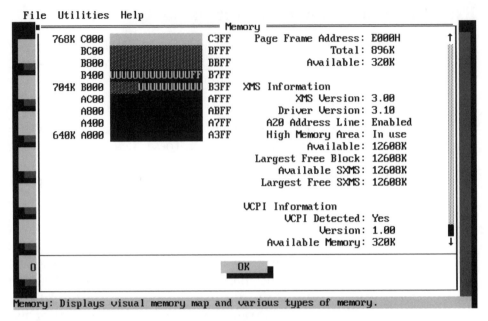

Figure 4.4 Press Page Down to see the lower section of the MSD memory report.

Because MSD uses segment notation, each column's hexadecimal address is 40h greater than the previous address. In Figure 4.3, for example, the first two blocks in the D800 row are in use. The first free block is at D880. Practice figuring out the addresses shown in the display until you're sure you understand how to specify the correct memory addresses. If necessary, you may want to review the material in Chapter 3.

Figure 4.4 shows the lower section of the upper memory area. This area is of special interest for memory management purposes. Table 4.1 shows why this area is so important for memory management.

As Table 4.1 shows, some of the addresses between A000 and BFFF are usually available for use as upper memory blocks. The key is knowing which areas are available. Since most modern PCs have VGA adapters, you can probably concentrate on the table listings for these adapters.

Let's assume you have a VGA adapter and a color monitor. Table 4.1 shows that in text mode, your video adapter uses addresses in the range

Table 4.1	Upper Memory Used by Video Adapters	
Adapter	**Mode**	**Address Range Used**
Monochrome	text	B000–B7FF
Monochrome graphics or Hercules	graphics	B000–B7FF or B000–BFFF
CGA	either	B800–BFFF
EGA or VGA	text	B800–BFFF (color) or B000–B7FF (monochrome)
EGA or VGA	graphics	A000–AFFF
Super VGA	graphics	A000–BFFF

B800–BFFF. In graphics mode, your video adapter uses addresses in the range A000–AFFF. This leaves the 32K block between B000 and B7FF as a potential area you can use to create an upper memory block. The MSD memory report can tell you whether this space is already in use, or whether it appears to be a good candidate. In Figure 4.4, the first 5K of this space is being used, but the remaining 27K has been used to create an upper memory block. The 32K block between B000 and B7FF is known as the *monochrome display adapter area*, and is usually at least partially available for use as an upper memory block.

Tip

If you are unable to start Windows in 386 enhanced mode after creating an upper memory block in the B000–B7FF range, add the line

```
DEVICE=MONOUMB.386
```

to the [386Enh] section of SYSTEM.INI in your Windows directory.

As you can see in Table 4.1 and Figure 4.4, there's an additional 64K block of memory addresses in the range A000–AFFF. This block is used by the VGA video adapter in graphics modes, but isn't used in text modes. You can take advantage of this to extend conventional memory to 704K by including the A000–AFFF range in the area managed by EMM386.EXE. Don't try running any applications that switch your system into a graphics mode, however, because your PC will lock up (or worse).

For more information on including specific memory areas, see Chapter 5 (MS-DOS 5), Chapter 6 (MS-DOS 6.x), or Chapter 7 (Novell DOS 7).

You may find it easier to work with a printed copy of the MSD memory report. Select File Print Report to display the Report Options screen (see Figure 4.5). It's a good idea to limit the printed report to specific items, such as memory, because the complete report will probably be well over twenty pages.

Looking Deeper at Memory

In addition to the normal memory display, MSD can show you exactly where each device driver, TSR, and free memory block is located. It can also search through memory to find specific text strings. This level of detail isn't usually necessary for memory management purposes, but if you're searching for every last byte of upper memory, you may find the information quite useful.

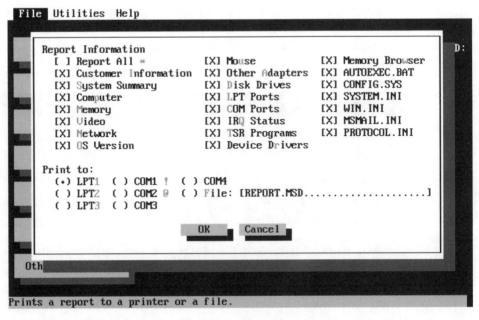

Figure 4.5   Select report options carefully.

Using the Memory Block Display

The memory block display shows the exact size and location of each device driver, TSR, and free memory block. To access this display, select the Utilities Memory Block Display command. Figure 4.6 shows a typical result.

As you move the highlight down the list of allocated memory, the memory map at the right side of the display shows the exact memory location of the currently highlighted item. In Figure 4.6, the location of the free memory block that starts at F9A7 is shown on the map by the area marked with vertical bars at each end, and a horizontal bar between.

Using the Memory Browser

You can use another MSD option, the memory browser, to locate text in ROM areas. Often, a much larger block of memory is allocated to a ROM than is really necessary. You may be able to locate the end of the areas that are actually in use by searching for phrases such as "end of code" or something similar. Later I'll show you how to use DEBUG to find holes in ROMs.

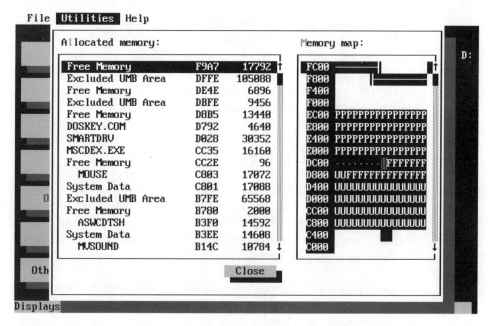

Figure 4.6   The memory block display shows detailed information.

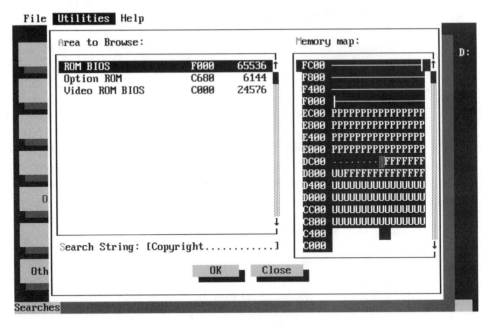

Figure 4.7   The memory browser finds text strings in ROM areas.

Another use for the memory browser is to find out who really made the ROMs in your system. This may be especially useful if you have a generic video adapter and want to know whose video drivers might work. Figure 4.7 shows the screen that is displayed after you select Utilities Memory Browser and enter **Copyright** as the text to search for. Figure 4.8 shows the result of searching the ROM BIOS for the word "Copyright."

What Else Can MSD Tell Me?

MSD can tell you quite a bit about your system, in addition to the memory management-related items already mentioned. For example, the video information tells you who made your video adapter board, how much memory it contains, and whether it supports the VESA standard. See Figures 4.2 and 4.5 for more information on the types of items MSD will report about.

Feel free to experiment with MSD's report options. Remember, though, that if you elect to print the MSD reports, you may end up with many pages of information. Be selective and you'll save quite a bit of time and paper.

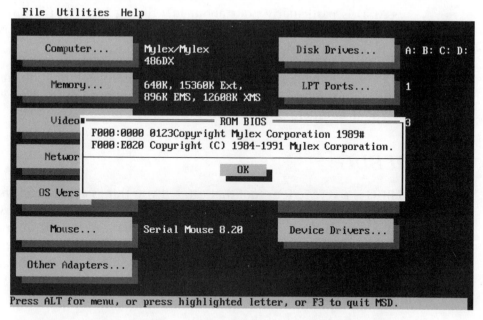

Figure 4.8   The result of searching for the word "Copyright."

What MSD May Lie About

But we must articulate our meaning before we begin to inquire; if not, the inquiry is on the border-line between being a search for something and a search for nothing.

—Aristotle, *Metaphysics*

Although MSD is a very good tool for examining your system, it's not perfect. The information MSD so confidently presents is often incorrect. There can be several reasons for this inaccuracy, and understanding those reasons can save you considerable grief.

- If you attempt to run MSD while Windows is running, much of the actual system information is hidden by Windows. Don't try to use MSD from within Windows!

- Some adapters, notably network adapters, aren't always visible to MSD unless they're in use.

- MSD is particularly poor about identifying IRQ status. Many adapter boards just won't show up on MSD's list, making it appear as though IRQs are available when they are already in use.

MSD can provide you with quite a lot of useful information. It's one of the important pieces in your memory management toolbox. Next we'll look at DEBUG, another powerful tool.

Using DEBUG

DEBUG is a very serious tool that can tell you things about your system that are very difficult to discover in any other manner. DEBUG is also a very dangerous tool, because it can do very serious damage if used improperly. If you're careless, DEBUG can wipe out files or entire disks. Don't get the idea that I'm trying to scare you away from using DEBUG to examine your system. Follow my instructions carefully, and you'll be rewarded with new insights into your PC's internal workings.

Even though I'm sure DEBUG is safe when used carefully, I'll understand if you prefer not to experiment. That's okay. You can use the tools we've already covered in this chapter to find most of your system's available memory. DEBUG will really find only relatively small additional amounts of memory anyway. This section is intended for those readers who want to find those last, lost bytes of memory, and are willing to work a little harder to find them.

Caution

Because the techniques presented in this section are very aggressive, always experiment using a boot diskette so you'll be able to restart your system from the hard disk if you make an error.

Looking at Memory

DEBUG enables you to peer directly into your PC's memory. With this tool, you can find information that isn't normally visible. Quite a bit of what's in memory is program code, which won't seem to make any sense. Some of what you'll see will be plain text, though. Don't worry about the parts you can't understand, but don't try to change them, either!

To begin using DEBUG, load the program by typing the command **DEBUG**. You'll know that DEBUG is loaded because the cursor will change to a dash (–). Now you're ready to look around.

Setting the Segment

In Chapter 2 you learned about segmented memory. You learned that a common way to talk about conventional memory is to divide the first 1M of address space into 16 memory pages, each 64K long. With DEBUG, this method is quite useful, because DEBUG can examine a maximum of 64K of memory at a time.

Each of these memory pages is designated beginning with a hexadecimal number between 0 and F, and followed by three zeros. The first page segment is 0000, the next 1000, and so on up to F000. There's nothing to prevent you from using any segment number you want, but following this 16-page convention will make it easier to keep track of what you're doing.

Once you've loaded DEBUG, you use the command **R** to examine the current register settings. (*Registers* are memory locations in the processor that hold special values, such as the location of the current program instruction.) For convenience, you can set the value of the CS (Code Segment) register to the page segment value. For example, to examine page F000, set the value of the CS register to F000 by entering the command **RCS** and then entering **F000** after the colon. Use the **R** command to again examine the current register settings to verify that your changes have been made (see Figure 4.9).

Dumping Memory

Dumping memory is the term used to describe displaying the contents of memory as text. By dumping successive memory addresses, you can examine what that memory contains. DEBUG uses the **D** command to dump memory. To specify which memory to dump, you add the segment and offset values to the command. Optionally, you can also add a length argument to specify how much memory to dump.

```
C:\>DEBUG
-R
AX=0000  BX=0000  CX=0000  DX=0000  SP=FFEE  BP=0000  SI=0000  DI=0000
DS=153E  ES=153E  SS=153E  CS=153E  IP=0100   NV UP EI PL NZ NA PO NC
  153E:0100 0F           DB     0F
-RCS
CS 153E
:F000
-R
AX=0000  BX=0000  CX=0000  DX=0000  SP=FFEE  BP=0000  SI=0000  DI=0000
DS=153E  ES=153E  SS=153E  CS=F000  IP=0100   NV UP EI PL NZ NA PO NC
F000:0100 05478B          ADD    AX,8B47
-
```

Figure 4.9   Set the CS register to the segment you want to examine.

Figure 4.10 shows a typical use of DEBUG to display the beginning of the F000 segment. This segment usually contains your system's ROM BIOS, and the beginning of the segment generally contains a copyright message.

Printing a Copy

If you want a printed copy of your DEBUG session, you can direct your printer to make a copy of everything displayed on the screen. Simply press **Ctrl-PrintScreen** or **Ctrl-P** to begin printer echo. Press the same keys to stop printer echo. When printer echo is enabled, you won't notice anything until something new is displayed on your screen. At that point, your printer will begin.

If you just want a copy of the current screen, press **Shift-PrintScreen**.

Finding Holes

In terms of memory management, the point of using DEBUG is to find *holes*—unused spaces in upper memory where you might be able to place an

```
C:\>DEBUG
-RCS
CS 153E
:F000
-DCS:00
F000:0000  30 31 32 33 43 6F 70 79-72 69 67 68 74 20 4D 79   0123Copyright My
F000:0010  6C 65 78 20 43 6F 72 70-6F 72 61 74 69 6F 6E 20   lex Corporation
F000:0020  31 39 38 39 23 FE FF 00-01 02 03 80 05 00 00 08   1989#..........
F000:0030  09 0A 0B 00 6E 01 8B 17-6E 1A 6E 01 B9 2E 75 01   ....n...n.n...u.
F000:0040  6E 01 6E 01 6E 01 A0 71-7B 01 21 FF A1 FF 21 55   n.n.n..q{.!...!U
F000:0050  A1 55 21 AA A1 AA 21 FF-A1 FF 20 11 21 08 21 04   .U!...!... .!.!.
F000:0060  21 01 21 FF A0 11 A1 70-A1 02 A1 01 A1 FF FA 2E   !.!....p........
F000:0070  8E 16 D0 66 2E 8E 1E C4-66 E4 64 A8 04 75 3B 80   ...f....f.d..u;.
-
```

Figure 4.10   Dumping the beginning of the F000 memory segment.

upper memory block. Some memory managers are better at finding these holes than others—some take a cautious approach and simply don't look in certain areas.

How can there be holes in upper memory? Often, more memory than is really needed will be allocated to a particular purpose. For example, the entire F000 segment is usually allocated for the ROM BIOS. Sometimes, though, the whole 64K isn't really used. Through careful searching, you may be able to find a block of unused memory large enough for one of your device drivers or TSRs, thus saving conventional memory.

The F000 segment isn't the only place you may find unallocated, unused memory. Sometimes you may find that part of the space set aside for an adapter card isn't being used. If the unused space is adjacent to an existing upper memory block, the benefits of adding the unused space to an existing upper memory block can be quite important. Sometimes a small increase in the size of an upper memory block is all you need to allow a device driver or TSR to fit into the block.

What to Look For

Unused memory is usually filled with a single filler character. Often this will be either FF or 00 (hexadecimal). It's not enough just to find memory filled with these characters, though. Sometimes, what seems like unused memory is simply memory that hasn't been used since you started your system, but that may be used at some point.

So how do you tell whether memory is really available, or simply hasn't been used yet? One trick is to run all of your normal programs, including Windows or any other environment you may use. If you're on a network, log onto and off of the network. Use anything in your system that has its own adapter board, such as a modem, a sound board, or a scanner. Once you've done all of this, start DEBUG (without restarting your system) and examine memory.

It's probably a fairly safe bet that any memory that remains unused after such a torture test really is unused. Sometimes, though, you'll find that the manufacturers of your system have left clues to help you know for certain. In the next example, you'll see what I mean.

An Example

DEBUG can search memory for specific text strings. In this example, you'll see one case where this ability is quite handy.

Figure 4.11 shows how to search the F000 segment for the word END. Why did I choose this word? Because Mylex, the manufacturer of my system's ROM BIOS, placed the phrase END OF CODE at the point in the ROM BIOS where unused memory begins. You may not be so lucky, and may simply have to dump the entire segment in your attempt to find some unused memory.

To search a memory segment, use the **S** command followed by the segment and offset for the beginning of the search. Next, add the letter **L** and the value **FFFF** to indicate that you want to search the entire length of the segment. Finally, enter the search text in quotes.

If the text is found, DEBUG will show the segment/offset address where the text begins. In this example, END was found twice, at F000:9CC4 and at

```
F000:0050  A1 55 21 AA A1 AA 21 FF-A1 FF 20 11 21 08 21 04   .U!...!... .!.!.
F000:0060  21 01 21 FF A0 11 A1 70-A1 02 A1 01 A1 FF FA 2E   !.!....p........
F000:0070  8E 16 D0 66 2E 8E 1E C4-66 E4 64 A8 04 75 3B 80   ...f....f.d..u;.
-SCS:00 L FFFF "END"
F000:9CC4
F000:AD30
-DCS:9CC0
F000:9CC0  00 45 58 54 45 4E 44 45-44 20 48 41 52 44 57 41   .EXTENDED HARDWA
F000:9CD0  52 45 20 49 4E 46 4F 52-4D 41 54 49 4F 4E 20 52   RE INFORMATION R
F000:9CE0  45 53 45 54 20 54 4F 20-44 45 46 41 55 4C 54 20   ESET TO DEFAULT
F000:9CF0  56 41 4C 55 45 53 0D 0A-00 48 41 52 44 57 41 52   VALUES...HARDWAR
F000:9D00  45 20 49 4E 46 4F 52 4D-41 54 49 4F 4E 20 44 4F   E INFORMATION DO
F000:9D10  45 53 20 4E 4F 54 20 4D-41 54 43 48 20 56 49 44   ES NOT MATCH VID
F000:9D20  45 4F 20 43 41 52 44 20-2D 20 52 55 4E 20 53 45   EO CARD - RUN SE
F000:9D30  54 55 50 0D 0A 00 43 4F-4C 4F 52 2F 4D 4F 4E 4F   TUP...COLOR/MONO
-DCS:AD30
F000:AD30  45 4E 44 20 4F 46 20 43-4F 44 45 28 43 29 43 4F   END OF CODE(C)CO
F000:AD40  50 59 52 49 47 48 54 20-4D 59 4C 45 58 20 43 4F   PYRIGHT MYLEX CO
F000:AD50  52 50 4F 52 41 54 49 4F-4E 20 31 39 38 33 2D 31   RPORATION 1983-1
F000:AD60  39 39 30 FF FF FF FF FF-FF FF FF FF FF FF FF FF   990.............
F000:AD70  FF FF FF FF FF FF FF FF-FF FF FF FF FF FF FF FF   ................
F000:AD80  FF FF FF FF FF FF FF FF-FF FF FF FF FF FF FF FF   ................
F000:AD90  FF FF FF FF FF FF FF FF-FF FF FF FF FF FF FF FF   ................
F000:ADA0  FF FF FF FF FF FF FF FF-FF FF FF FF FF FF FF FF   ................
-
```

Figure 4.11   Searching for the beginning of unused memory.

F000:AD30. Use the **D** command to dump the addresses where the text was found to see if you've found what you want. The second address was the correct one in Figure 4.11.

Once you find the beginning of apparently unused memory, note the address and then use the **D** command to continue dumping memory from that point on. If you're lucky, you may find a fairly large block. Remember, any deviation from the filler character probably indicates the end of the unused block. Figure 4.12 shows that address F000:DD0F seems to be the end of the unused memory block.

Now you'll have to use the segment/offset information you learned in Chapter 2. First, convert the starting address to a segment address with an offset of zero. Since the beginning of the block in this example was at F000:AD30, you can specify this as address FAD3:0000. You only need to remember the segment, however. Next, convert the ending address to FDD0:0000.

You now have the address range of the memory block you want to include as an upper memory block, FAD3–FDD0. Using the hexadecimal math you

```
F000:DC50   FF FF FF FF FF FF FF FF-FF FF FF FF FF FF FF FF    ................
F000:DC60   FF FF FF FF FF FF FF FF-FF FF FF FF FF FF FF FF    ................
F000:DC70   FF FF FF FF FF FF FF FF-FF FF FF FF FF FF FF FF    ................
F000:DC80   FF FF FF FF FF FF FF FF-FF FF FF FF FF FF FF FF    ................
F000:DC90   FF FF FF FF FF FF FF FF-FF FF FF FF FF FF FF FF    ................
F000:DCA0   FF FF FF FF FF FF FF FF-FF FF FF FF FF FF FF FF    ................
-D
F000:DCB0   FF FF FF FF FF FF FF FF-FF FF FF FF FF FF FF FF    ................
F000:DCC0   FF FF FF FF FF FF FF FF-FF FF FF FF FF FF FF FF    ................
F000:DCD0   FF FF FF FF FF FF FF FF-FF FF FF FF FF FF FF FF    ................
F000:DCE0   FF FF FF FF FF FF FF FF-FF FF FF FF FF FF FF FF    ................
F000:DCF0   FF FF FF FF FF FF FF FF-FF FF FF FF FF FF FF FF    ................
F000:DD00   FF FF FF FF FF FF FF FF-FF FF FF FF FF FF FF FF    ................
F000:DD10   34 38 36 44 58 2F 53 58-20 49 53 41 20 42 49 4F    486DX/SX ISA BIO
F000:DD20   53 20 56 65 72 73 69 6F-6E 20 36 2E 31 32 20 30    S Version 6.12 0
-D
F000:DD30   32 2F 30 37 2F 39 32 20-0D 0A 20 0D 0A 0A 00 00    2/07/92 .. .....
F000:DD40   00 00 00 00 00 00 00 00-00 00 00 00 00 00 00 00    ................
F000:DD50   00 00 00 00 00 00 00 00-00 00 00 00 00 00 00 00    ................
F000:DD60   00 00 00 00 00 00 00 00-00 00 00 00 00 00 00 00    ................
F000:DD70   00 00 00 00 00 00 00 00-00 00 00 00 00 00 00 00    ................
F000:DD80   00 00 00 00 00 00 00 00-00 00 00 00 00 00 00 00    ................
F000:DD90   00 00 00 00 00 00 00 00-00 00 00 00 00 00 00 00    ................
F000:DDA0   00 00 00 00 00 00 00 00-00 00 00 00 00 00 00 00    ................
-
```

Figure 4.12   The apparent end of the unused memory block.

learned in Chapter 2, you know this is a block of memory of 12,240 bytes, or nearly 12K. Without DEBUG, you'd never know the block was there. With DEBUG, you may have found a way to save nearly 12K of conventional memory by providing space in upper memory for another device driver or TSR.

The later chapters on specific memory managers will show you how to specify a block of memory to use for upper memory blocks.

When a Hole Isn't Real

It's possible that what appears to be a block of unused memory really isn't available. The hole you worked so hard to find might have some unknown purpose, and your system may lock up or act strangely once you actually try to use the block. Remember, I told you at the beginning of the section on DEBUG that this technique was for the brave. Because this technique does present a risk of locking up your system, always remember to try changes in memory allocation using a boot diskette before making those changes on your hard disk. If you have a problem, remove the boot diskette and restart from the hard disk.

Quitting DEBUG

Once you're done examining memory, use the **Q** command to exit from DEBUG. You'll be returned to the DOS prompt, and you can begin your experiments.

Summary

Effective memory management begins with finding all of your system's available memory. There's no sense in wasting memory—you probably paid too much for it to want to waste any. The tools and techniques presented in this chapter have shown you how to find as much memory as possible.

Each of the major DOS versions in common use today has its own, unique requirements for applying advanced memory management techniques. To make your memory management task as straightforward as possible, the following chapters present the complete information needed for each of these DOS versions. Chapter 5 covers MS-DOS 5, Chapter 6 covers MS-DOS 6.x, and Chapter 7 covers Novell DOS 7. You don't have to wade through material on any DOS version other than your own. I hope you appreciate this approach.

Chapter 5

Managing Your Memory with MS-DOS 5

This chapter is about memory management using the tools included in MS-DOS 5, which was the first version of DOS that included the tools needed for memory management. Earlier DOS versions simply didn't take advantage of upper memory, the high memory area, or even extended memory.

> 'Tis easy to see, hard to foresee.
>
> —Benjamin Franklin, *Poor Richard's Almanack*

In this chapter I'll show you how to use all of MS-DOS 5's memory management options. I'll also explain why you might want to use some of the more obscure options, and what effect they'll have on your PC.

Memory management in MS-DOS 5 can be broken down into three areas:

- The first area consists of the commands and directives you'll use in CONFIG.SYS. This file presents the first system configuration opportunity on any PC, because this is the first user file processed whenever you start your system.

111

Why MS DOS 5 Was a Revolutionary Product

One major problem with advanced memory management was solved by the introduction of MS-DOS 5. This was the compatibility problem caused by the lack of real standards for the use of memory outside the normal 640K conventional memory space. For example, several different methods of using extended memory for extending DOS beyond 640K were developed. If you used DOS-extended programs, you ran a very real risk of major incompatibilities between your programs. Throw one of the early third-party memory managers into the mix, and you could have a real mess.

The introduction of MS-DOS 5 provided the average PC user with the first opportunity to enhance system operation through the use of upper memory, the high memory area, and the XMS memory standard for extended memory. For the first time, DOS itself provided standard ways to access these additional resources. MS-DOS 5 also represented DOS's first break with the PC's past—taking advantage of all of MS-DOS 5's new features required at least an 80386 processor. Users could still upgrade to MS-DOS 5 on their old PCs, but memory management was no longer hampered by ancient technology.

- The second area consists of the commands you'll use in AUTOEXEC.BAT. This is the second user file processed during startup.

- The third area of MS-DOS 5 memory management is something I call the *load order juggling act*. Often, this is the most difficult area to understand, but one that can produce quite impressive results.

Note

Advanced memory management techniques require an understanding of the subjects presented in the earlier chapters of this book. If you aren't comfortable with some of the topics covered earlier, please take the time to review any matter that doesn't seem clear before you begin experimenting with your system's configuration.

Using CONFIG.SYS Options

CONFIG.SYS is a very important file. If CONFIG.SYS exists in the root directory of the boot disk, any commands or directives it contains are read and executed as part of the system startup process. Many of the system configuration options can be used only when placed in CONFIG.SYS; you cannot exercise these options any other way.

Because most of the CONFIG.SYS system configuration options cannot be executed at the command line, it's often difficult to see exactly what happens as they are processed. Error or information messages displayed during the processing of CONFIG.SYS usually scroll by so quickly that you might miss important details. If you're not watching your screen closely, and if you're not a speed reader, you might never realize that something is wrong. This makes it even more important to make certain that your CONFIG.SYS file is correctly structured, and that every line it contains is absolutely correct.

Caution

Experimenting with system configuration options can result in serious problems, including a system that cannot be started. Always try your proposed changes on a boot diskette first, and copy them to your hard disk only after you've verified that a new configuration works correctly. For information on making a boot disk, see Chapter 3.

For MS-DOS 5 memory management purposes, two device drivers, HIMEM.SYS and EMM386.EXE, are the two most important items that appear in CONFIG.SYS. It's very important to understand how to use these two device drivers; otherwise, you won't be able to apply any of the other MS-DOS 5 advanced memory management techniques. Because of this importance, I'll start the discussion of CONFIG.SYS options by looking at each of these two device drivers in detail.

Understanding HIMEM.SYS's Options

HIMEM.SYS is the MS-DOS 5 XMS memory manager. It must be loaded before EMM386.EXE, and is usually the first device driver listed in CONFIG.SYS. Until HIMEM.SYS is loaded, no XMS memory is available, the high memory area is not available, and no upper memory can be made available. In fact, without HIMEM.SYS, your PC is limited to accessing the 640K of conventional memory.

Although some of the CONFIG.SYS commands such as BREAK and BUFFERS can precede the line that loads the HIMEM.SYS device driver, it's usually best to place this line as the first line in CONFIG.SYS. If your DOS files are in C:\DOS, the following CONFIG.SYS line loads the HIMEM.SYS device driver without specifying any optional parameters:

```
DEVICE=C:\DOS\HIMEM.SYS
```

The exception to the rule of loading the HIMEM.SYS device driver first is for systems that use special device drivers to access their hard disk. Usually, such device drivers must be loaded first, before any memory manager is loaded. For example, systems with SCSI hard disks and adapters may include a command similar to

```
DEVICE=C:\UTILITY\ASPI4DOS.SYS
```

If your system includes a similar device driver as the first line in your existing CONFIG.SYS file, it's usually best simply to add the HIMEM.SYS device driver as the second device driver.

Note

The discussions of HIMEM.SYS and EMM386.EXE in this chapter are based upon the versions shipped with MS-DOS 5. If you've installed Windows 3.1 or Windows for Workgroups, you probably have newer versions of HIMEM.SYS and EMM386.EXE that were supplied with Windows. These newer versions of HIMEM.SYS and EMM386.EXE are discussed in Chapter 6.

If you don't use any options, HIMEM.SYS allocates all extended memory as XMS memory, and default settings are used for all HIMEM.SYS options. In most cases the default settings will work adequately, but you may find that using one or more of HIMEM.SYS's options is necessary or at least desirable. In some cases, the only way you'll be able to use certain software will be to specify certain options. In other cases, using certain options will actually make your PC run faster. Let's have a look at the options in the MS-DOS 5 version of HIMEM.SYS.

Why You Might Need the /HMAMIN Option

The /HMAMIN=n option specifies how much memory, in K, a program must use before it can take over the high memory area (HMA). You can specify a value between 0 and 63, and the default is 0.

The high memory area is a very useful, but limited, extension to the memory your PC can access in real mode. At just under 64K in size, this special section of memory can be used almost like conventional memory for loading a memory-resident program. Generally, the most common use for the high memory area in MS-DOS 5 is to hold part of the DOS kernel, reducing the amount of conventional memory used by DOS itself.

The high memory area suffers from one major limitation, however, and it is the reason the /HMAMIN=n option is available. Only one program at a time can use the high memory area, and any leftover space in the high memory area is simply wasted.

For example, suppose a program that uses 12K of memory is loaded into the high memory area. The remaining 52K of space is simply wasted, because no other program can use the high memory area once the first program is loaded. In such a case, specifying **/HMAMIN=13** would prevent the 12K program from loading into the high memory area, and allow a larger program access.

The reason the /HMAMIN=n option may be needed is that some programs automatically load themselves into the high memory area if it is available. For example, certain network drivers try to use this area if possible. If you have several such programs, you'll use the /HMAMIN=n option to make certain only the largest possible program can use high memory.

You don't need to use the /HMAMIN=n option if the DOS kernel is the only program on your system that uses high memory.

Why You Might Need the /NUMHANDLES Option

The /NUMHANDLES=n option specifies the number of extended memory block handles that can be used at the same time. You can specify any number between 1 and 128; the default is 32. Each extended memory block handle uses 6 bytes of memory, so the default number uses 192 bytes, while the maximum uses 768 bytes.

An XMS memory manager allocates extended memory by providing *extended memory block handles*—which are basically the means to temporarily access blocks of extended memory—to programs that request extended memory. If too many extended memory block handles are requested at the same time, some of those requests will fail, and the requesting program may wait and try again, display an error message, or simply crash.

Normally, the default of 32 handles should be sufficient, but if you run a large number of programs that use XMS memory at the same time, such as a large number of Windows programs, you may need to increase the number of handles. Most well-behaved programs will display an error message rather than crashing your system, but if you experience an unusual number of system crashes, you may want to increase the number of handles to see if the problem is reduced or eliminated. Adding additional handles really doesn't cost you very much memory—doubling the number to 64 consumes only an extra 192 bytes.

Why You Might Need the /INT15 Option

The /INT15=*nnnn* option specifies how much extended memory, in K, is reserved for access through the interrupt 15h interface method. You can specify a value between 64 and 65,536. The default is zero.

Older programs that use their own DOS extenders usually cannot use XMS memory, but instead often use a method of allocating extended memory through a DOS service called the *interrupt 15h interface*. If you use these types of programs, you must use the /INT15=*nnnn* option to enable them to access extended memory.

Any extended memory allocated through the interrupt 15h interface cannot also be used as XMS memory. This conflict between methods of accessing extended memory can usually be eliminated by upgrading to newer versions of your application programs, since most programs that use extended memory now recognize the XMS standard.

If you are unable or unwilling to upgrade to an XMS-aware program, you may want to consider one of the multiple configuration options discussed in Chapter 3. When you need to use the old DOS extended program, boot using a special configuration that supplies extended memory through the interrupt 15h interface. When you aren't using the DOS extended program, boot your system using a configuration that supplies all extended memory through the XMS standard. This will allow you to run Windows, SmartDrive, and other modern XMS-aware programs.

Why You Might Need the /MACHINE Option

The /MACHINE:*xxxx* option specifies the type of computer you're using, so HIMEM.SYS can properly access extended memory. Usually HIMEM.SYS can work correctly without having this option specified, but in some cases, specifying the type of system is necessary, or may improve performance.

HIMEM.SYS uses something called an *A20 handler* to access extended memory. *A20* refers to the twenty-first memory address line, the first memory address line that accesses memory above the 1M address. The first twenty memory address lines, A0–A19, are present on all PCs, regardless of their processors. The A20 line is available only on systems with an 80286 or higher processor.

Table 5.1 shows the different codes and numbers you can specify for your system. You can specify either the code or the corresponding number, but not both. The default A20 handler is the standard IBM AT handler.

It may be difficult to determine whether your system needs to have the A20 handler specified. If HIMEM.SYS cannot access the A20 handler correctly, you may see an error message while the system is booting, or your system may be prone to crashing when DOS is loaded into the high memory area.

You should probably assume that if your system is specifically listed in Table 5.1, specifying the A20 handler is required. If your system is not listed in Table 5.1, but you see an error message from HIMEM.SYS, or your system becomes unstable when DOS is loaded high, try the AT1, AT2, or AT3 settings, or select a setting for a system similar to your PC.

Why You Might Need the /A20CONTROL Option

The /A20CONTROL:*on|off* option specifies whether HIMEM.SYS should attempt to take control of the A20 memory address line, even if another program has already taken control of the line when HIMEM.SYS is loaded. If you specify /**A20CONTROL:off**, HIMEM.SYS can take control only if no other program is already using the A20 memory address line.

The use of the /A20CONTROL:*on|off* option is a very difficult issue to resolve. Generally, only memory managers and DOS extenders will attempt to control the A20 memory address line. If you're using HIMEM.SYS to manage extended memory, it's quite unlikely you'll ever have a need for this option. If you use a third-party memory manager, you probably don't have any reason to load HIMEM.SYS in addition to the other memory manager. Finally, if you use programs that use their own DOS extenders, you'll proba-

Table 5.1 Values for the /MACHINE:xxxx Option		
System	**Code**	**Number**
Acer 1100	ACER1100	6
AT&T 6300 Plus	ATT6300PLUS	5
CSS Labs	CSS	12
HP Vectra	FASTHP	14
HP Vectra (A & A+)	HPVECTRA	4
IBM AT or 100% compatible	AT	1
IBM PC/AT (alternative delay)	AT1	11
IBM PC/AT (alternative delay)	AT2	12
IBM PC/AT (alternative delay)	AT3	13
IBM PS/2	PS2	2
Philips	PHILIPS	13
Phoenix Cascade BIOS	PTLCASCADE	3
Toshiba 1600 & 1200XE	TOSHIBA	7
Tulip SX	TULIP	9
Wyse 12.5 Mhz 286	WYSE	8
Zenith ZBIOS	ZENITH	10

bly use the /INT15 option to supply extended memory to the DOS extended program.

If you do specify **/A20CONTROL:on**, HIMEM.SYS will attempt to take control of the A20 memory address line, regardless of any other program's existing control of the line. Doing so will probably disable the other program.

Why You Might Need the /SHADOWRAM Option

The /SHADOWRAM:*on|off* option specifies whether HIMEM.SYS should attempt to switch off *shadow RAM*—the process of copying the system's ROM BIOS into RAM for faster execution. HIMEM.SYS cannot always control whether shadow RAM is enabled, so this option may not accomplish anything on some systems.

Your system uses the ROM BIOS to hold basic system operating instructions. These very basic instructions are executed frequently, so PC manufacturers often copy them from ROM, which has quite slow access, to RAM, which can be accessed much faster. Before MS-DOS 5 made access to upper memory available, this was usually a very good idea, because it allowed for a small performance boost through the use of largely unused memory. Today, however, access to additional memory is usually more important than the small increase in performance achieved through the use of shadow RAM.

It's usually a good idea to trade a little speed for the extra memory that may be made available by using the **/SHADOWRAM:off** switch. Keep in mind, however, that since HIMEM.SYS cannot always control shadow RAM, this switch may have no effect on your system.

Why You Might Need the /CPUCLOCK Option

The /CPUCLOCK:*on|off* option is used to specify whether HIMEM.SYS affects your system's internal clock. If your PC runs slower when HIMEM.SYS is loaded, specifying **/CPUCLOCK:ON** might correct the problem.

Be aware, however, that specifying **/CPUCLOCK:ON** makes HIMEM.SYS itself a little slower, so if you feel HIMEM.SYS is slowing your PC's clock, you may want to experiment to see whether adding this switch helps, or whether it makes your PC run even more slowly.

This switch is most useful on some of the systems that have a "turbo" switch that switches the processor between high- and low-speed operation. If your PC has such a switch, and booting your system and loading HIMEM.SYS switches to the lower speed, try the **/CPUCLOCK:ON** option to see if it removes the problem.

Understanding EMM386.EXE's Options

EMM386.EXE is the MS-DOS 5 EMS memory manager and upper memory block provider. EMM386.EXE requires access to XMS memory, and therefore must be loaded after HIMEM.SYS. You cannot use EMM386.EXE without also loading HIMEM.SYS (or another XMS memory manager).

Because EMM386.EXE requires an 80386 or higher processor, you cannot use it to provide either EMS memory or upper memory blocks on a system with an 80286 or lower processor. HIMEM.SYS can be used on an 80286 system to provide XMS memory, but MS-DOS 5 does not include a comparable EMS memory manager and upper memory block provider for these types of systems.

You can use EMM386.EXE to provide either EMS memory or upper memory blocks individually, or to provide access to both types of memory at the same time. EMM386.EXE also provides some additional memory management functions, which are controlled through the use of its optional switches.

Why You Might Need the /P Option

The /P*xxxx* option specifies the starting address for the 64K EMS page frame. You can specify segment addresses in the range 8000h to 9000h, and C000h through E000h, using 400h increments. For example, you can specify **/P8000** or **/P8400**, but you cannot specify **/P8200**.

Note
Don't confuse the /P*xxxx* option with the P*n*=*xxxx* option. /P*xxxx* specifies the beginning of a contiguous 64K page frame, while P*n*=*xxxx* specifies the beginning of a specific page.

Specifying the starting address of the page frame provides control over the size of upper memory blocks. Usually, you'll want to create the largest possible upper memory blocks, so you'll want to place the page frame in a location that does not break an upper memory block into two noncontiguous pieces.

Why You Might Need the A Option

The A=*n* option specifies how many fast alternate register sets to allocate to EMM386.EXE. Fast alternate register sets are used for multitasking, which is running more than one program on your system at the same time. You can specify values between 0 and 254; by default, 7 fast alternate register sets are allocated to EMM386.EXE.

Each fast alternate register set allocated to EMM386.EXE uses about 200 bytes of memory, so don't increase the number allocated to EMM386.EXE unless you are specifically directed to do so by a program's documentation. If memory is very tight on your system, you can experiment with reducing the size of memory used by EMM386.EXE by specifying a smaller number of fast alternate register sets. Normally, however, you'll have little need to use this switch.

Why You Might Need the B Option

The B=*xxxx* option specifies the lowest segment address available for swapping EMS memory pages. You can specify any value between 1000h and 4000h.

You can make EMS memory pages available to programs by making them appear to be located in conventional memory. Normally, pages are swapped above the 256K address, but this switch can permit the swapping to occur at a lower address. Unless you are specifically directed to do so by a program's documentation, you won't need to use this switch.

Why You Might Need the D Option

The D=*nnn* option specifies how much memory, in K, to reserve for buffered direct memory access, or DMA. You can specify values between 16 and 256. The default is 16.

DMA transfers are used by some types of adapters, such as SCSI adapters. This is especially true if you have a CD-ROM drive installed in your system. Many CD-ROM drives require at least 64K for DMA.

If you don't have enough memory reserved for DMA transfers, your system will probably lock up at some point and display a message similar to the following:

```
EMM386 DMA buffer is too small.
Add D=nn parameter and reboot.
```

If you see this message, you'll have to increase the amount of DMA memory by specifying a larger number with the D=*nnn* option. Unfortunately, it's possible to see this error message while you're starting your system, making it impossible to correct the problem unless you can boot from another disk. This possibility should be enough to convince you to keep an emergency boot diskette handy, especially if you add new hardware to your system.

Why You Might Need the Frame Option

The FRAME=*xxxx* option specifies the base address for the 64K EMS page frame. You can specify segment addresses in the range 8000h to 9000h, and C000h through E000h, using 400h increments. For example, you can specify **FRAME=8000** or **FRAME=8400**, but you cannot specify **FRAME=8200**.

Specifying the starting address of the page frame provides control over the size of upper memory blocks. Usually, you'll want to create the largest possible upper memory blocks, so you'll want to place the page frame in a location that does not break an upper memory block into two noncontiguous pieces.

The FRAME=*xxxx* option and /P*xxxx* option serve the same purpose. You can use either option if you want to specify the EMS page frame address.

Why You Might Need the H Option

The H=*nn* option specifies how many handles EMM386.EXE can use. You can specify a number between 2 and 255. The default is 64.

Unless specifically directed to change this value by a program's documentation, there's really no reason to use the H=*nn* option.

Why You Might Need the I Option

The I=*xxxx-xxxx* option specifies a range of segment addresses in the range A000h to FFFFh to use for upper memory blocks or the EMS page frame. Values are rounded down to the nearest 4K boundary.

The I=*xxxx-xxxx* option is one of the most useful of EMM386.EXE's options. Normally, EMM386.EXE is quite conservative in selecting areas of upper memory for upper memory blocks and the EMS page frame. As you learned in Chapter 4, there are often additional sections of upper memory that can be used for these purposes. For example, to include the monochrome display page memory, you would use the following syntax:

```
I=B000-B7FF
```

You can include more than one section of upper memory by placing more than one I=*xxxx-xxxx* switch in the EMM386.EXE command line.

Generally, it is best to create the largest contiguous upper memory blocks possible. Since some device drivers and TSRs require more memory to load than their memory image size, it's desirable to have upper memory blocks large enough to allow loading such device drivers and TSRs; otherwise, they will be loaded into conventional memory.

Note

If you attempt to include upper memory as upper memory blocks or as the EMS page frame, and that memory is already in use, your system may crash. Make certain you have an emergency boot diskette available when you experiment with including extra upper memory.

It's also possible to include the first section of upper memory as an extension to conventional memory, if you have an EGA or VGA adapter but don't use any graphics modes. The switch **I=A000-AFFF** will increase conventional memory to 704K, but your system will lock up as soon as it attempts to enter a graphics mode. Purely text mode programs, however, can usually function correctly with this memory added to the top of conventional memory.

Two areas of upper memory are usually safe to include even if you use programs that use graphics modes. In addition to the B000–B7FF range mentioned above, the E000–EFFF range is usually safe to use on most systems. If these two ranges are not already being used by EMM386.EXE, explicitly including them can add up to 96K of additional upper memory for upper memory blocks and the EMS page frame.

Why You Might Need the L Option

The L=*nnn* option specifies an amount of XMS memory, in K, that must remain available after EMM386.EXE is loaded. By default, EMM386.EXE uses as much memory as is necessary to provide the amount of EMS memory you request.

If you use programs that require XMS memory, you can use the L=*nnn* option to ensure that those programs have access to a specified minimum amount of XMS memory. If you don't include the L=*nnn* option, your programs may not be able to access any XMS memory, because EMM386.EXE may convert all XMS memory into EMS memory.

Why You Might Need the M Option

The M*x* option specifies the location of the EMS page frame. Table 5.2 shows the values of *x* to use to specify the address.

Table 5.2	Page Frame Address Values for the Mx Option
Address	**X**
C000	1
C400	2
C800	3
CC00	4
D000	5
D400	6
D800	7
DC00	8
E000	9
8000	10*
8400	11*
8800	12*
8C00	13*
9000	14*

*Do not use values 10–14 on systems with 640K of memory. These values should be used only on systems with 512K of memory.

The M*x* option is similar to the FRAME=*xxxx* and /P*xxxx* options, but may be a better choice because you are less likely to enter an incorrect address when using the M*x* option. Usually, you'll want to specify the starting address of the page frame so that you create the largest possible upper memory blocks. Place the page frame in a location that does not break an upper memory block into two noncontiguous pieces.

Why You Might Need the Memory Option

The *memory* option specifies how much XMS memory, in K, to allocate to EMM386.EXE. You can specify a value between 16 and 32768. The default is 256. Any value you specify is rounded down to the nearest 16K.

If you use programs that require EMS memory, you may find that the default of 256K of EMS memory is inadequate. If so, use the *memory* argument to specify an additional amount of EMS memory.

On the other hand, if the programs that use EMS memory aren't using the entire 256K of default EMS memory, specify a smaller size. Keep in mind, however, that regardless of the amount of EMS memory you allocate, if you provide any EMS memory, 64K of upper memory will be used for the page frame.

This presents an interesting challenge, because you could be wasting memory by providing EMS memory. Suppose, for example, that one of your device drivers uses EMS memory for its buffers. By watching the screen messages when the driver loads, you can see that the driver uses only 32K of EMS memory for its buffers. If no other programs need EMS memory, the device driver's buffers are using at least 64K of upper memory to hold only 32K of buffers. In addition, whatever amount of XMS memory you specify using the *memory* argument is also being used. If you specify 32K, then 32K of XMS memory, plus 64K of upper memory is being used to hold one device driver's 32K of buffers. Don't you wish the manufacturers would get off their behinds and modernize their device drivers so they could use XMS memory?

Rather than wasting 96K of memory for the device driver's buffers, you may want to try some alternatives. Consider not providing EMS memory to the device driver so it places its buffers in conventional memory instead of in EMS memory. This might allow you to do away with the EMS page frame, and have an extra 64K of upper memory for loading device drivers and TSRs. You might find that you can move enough device drivers and TSRs into upper memory blocks to more than offset the extra conventional memory used by the offending device driver's buffers. You may also want to call the manufacturer's customer support line, especially if it's an 800 number, and complain about the device driver's using EMS instead of XMS memory.

Why You Might Need the NOEMS Option

The NOEMS option tells EMM386.EXE to provide upper memory block support, but not to provide EMS (or Virtual Control Program Interface—VCPI) memory. You must still use the CONFIG.SYS directive DOS=UMB (or DOS=HIGH,UMB) to activate upper memory blocks.

EMS memory is becoming far less important as software manufacturers upgrade their software to use XMS memory. If you don't need to provide EMS memory to any of your programs, use the NOEMS option to prevent EMM386.EXE from using 64K of upper memory for the EMS page frame. If there is no page frame, more upper memory will be available for upper memory blocks. You'll have more room to load device drivers and TSRs, and may end up with more free conventional memory.

Using the NOEMS option may be even more effective than you may think. The EMS page frame is usually taken out of the largest upper memory block. If there is no EMS page frame, the largest upper memory block may grow by 64K, making it possible to load into upper memory device drivers or TSRs that require more than their memory image size to load.

Keep in mind that Windows and Windows programs do not use EMS memory. If you use primarily Windows programs, there may be no reason to provide EMS memory.

Why You Might Need the ON, OFF, and AUTO Options

The ON, OFF, and AUTO options are related, mutually exclusive options. They specify whether EMS memory support is initially set to on or to off, or is available only when requested by a program. You can use these same options at the DOS command line or in a batch file to switch the state of EMS support.

By default, EMS support is set to on. Some programs, however, are unable to function correctly when EMS support is enabled. You can use these options to supply EMS support only as needed. For example, if you use only one program that requires EMS memory, you can set EMS off initially. You can then start the program using a batch file that includes the line **EMM386 ON** before the command that starts the program, and **EMM386 OFF** after the program exits.

Why You Might Need the Pn Option

The P*n*=*xxxx* option specifies the base segment address of an EMS page. *N* specifies the page, which can be 0 to 255, and *xxxx* specifies the segment address, which can be in the ranges 8000h to 9C00h or C000h to EC00h, in 400h increments.

If you specify values for pages 0 through 3, they must be contiguous.

Most programs only use the first four contiguous EMS pages. It's possible, however, to use up to 256 EMS pages, each of which is 16K in length. Generally, though, the P*n*=*xxxx* option is of little use to the average PC user. If you need to use this option, you can be certain that your program documentation will advise you about the values you must use.

Why You Might Need the RAM Option

The RAM option provides access to both EMS memory and the upper memory area. You must still include the CONFIG.SYS directive DOS=UMB (or DOS=HIGH,UMB) to activate upper memory block support.

You must use either the RAM or the NOEMS option to provide access to upper memory.

When you specify the RAM option, EMM386.EXE allocates a 64K contiguous block of upper memory as the EMS page frame. This reduces the amount of upper memory that is available for upper memory blocks.

If your programs require either EMS or Virtual Control Program Interface (VCPI) memory, you must use the RAM option to enable this support. If you include this option but EMM386.EXE cannot allocate a 64K contiguous block of upper memory as the EMS page frame, you'll see an error message when you start your system, and no EMS memory will be made available.

If you don't need EMS memory, use the NOEMS option instead of the RAM option.

Why You Might Need the W Option

The W=*on|off* option enables or disables support for the Weitek math coprocessor. The default is off.

The Weitek math coprocessor is a special, high-performance math coprocessor sometimes used to speed up complex calculations. This math coprocessor is very uncommon—you should not confuse it with a math coprocessor like the 80287 or 80387, neither of which needs this option turned on.

Note

Only the Weitek math coprocessor needs this option turned on. All other brands of math coprocessors, including Intel and Cyrix, do not use this switch.

Why You Might Need the X Option

The X=*xxxx-xxxx* option specifies a range of upper memory segment addresses that EMM386.EXE should not use for upper memory blocks or the EMS page frame. You can specify addresses in the range A000 to FFFF, and they are rounded down to the nearest 4K boundary. If you specify both X=*xxxx-xxxx* and I=*xxxx-xxxx*, the X=*xxxx-xxxx* takes precedence if you specify overlapping ranges.

Sometimes EMM386.EXE is unable to determine that a range of addresses cannot be used safely, and includes that range in upper memory. This can happen for several reasons. One of the most common is an adapter card, such as a network card, that doesn't initialize its memory space until the card is activated. Since EMM386.EXE loads before the card is used, the card remains invisible during the process of allocating upper memory.

Generally, it's fairly easy to find out the beginning address used by an adapter card, but it may be more difficult to determine how large a space to reserve for the card. The beginning address is usually listed as the *base address*. Network adapter cards often use a base address like D800 (which you may also see as D8000). Chapter 4 showed you how to use tools such as MSD and DEBUG to search through memory, but even those tools sometimes have difficulty showing how much memory space to reserve for an adapter card. So how do you determine exactly how much space to reserve for such an adapter card?

It's important to remember that both the X=*xxxx-xxxx* and I=*xxxx-xxxx* options round down to the nearest 4K boundary. In effect, this means that you can include or exclude memory space in 4K sections. This fact makes determining how much space to exclude for an adapter card much easier, because there are a limited number of 4K blocks in upper memory. Suppose, for example, that you've determined that your network adapter card has a base address of D800. Starting from this address, the next three successive 4K boundaries are located at D900, DA00, and DB00. The end of each 4K block is at D8FF, D9FF, DAFF, and DBFF.

It's safest to start by allocating at least 16K to an adapter board. Therefore, you should start by excluding the range from D800 through DBFF, using the command **X=D800-DBFF**. Once you've included this option in the EMM386.EXE device driver line, you can save CONFIG.SYS, and then reboot your system. (Don't forget to reboot every time you try a changed setting—otherwise, you won't really be using the new setting.) Once the system has restarted, make certain everything is working correctly and no error messages are displayed. Be sure you test the network adapter card by logging onto the network and making certain it works, too.

If excluding the range from D800 through DBFF works correctly, you can either accept the current setup as adequate, or you can experiment to see whether reserving less space for the adapter card works. You may have to spend quite a bit of time adjusting the settings, saving your work, rebooting, and checking the results, but doing so may give you additional upper memory that otherwise wouldn't be available. If you do decide to experiment further, remember to change the ranges in 4K increments. To reserve 12K instead of 16K, use **X=D800-DAFF**.

EMM386.EXE's options give you a great amount of control over upper memory. By using these options carefully, you can increase the amount of upper memory block space, reducing the amount of conventional memory needed for device drivers and TSRs. In the rest of this section, we'll examine more of the commands you can use in CONFIG.SYS to further enhance your system's configuration.

Using the BREAK Command

The BREAK=*on|off* command specifies whether your system should do extended testing for the Ctrl-C (or Ctrl-Break) key combination. By default, BREAK is off, which means that your PC looks for Ctrl-C only when it normally reads from the keyboard, or when writing to the screen or your printer.

The setting of the BREAK command doesn't have any memory management effects, but it can have a system performance effect. If BREAK is set to on, your system must spend more time looking for the Ctrl-C key combination, so normal operations may be a little slower than usual.

The main reason for setting BREAK to on is to enable you to interrupt a program that isn't responding. You may want to include the command **BREAK=ON** in CONFIG.SYS while you're testing system configuration options, and later remove the command for slightly improved performance.

Using the BUFFERS Command

The BUFFERS=*n,m* command specifies the number of primary and secondary disk buffers your system should reserve. Primary buffers, *n*, can be between 1 and 99. Secondary buffers, *m*, can be between 1 and 8.

Disk buffers are a DOS system structure used to improve disk performance by storing data in memory. If the same data is needed a second time and is still in a buffer, the system does not have to read the data from disk, and considerable time is saved.

Buffers are far less important to system performance when disk caching software, such as SmartDrive, is being used. Although disk caching software performs a similar function to disk buffers, disk caching software is much more efficient, and provides a much larger improvement in system performance.

Each buffer uses approximately 532 bytes of memory. The default buffer setting, which is 15 on a 640K system, uses nearly 8K of conventional memory. The maximum setting of 99 primary and 8 secondary buffers would eat up nearly 56K of conventional memory. Fortunately, you don't need to use such a large number of buffers, and it's possible to reduce the conventional memory used by buffers to a very small amount.

If HIMEM.SYS is loaded and the command DOS=HIGH is included in CONFIG.SYS, the DOS kernel is placed into the high memory area. The DOS kernel doesn't use the entire high memory area, but the unused space doesn't have to go to waste. Even though only one program at a time can use the high memory area, the unused space in the high memory area can be used to hold the disk buffers if you don't allocate too many. The reason this works is that buffers are a DOS system structure, and therefore are considered part of DOS itself.

Generally, there's room for about 24 buffers along with the DOS kernel in the high memory area. The exact number of buffers you allocate usually isn't too critical, so allocating a number that will fit into the high memory area makes good sense from a memory management perspective. This is especially true if you use disk caching software, because the disk buffers you allocate really won't add very much performance.

Note

If you use the high memory area for purposes other than loading the DOS kernel, the disk buffers will use conventional memory. If you also use disk caching software, reduce the number of buffers to about 3 to minimize the amount of conventional memory used by the buffers.

Usually it's unnecessary to change the secondary buffers from the default of 1. To set the primary buffers to 24, use the command

```
BUFFERS=24
```

Using the COUNTRY Command

The COUNTRY command configures your system to recognize international date, time, currency, case, and decimal separator conventions. Your MS-DOS manual includes complete information on using this command.

The COUNTRY command has one memory management implication—it increases the size of DOS in memory. If you use this command, available conventional memory will probably be reduced because of this larger size for DOS. Therefore, unless you really need to use the international conventions on your system, it's better to forego using the COUNTRY command, at least from a memory management standpoint.

Using the DEVICE Command

The DEVICE command loads a device driver into conventional memory. Device drivers are special programs that provide capabilities not built into DOS itself. These include management of memory outside the 640K conventional memory space, such as upper memory, extended memory, and expanded memory. Other device drivers may provide the ability to access hardware such as SCSI adapters, sound boards, network adapters, and so on.

Because the DEVICE command loads device drivers into conventional memory, it's usually preferable to use the DEVICEHIGH command instead of the DEVICE command. Some device drivers, however, cannot be placed outside of conventional memory. The two MS-DOS 5 memory managers, HIMEM.SYS and EMM386.EXE, are examples of device drivers that must be loaded into conventional memory. In the case of these two device drivers, there's really no other choice, because before the two of them are loaded, your system cannot access any memory other than conventional memory.

Occasionally, you'll find other device drivers that cannot be loaded into upper memory. Usually, the program documentation supplied with the device driver will inform you if the device driver must be loaded into conventional memory. For these types of device drivers, you must use the DEVICE command to load the device driver.

Using the DEVICEHIGH Command

The DEVICEHIGH command loads a device driver into upper memory if possible; otherwise, it loads the device driver into conventional memory. By loading device drivers into upper memory, you can conserve conventional memory for other uses. This make the DEVICEHIGH command one of the most important CONFIG.SYS commands for memory management.

You can optionally include an argument that specifies how much memory a device driver requires. If no upper memory block contains at least the specified amount of free memory, the device driver will be loaded into conventional memory instead of upper memory. This optional argument is of the most value for device drivers that expand after they're loaded into memory. Very few device drivers do this, but the SIZE=*xxxx* argument is available if it becomes necessary. If you use this argument, you must place it between the DEVICEHIGH command and the name of the device driver, and you must specify the memory size in hexadecimal format. For example, to specify that the device driver C:\UTILITY\MYDRV.SYS be loaded in upper memory only if 16K of contiguous upper memory is available, you would use the following command line:

```
DEVICEHIGH SIZE=4000 C:\UTILITY\MYDRV.SYS
```

If more than one upper memory block is available, the DEVICEHIGH command will load each device driver into the upper memory block that has the largest free block. For example, if two upper memory blocks have 45K and 20K free, the 45K block is used first, regardless of the size of the device driver being loaded. This can cause the upper memory blocks to be used in a less than optimum manner. The section on "Performing the Load Order Juggling Act," later in this chapter, suggests methods of working around this problem.

Occasionally, you'll encounter device drivers that cannot be loaded into upper memory.

- Some device drivers cannot be loaded into upper memory because they don't work correctly unless they're loaded in conventional memory. If these types of device drivers are loaded into upper memory, you may lock up your system, or you may experience intermittent crashes.

- Some device drivers cannot be loaded into upper memory because they require more memory to load than their memory image size. In some cases, it's possible to load such device drivers into upper memory if you can free a large enough block of contiguous memory, but sometimes it's just not possible to create a large enough upper memory block.

- Some device drivers cannot be loaded into upper memory because upper memory simply isn't available when they're loaded. HIMEM.SYS and EMM386.EXE are two such device drivers, but device drivers that must be loaded before any memory managers are loaded also fall into this category.

It's important to remember that the DEVICEHIGH command does not fail to load a device driver if upper memory isn't available. Instead, the DEVICE-HIGH command is treated as though you issued the DEVICE command, and the device driver is loaded into conventional memory. As a result, it's not safe to assume that just because you used the DEVICEHIGH command, the device driver actually loaded into upper memory.

Using the DOS Command

The DOS command performs two functions. Used with the UMB parameter, the DOS command enables the use of upper memory—if an upper memory block provider like EMM386.EXE is loaded. Used with the HIGH parameter, the DOS command loads the DOS kernel into the high memory area—if the high memory area is available.

You can combine the HIGH and UMB parameters in the same command, as in

```
DOS=HIGH,UMB
```

Placing the DOS kernel in the high memory area increases the amount of conventional memory available to applications by reducing the amount of conventional memory used by DOS. Not only does the DOS=HIGH command move the DOS kernel into the high memory area, but it also moves the DOS disk buffers into the high memory area if the buffers will fit in the high memory area. (Usually, there's room for about 24 buffers in the high memory area.)

Enabling access to upper memory allows device drivers and TSRs to be loaded into upper memory blocks. This, too, increases the amount of conventional memory available to applications.

Before you can use either the HIGH or UMB parameters, you must first load HIMEM.SYS. In addition, the UMB parameter requires that EMM386.EXE be loaded before you use the DOS command.

Loading the DOS kernel into the high memory area and enabling upper memory block access are two very important steps in advanced memory management. These steps ensure that more conventional memory can be made available for applications.

> **Note**
>
> If you're on a network, you may find that your network software requires access to the high memory area. If so, you will not be able to use the HIGH parameter with the DOS command, because only one program can use the high memory area at a time. You can still use the UMB parameter to enable access to upper memory, however.

Using the DRIVPARM Command

The DRIVPARM command defines the standard configuration of a disk drive that is not automatically recognized correctly by DOS. You can also use this command to define the parameters for other types of block devices, such as tape drives that are accessed using a drive letter.

A common use for the DRIVPARM command is to help a system recognize types of disk drives not originally available on the system. For example, if you add 3.5-inch diskette drives on some systems, the PC will assume that the drive is a 360K, 5.25-inch diskette drive. The DRIVPARM command tells the system how to access the drive correctly.

The DRIVPARM command is not a memory management command, but using this command slightly increases the size of DOS in memory, so you should avoid using the DRIVPARM command if possible. One way to test whether the DRIVPARM command is needed is to insert a new, unformatted, high-density diskette in the drive, and then format the diskette without specifying the diskette size, and without having DRIVPARM loaded. If the diskette if formatted to its full capacity, you don't need to use the DRIVPARM command. If the diskette is formatted at a lower capacity, use the DRIVPARM command to specify the drive's specifications.

Using the FCBS Command

The FCBS command specifies the number of file control blocks that can be open at one time. You can specify a value between 1 and 255; the default is 4.

File control blocks are an obsolete method of accessing files. Programmers have been discouraged from using this method of file access since MS-DOS 2.x, so there's really no excuse for a modern program to require the use of file control blocks.

Each additional file control block uses conventional memory. You can save a small amount of memory by including the following command in CONFIG.SYS:

```
FCBS=1
```

Using the FILES Command

The FILES command specifies the number of files that can be open at one time. You can use values between 8 and 255. The default is 8.

Each additional file you specify with the FILES command uses some conventional memory, so you might assume that you would want to save memory by specifying the smallest possible value. In reality, however, you must specify a large enough value to accommodate the needs of every program that may be running simultaneously. Unfortunately, it can be difficult to determine how many files each program may attempt to open. One method of determining how many files you must specify is to start with a very low value, such as 8, and try running all of your applications. If you receive an error message telling you that the program is unable to open enough files, you'll know you must increase the number of files that can be open at one time.

This trial and error approach to specifying the number of files that can be open at one time may work, but it may also create difficult problems. Suppose, for example, that you try a low value for the files, and everything seems to be working. A few weeks later, after working for several hours, you try to update a data file, only to be greeted with an error message telling you the data can't be saved because too many files are open. The few bytes of memory you saved by specifying a minimum number of files won't seem quite so important at that point, will they?

A good compromise is possible without applying the trial and error approach. In most cases, 20 files would be adequate for users who run only DOS programs. If you use Windows, or some other environment that allows several programs to run at the same time, you'll need a setting of at least 40. In either case, the 1K or 2K of memory used by the FILES command is good insurance against the problem of being unable to open files when necessary.

> ### Note
>
> Some programs have even higher requirements. Be sure to check the program documentation when you install new software to see whether the FILES setting should be increased.

MS-DOS 5 always places the structures for open files in conventional memory. This is true even when the DOS kernel is loaded into the high memory area.

Using the INSTALL Command

The INSTALL command loads TSR programs into conventional memory. Generally, INSTALL is used to load TSRs that should be loaded only once per DOS session. For example, if you use the FASTOPEN program, the program can be loaded only once each time you boot your system.

Although you could load TSR programs using commands in AUTOEXEC.BAT or at the DOS command prompt, loading them using the INSTALL command in CONFIG.SYS uses slightly less memory. This is because INSTALL does not create an environment for the TSR. Thus, TSRs loaded using the INSTALL command cannot use environment variables. They also cannot use shortcut keys, or require COMMAND.COM for handling critical errors. Some TSRs do not function properly if you load them using the INSTALL command.

TSRs that are loaded at the DOS command prompt, or in a batch file such as AUTOEXEC.BAT, receive a copy of the DOS environment. By default, MS-DOS 5 reserves 256 bytes for the environment. If you use the default environment size, loading four TSRs using the INSTALL command in CONFIG.SYS would save 1K of conventional memory, compared to loading those same TSRs in AUTOEXEC.BAT or at the DOS command prompt.

All DEVICE and DEVICEHIGH commands are processed and executed before any INSTALL commands are processed and executed. You cannot load a TSR before a device driver by placing an INSTALL ahead of the DEVICE and DEVICEHIGH commands.

Using the INSTALLHIGH Command

The INSTALLHIGH command loads TSR programs into upper memory if it is available; otherwise, it loads them into conventional memory. The INSTALL-HIGH command is used for exactly the same purposes as the INSTALL command.

The INSTALLHIGH command is not shown in the documentation provided with MS-DOS 5, but you can use the command just as you would the INSTALL command. The same restrictions that apply to the INSTALL command also apply to the INSTALLHIGH command. Like the INSTALL command, the INSTALLHIGH command is processed after all DEVICE and DEVICEHIGH commands.

If your TSR programs can function correctly without a copy of the DOS environment, without shortcut keys, and without using COMMAND.COM as a critical error handler, loading them using the INSTALLHIGH command is a good way to save memory. Since TSRs loaded with the INSTALLHIGH command don't receive a copy of the DOS environment, they can fit into a slightly smaller upper memory block than is possible if you load them in AUTOEXEC.BAT or at the DOS command prompt. This especially important if you increase the environment size, because each TSR loaded using the INSTALLHIGH command saves an amount of memory equal to the environment size.

The INSTALLHIGH command is an important part of your advanced memory management toolkit. Sometimes, even a very small amount of additional space in upper memory blocks makes the difference between being able to load everything you want into upper memory, and loading some items into conventional memory.

Using the LASTDRIVE Command

The LASTDRIVE command specifies the maximum number of disk drives you can access. You can specify any drive letter between A and Z. By default, DOS allocates structures for one drive following the last physical drive in your system.

You must specify drive letters at least as high as the last drive letter you want to access as a substituted drive or on a network. For example, if you create three substituted drives on a PC that has two diskette drives and a hard disk, you must specify a LASTDRIVE of at least F.

Networks often use drive M: as a network drive, especially if email is in use on the network. You must specify a LASTDRIVE high enough to allow access to the last network drive letter you intend to map.

MS-DOS creates data structures in conventional memory for each drive letter you specify. Allocating too many drive letters simply wastes memory. For example, setting LASTDRIVE to Z uses slightly over 2K of conventional memory, while providing no extra benefits compared to a more appropriate setting. Unless you are connected to a network or use substituted drives, it's usually best to allow DOS to allocate the default number of drive letters.

Using the REM Command

The REM command indicates a comment line in CONFIG.SYS. Normally, REM is used to document CONFIG.SYS, but it has an even more important purpose when you are experimenting with system configurations. Rather than deleting lines you don't want executed, you can add REM and a space at the beginning of the line. Of course, adding a real comment line to remind you of the purpose of each change you make can be quite helpful, too.

CONFIG.SYS lines that start with REM aren't displayed when CONFIG.SYS is processed unless you add the command **ECHO ON** to an earlier line in the file. Use **ECHO OFF** to turn off echoing of command lines you've disabled with REM—otherwise, it's easy to become confused about which lines are actually being executed, and which are simply comment lines.

Once you've determined the optimum configuration for your system, you may want to remove the extra command lines you turned into comment lines using REM. These extra lines increase the size of CONFIG.SYS, and even though comment lines are not executed, they will slow the boot process slightly. In addition, the fewer commented-out command lines you have in

CONFIG.SYS, the easier it will be to understand the overall flow of your CONFIG.SYS file.

Using the SHELL Command

The SHELL command specifies the name and location of the command interpreter, which is usually COMMAND.COM. Used in combination with COMMAND, the SHELL command can also be used to specify the DOS environment size. For example, the following command specifies C:\DOS as the location of COMMAND.COM, the command interpreter, and increases the environment size to 384 bytes (the /E:*nnn* sets the environment size):

```
SHELL=C:\DOS\COMMAND.COM C:\DOS\ /E:384 /P
```

Increasing the environment size has serious implications for memory management. Each TSR and program loaded at the command prompt, or in a batch file such as AUTOEXEC.BAT, inherits a copy of the DOS environment. If you increase the environment size, the amount of memory used by each of these TSRs and programs increases by the amount of the increase in the environment size. If the environment size is 256 bytes too large, each TSR and program uses 256 bytes more memory than necessary.

It's important, therefore, to make certain you don't increase the environment size any more than necessary. To determine how large the environment should be, enter the following commands at the DOS prompt:

```
SET > SETSIZE.TXT
DIR SETSIZE.TXT
```

The size displayed for SETSIZE.TXT indicates the amount of memory used by the DOS environment variables currently allocated. To minimize the amount of memory wasted by setting the environment size too large, set your environment slightly larger than the size of SETSIZE.TXT. The environment size should be set to a multiple of 16 bytes. To determine the minimum size for your environment, divide the size of SETSIZE.TXT by 16, round the result up to the next integer value, and multiply that value by 16.

For example, if SETSIZE.TXT is listed as 344 bytes, divide 344 by 16 to obtain the value of 21.5. Round this up to 22, and multiply by 16 to obtain the correct value of 352 bytes for the environment size.

Note

Setting a minimal size for the DOS environment allows very little room for additional environment variables. Sometimes batch files or other programs create temporary environment variables that may not be visible using the technique noted above. If you receive the message "Out of environment space" when you run a batch file or an application program, increase the size of the DOS environment slightly. Remember to increase the environment size in 16-byte increments.

Using the STACKS Command

The STACKS=n,s command specifies the number of data stacks your system should allocate for programs to handle hardware interrupts. You can specify 0 or 8 through 64 for n (the number of stacks), and 0 or 32 through 512 for s (the size of the stacks in bytes). Except for 8088-based systems, the default is STACKS=9,128.

A common setting for STACKS is 9,256, which allocates 9 stacks of 256 bytes each, using almost 3K of conventional memory. You may be able to specify STACKS=0,0 to save the memory otherwise allocated for this system structure.

It's difficult to determine whether the 0,0 setting is working correctly, because the standard description states that the "computer becomes unstable" when the values are set too low. Unless you are prepared to do extensive testing after making this single change, it's nearly impossible to know whether STACKS=0,0 will work correctly on your PC. This is one case where you're truly on your own, so good luck!

Many of the CONFIG.SYS options have memory management implications that go far beyond what you might normally expect. Even small changes are often multiplied as they spread their effects across the broad range of device drivers and TSRs you load each time you start your system. Next we'll look at how your AUTOEXEC.BAT file further affects your system.

Using AUTOEXEC.BAT Options

After CONFIG.SYS, AUTOEXEC.BAT is the second special user-created config-uration file your system reads each time you start your PC. Once the com-mands in CONFIG.SYS have been executed, those in AUTOEXEC.BAT are processed. Both files can contain commands that configure your system, but only CONFIG.SYS can be used to load device drivers. Both files can contain commands that load TSRs, but only AUTOEXEC.BAT can be used to load TSRs that need a copy of the DOS environment.

From a memory management perspective, there are relatively few changes you can make in AUTOEXEC.BAT that affect the amount of available mem-ory. You may be able to adjust the parameters passed to some TSRs you load in AUTOEXEC.BAT, but in most cases these changes will have little effect on memory usage. Let's have a look at what you can do in AUTOEXEC.BAT to enhance your memory utilization.

Using the LOADHIGH Command

The LOADHIGH command, which you can abbreviate as LH, is the one MS-DOS 5 memory management command you can use at the DOS prompt or in a batch file such as AUTOEXEC.BAT. This command loads a TSR into upper memory if possible; otherwise, the TSR is loaded into conventional memory.

To use the LOADHIGH command, simply add the command to the begin-ning of a line in AUTOEXEC.BAT that loads a TSR program. If a large enough contiguous upper memory block is available, the TSR is loaded into upper memory. The LOADHIGH command does not fail if no upper memory block is large enough to load the TSR; instead, the TSR program is simply loaded into conventional memory—no error message is displayed.

Each TSR program you can load into upper memory instead of conven-tional memory increases the amount of free conventional memory. Most TSRs can function correctly in upper memory, so you should load as many TSRs using the LOADHIGH command as possible.

Before you can use the LOADHIGH command successfully, three com-mands must be executed in CONFIG.SYS:

1. The HIMEM.SYS device driver must be loaded.

2. The EMM386.EXE device driver must be loaded.

3. The DOS=UMB (or DOS=HIGH,UMB) command must be executed.

Consider the INSTALLHIGH Option

Instead of loading TSRs into upper memory using the AUTOEXEC.BAT command LOADHIGH, you may want to consider loading them using the CONFIG.SYS command INSTALLHIGH. Although the two commands serve a similar purpose, TSRs loaded using the INSTALLHIGH command may use slightly less memory because they don't receive their own copy of the DOS environment, as they do when loaded using LOADHIGH.

TSRs that require a copy of the DOS environment, that use shortcut keys, or that depend upon COMMAND.COM to handle critical errors cannot be loaded using the INSTALLHIGH command, however, so LOADHIGH is the only way to load these TSRs into upper memory. See the earlier section on CONFIG.SYS options for more information in the INSTALLHIGH command.

Performing the Load Order Juggling Act

Once you've applied all the memory management tricks you've learned so far, you probably have more conventional memory available than you ever had before. But now that you have a feel for advanced memory management, you're probably also a little frustrated because you haven't been able to accomplish quite as much as you'd like. You probably still have one or two device drivers or TSRs in conventional memory that you'd like to load into upper memory. It's time to bring out the last "big gun" of MS-DOS 5 advanced memory management techniques, the load order juggling act.

Reordering Device Drivers and TSRs

The *load order juggling act* is the term I use to describe the process of making better use of memory resources by changing the order in which device drivers and TSRs are actually loaded into memory. You may wonder how changing the order in which device drivers and TSRs are loaded into memory can affect memory usage. After all, simply changing the order in which device drivers and TSRs are loaded doesn't change the amount of memory they use, does it?

It's true that device drivers and TSRs will still use the same amount of memory no matter what order they're loaded in. What changes along with load order, though, is how the device drivers and TSRs fit together in memory. To understand how changing the load order can have this effect, think of the pieces of a jigsaw puzzle. If you line up the puzzle pieces in a row, the row will be longer if the pieces are arranged at random than it will if the pieces are arranged so they fit together.

Of course, device drivers and TSRs don't fit together like jigsaw puzzle pieces, but the order in which they're loaded can result in a similar effect. There are several reasons for this:

- Device drivers and TSRs you load into upper memory always use the largest available upper memory block, whether they need a block that large or not. If a small device driver or TSR uses part of an upper memory block, the remaining space may not be of sufficient size to load a larger device driver or TSR you load later.

- Some device drivers and TSRs require more memory to load than their memory image size. If a device driver or TSR cannot find an upper memory block large enough for its load size, the device driver or TSR will load into conventional memory.

- TSR programs loaded using the INSTALLHIGH command in CONFIG.SYS use slightly less memory than if the same TSR program is loaded using the LOADHIGH command in AUTOEXEC.BAT. Sometimes this small difference can be enough to leave just the extra amount of memory that allows another TSR to load into upper memory instead of into conventional memory.

Let's consider some examples that show how these factors affect your memory management scheme.

First, imagine that you have two device drivers, DRV1.SYS and DRV2.SYS, that use 12K and 45K of memory, respectively. If you have two upper memory blocks of 16K and 50K, both device drivers can be loaded into upper memory, but only if the 45K DRV2.SYS is loaded first. If the 12K DRV1.SYS is loaded first, it will use the 50K upper memory block, even though the 16K upper memory block is large enough to hold DRV1.SYS. Because the 50K upper memory block will only have 38K of free space after DRV1.SYS is loaded, DRV2.SYS can load only into conventional memory. To optimize your memory management scheme, you should take one of two steps, depending on the situation. If the two device drivers are independent of each other, simply load DRV2.SYS first, and then load DRV1.SYS. Both device drivers will fit into the correct upper memory blocks, and they won't use any conventional memory. If the two device drivers aren't independent of each other, and DRV2.SYS requires that DRV1.SYS be loaded first, use the DEVICE command to load DRV1.SYS into conventional memory. Then use DEVICEHIGH to load DRV2.SYS into upper memory. You'll use 12K of conventional memory for DRV1.SYS, but because DRV2.SYS is loaded into upper memory, you'll save the 45K of conventional memory it would use. Changing the first DEVICEHIGH command to a DEVICE command saves a net of 33K of conventional memory in this case.

Next, suppose you load a device driver, DRV3.SYS, that takes 55K of memory to load, but has a memory image size of 18K. In addition, you load another device driver, DRV4.SYS, that requires 37K of memory, both during and after loading. If you have an upper memory block that's 57K in size, you can load the two device drivers into the upper memory block only if you load DRV3.SYS before you load DRV4.SYS. Once again, though, you have to consider whether the two device drivers are truly independent of each other. If DRV3.SYS must be loaded before DRV4.SYS, consider the memory image size of each to determine which makes better use of upper memory. Load the device driver with the smallest memory image size into conventional memory.

Finally, suppose you load several TSR programs that don't require a copy of the DOS environment, shortcut keys, or COMMAND.COM's critical error handler. In addition, you use the SHELL= command in CONFIG.SYS to increase the DOS environment size to 1024 bytes. By using the INSTALL-HIGH command in CONFIG.SYS, you'll save 1K of upper memory for each TSR. This small saving may be just enough to allow an additional TSR to fit into an upper memory block, compared to loading the same TSRs using LOADHIGH in AUTOEXEC.BAT. By moving the loading of these TSRs from AUTOEXEC.BAT to CONFIG.SYS, you've saved the conventional memory that would normally be used by one of the TSRs.

Limitations to Reordering

There are some limitations to what you can accomplish through reordering the loading sequence of your device drivers and TSRs. These limitations can sometimes prevent you from accomplishing your goal of placing all device drivers and TSRs into upper memory, leaving the maximum possible free conventional memory.

- Device drivers are always loaded before TSR programs. You cannot change this by placing INSTALLHIGH commands before DEVICEHIGH commands in CONFIG.SYS.
- Some device drivers and TSRs require a certain load order. In some cases, a device driver or TSR depends on another device driver or TSR that must be loaded first. In other cases, device drivers or TSRs cannot function correctly if certain other device drivers or TSRs have already been loaded.
- A few device drivers cannot be loaded once a memory manager has been loaded. One example is certain SCSI adapter device drivers that must be placed first in CONFIG.SYS.

As you experiment with changing the load order of device drivers and TSRs, use the MEM command options you learned in Chapter 4 to track your success. Printed copies of each version of CONFIG.SYS and AUTOEXEC.BAT, along with printed copies of the MEM reports, will provide good documentation of your progress. Don't forget to write the current date and time on each set of printouts.

Summary

MS-DOS 5 introduced the concept of advanced memory management to the average PC user. For the first time, MS-DOS included the tools you needed to make better, more efficient use of your system's memory resources.

Actually using the MS-DOS 5 memory management tools wasn't an easy task, however. Not only was the documentation provided with the operating system overly technical, but it was also quite short on really useful information. MS-DOS 5 memory management has often been relegated to the realm of the computer wizard or the technical nerd. In this chapter you learned that MS-DOS 5's memory management tools really can be used by the average PC user. You actually can improve the way your system operates, and feel good about your ability to relate to one of the more complicated parts of your computer.

Chapter 6

Managing Your Memory with MS-DOS 6

Although MS-DOS 5 was the first version of DOS that included the tools needed for memory management, MS-DOS 6 was the first version of DOS that made advanced memory management truly available to the average PC user. This chapter is about memory management using the tools included in MS-DOS 6.

The memory management tools included in MS-DOS 6 are, for the first time, strong enough to compete with third-party memory managers such as QEMM and 386MAX. In most cases, there is little you can gain from those third-party memory managers compared to what comes with MS-DOS 6. If you're moving up from MS-DOS 5, you'll probably be surprised at how much more powerful the memory management tools in MS-DOS 6 actually are than their MS-DOS 5 counterparts.

Prior to the introduction of MS-DOS 5, advanced memory management suffered from a major problem of compatibility. This problem was caused by the lack of real standards for the use of memory outside the normal 640K conventional memory space. By the time MS-DOS 6 was introduced, the standards established in MS-DOS 5 were well accepted in the PC industry.

Memory management technique conflicts are far less common today than they were just a few years ago, simply because these standards have become so well accepted.

As with MS-DOS 5, taking advantage of all of MS-DOS 6's new features requires at least an 80386 processor in your system. MS-DOS 6 did not introduce any new memory specifications, but it offered full support of upper memory, the high memory area, and the XMS memory standard for extended memory on modern PCs.

The advanced memory management tools in MS-DOS 6 are really greatly enhanced compared to those in MS-DOS 5. They're easier to use and have more powerful capabilities, as well. Many of the memory management options introduced in MS-DOS 5 remain available in MS-DOS 6, but you're less likely to need to use them manually. Some of the memory management options introduced in MS-DOS 5 have been changed slightly, making it even more important to understand how those options work when you upgrade. Finally, a few memory management options are simply no longer necessary.

In this chapter I'll show you how to use all of MS-DOS 6's (and MS-DOS 6.2's) memory management options. I'll also explain why you might want to use some of the more obscure options, and what effect they'll have on your PC.

Memory management in MS-DOS 6 can be broken down into four areas:

- The first area consists of the commands and directives you'll use in CONFIG.SYS. This file presents the first system configuration opportunity on any PC, because this is the first user file processed whenever you start your system.

- The second area consists of the commands you'll use in AUTOEXEC.BAT. This is the second user file processed during startup.

- The third area consists of using MemMaker, the automated memory optimizer.

- The fourth area of MS-DOS 6 memory management is something I call the *load order juggling act*. Often, this is the most difficult area to understand, but one that can produce quite impressive results.

> **Note**
>
> Advanced memory management techniques require an understanding of the subjects presented in the earlier chapters of this book. If you aren't comfortable with some of the topics covered earlier, please take the time to review any matter that doesn't seem clear before you begin experimenting with your system's configuration.

Using CONFIG.SYS Options

CONFIG.SYS is very important in configuring your system. If CONFIG.SYS exists in the root directory of the boot disk, any commands or directives it contains are read and executed as part of the system startup process. Many of the system configuration options can be used only when placed them in CONFIG.SYS; you cannot exercise these options any other way.

Because most of the CONFIG.SYS system configuration options cannot be executed at the command line, it's often difficult to see exactly what happens as they are processed. Error or information messages displayed during the processing of CONFIG.SYS usually scroll by so quickly that you might miss important details. If you're not watching your screen closely, and if you're not a speed reader, you might never realize that something is wrong. This makes it even more important to make certain that your CONFIG.SYS file is correctly structured, and that every line it contains is absolutely correct.

Fortunately, an important modification to one of the MS-DOS system files, IO.SYS, was incorporated in MS-DOS 6. If you press the F8 key when you see the message "Starting MS-DOS..." while your system is booting, you will be prompted before each line in CONFIG.SYS is executed. This makes it much easier to see any error or information messages that may be displayed.

In MS-DOS 6, you can bypass CONFIG.SYS and AUTOEXEC.BAT entirely by pressing the F5 key when the message "Starting MS-DOS..." is displayed. MS-DOS 6 and MS-DOS 6.2 both use the F5 key the same way, but they differ in their use of the F8 key. While both MS-DOS 6 and MS-DOS 6.2 allow you to confirm each CONFIG.SYS line after you press the F8 key, only MS-DOS 6.2 allows you to confirm each line in AUTOEXEC.BAT. MS-DOS 6 simply gives you the option of processing or bypassing the entire AUTOEXEC.BAT file.

Note

In MS-DOS 6.2, you can also bypass the loading of DBLSPACE.BIN by pressing Ctrl-F5 or Ctrl-F8, but since DBLSPACE.BIN is required for accessing compressed drives, this is not recommended except in an emergency.

Even though the F5 and F8 key methods of controlling the processing of CONFIG.SYS and AUTOEXEC.BAT commands make experimenting with system configuration options much safer in MS-DOS 6 than in earlier DOS versions, it's always best to play it safe. Always try your proposed changes on a boot diskette first, and copy them to your hard disk only after you've verified that a new configuration works correctly.

For MS-DOS 6.x memory management purposes, two device drivers, HIMEM.SYS and EMM386.EXE, are the two most important items that appear in CONFIG.SYS. If you've upgraded from MS-DOS 5, many of the options for these two device drivers will seem familiar, but there are some very important differences in the newer versions of these device drivers. It's very important to understand how to use these two device drivers, especially if you've upgraded from an earlier DOS version. Otherwise, you won't be able to apply any of the other MS-DOS 6.x advanced memory management techniques, and you may not be taking advantage of the upgraded options in the newer versions. Because of this importance, I'll start the discussion of CONFIG.SYS options by looking at each of these two device drivers in detail.

Understanding HIMEM.SYS's Options

HIMEM.SYS is the MS-DOS 6 XMS memory manager. It must be loaded before EMM386.EXE, and is usually the first device driver listed in CONFIG.SYS. Until HIMEM.SYS is loaded, no XMS memory is available, the high memory area is not available, and no upper memory can be made available. In fact, without HIMEM.SYS, your PC is limited to accessing the 640K of conventional memory.

The discussions of HIMEM.SYS and EMM386.EXE in this chapter are based upon the versions shipped with MS-DOS 6, Windows 3.1, or Windows for Workgroups. You should always use the newest versions of HIMEM.SYS and EMM386.EXE that are available.

Although some of the CONFIG.SYS commands, such as BREAK and BUFFERS, can precede the line that loads the HIMEM.SYS device driver, it's usually best to place this line as the first line in CONFIG.SYS. If your DOS files are in C:\DOS, the following CONFIG.SYS line loads the HIMEM.SYS device driver without specifying any optional parameters:

```
DEVICE=C:\DOS\HIMEM.SYS
```

The exception to the rule of loading the HIMEM.SYS device driver first is for systems that use special device drivers to access their hard disk. Usually, such device drivers must be loaded first, before any memory manager is loaded. For example, systems with SCSI hard disks and adapters may include a command similar to

```
DEVICE=C:\UTILITY\ASPI4DOS.SYS
```

If your system includes a similar device driver as the first line in your existing CONFIG.SYS file, it's usually best simply to add the HIMEM.SYS device driver as the second device driver.

If you don't use any options, HIMEM.SYS allocates all extended memory as XMS memory, and default settings are used for all HIMEM.SYS options. In most cases, the default settings will work adequately, but you may find that using one or more of HIMEM.SYS's options is necessary, or at least desirable. In some cases, the only way you'll be able to use certain software will be to specify certain options. In other cases, using certain options will actually make your PC run faster. Let's have a look at the options in the MS-DOS 6 version of HIMEM.SYS.

Why You Might Need the /A20CONTROL Option

The /A20CONTROL:*on|off* option specifies whether HIMEM.SYS should attempt to take control of the A20 memory address line even if another program has already taken control of the line when HIMEM.SYS is loaded. If you specify /**A20CONTROL:off**, HIMEM.SYS can take control only if no other program is already using the A20 memory address line.

The use of the /A20CONTROL:*on|off* option is a very difficult issue to resolve. Generally, only memory managers and DOS extenders will attempt to control the A20 memory address line. If you're using HIMEM.SYS to manage extended memory, it's quite unlikely that you'll ever have a need for this option. If you use a third-party memory manager, you probably don't have any reason to load HIMEM.SYS in addition to the other memory manager. Finally, if you use programs that use their own DOS extenders, you'll probably use the /INT15 option to supply extended memory to the DOS extended program.

If you do specify /**A20CONTROL:on**, HIMEM.SYS will attempt to take control of the A20 memory address line, regardless of any other program's existing control of the line. Doing so will probably disable the other program.

Why You Might Need the /CPUCLOCK Option

The /CPUCLOCK:*on|off* option is used to specify whether HIMEM.SYS affects your system's internal clock. If your PC runs slower when HIMEM.SYS is loaded, specifying /**CPUCLOCK:ON** might correct the problem.

Be aware, however, that specifying /**CPUCLOCK:ON** makes HIMEM.SYS itself a little slower, so if you feel HIMEM.SYS is slowing your PC's clock, you may want to experiment to see whether adding this switch helps, or whether it makes your PC run even more slowly.

This switch is most useful on some of the systems that have a "turbo" switch that switches the processor between high- and low-speed operation. If your PC has such a switch, and booting your system and loading HIMEM.SYS switches to the lower speed, try the /**CPUCLOCK:ON** option to see whether it removes the problem.

Why You Might Need the /EISA Option

The /EISA option specifies that HIMEM.SYS should allocate all available extended memory on a system with an EISA (Extended Industry Standard

Architecture) bus and more than 16M of memory. This option serves no purpose on any other type of system, because HIMEM.SYS automatically allocates all available extended memory on any other type of system.

Occasionally, memory access conflicts may arise on systems with more than 16M of memory and certain types of adapters that use DMA (Direct Memory Access), such as some SCSI adapters. If your system has more than 16M of memory and uses the EISA bus, you may need to experiment with the /EISA option to determine whether you need to use this option.

Why You Might Need the /HMAMIN Option

The /HMAMIN=*n* option specifies how much memory, in K, a program must use before it can take over the high memory area (HMA). You can specify a value between 0 and 63, and the default is 0.

The high memory area is a very useful, but limited, extension to the memory your PC can access in real mode. At just under 64K in size, this special section of memory can be used almost like conventional memory for loading a memory-resident program. Generally, the most common use for the high memory area in MS-DOS 6 is to hold part of the DOS kernel, reducing the amount of conventional memory used by DOS itself.

The high memory area suffers from one major limitation, however, and it is the reason the /HMAMIN=*n* option is available. Only one program at a time can use the high memory area, and any leftover space in the high memory area is simply wasted.

For example, suppose a program that uses 12K of memory is loaded into the high memory area. The remaining 52K of space is simply wasted, because no other program can use the high memory area once the first program is loaded. In such a case, specifying /**HMAMIN=13** would prevent the 12K program from loading into the high memory area, and allow a larger program that access.

The reason the /HMAMIN=*n* option may be needed is that some programs automatically load themselves into the high memory area if it is available. For example, certain network drivers try to use this area if possible. If you have several such programs, you'll use the /HMAMIN=*n* option to make certain only the largest possible program can use high memory.

You don't need to use the /HMAMIN=*n* option if the DOS kernel is the only program on your system that uses high memory.

Why You Might Need the /INT15 Option

The /INT15=*nnnn* option specifies how much extended memory, in K, is reserved for access through the interrupt 15h interface method. You can specify a value between 64 and 65,535. The default is zero.

Older programs that use their own DOS extenders usually cannot use XMS memory, but instead often use a method of allocating extended memory through a DOS service called the *interrupt 15h interface*. If you use these types of programs, you must use the /INT15=*nnnn* option to enable them to access extended memory.

Any extended memory allocated through the interrupt 15h interface cannot also be used as XMS memory. This conflict between methods of accessing extended memory can usually be eliminated by upgrading to newer versions of your application programs, since most programs that use extended memory now recognize the XMS standard.

If you are unable or unwilling to upgrade to an XMS-aware program, you may want to consider one of the multiple configuration options discussed in Chapter 3. When you need to use the old DOS extended program, boot using a special configuration that supplies extended memory through the interrupt 15h interface. When you aren't using the DOS extended program, boot your system using a configuration that supplies all extended memory through the XMS standard. This will allow you to run Windows, SmartDrive, and other modern XMS-aware programs.

Why You Might Need the /NUMHANDLES Option

The /NUMHANDLES=*n* option specifies the number of extended memory block handles that can be used at the same time. You can specify any number between 1 and 128; the default is 32. Each extended memory block handle uses 6 bytes of memory, so the default number uses 192 bytes, while the maximum uses 768 bytes.

An XMS memory manager allocates extended memory by providing *extended memory block handles*—which are basically the means to temporarily access blocks of extended memory—to programs that request extended memory. If too many extended memory block handles are requested at the same time, some of those requests will fail, and the requesting program may wait and try again, display an error message, or simply crash.

Normally, the default of 32 handles should be sufficient, but if you run a large number of programs that use XMS memory at the same time, such as a large number of Windows programs, you may need to increase the number of handles. Most well-behaved programs will display an error message rather than crashing your system, but if you experience an unusual number of system crashes, you may want to increase the number of handles to see if the problem is reduced or eliminated. Adding additional handles really doesn't cost you very much memory—doubling the number to 64 consumes only an extra 192 bytes.

Why You Might Need the /MACHINE Option

The /MACHINE:*xxxx* option specifies the type of computer you're using so HIMEM.SYS can properly access extended memory. Usually, HIMEM.SYS can work correctly without having this option specified, but in some cases, specifying the type of system is necessary, or may improve performance.

HIMEM.SYS uses something called an *A20 handler* to access extended memory. A20 refers to the twenty-first memory address line, the first memory address line that accesses memory above the 1M address. The first 20 memory address lines, A0–A19, are present on all PCs, regardless of their processors. The A20 line is available only on systems with an 80286 or higher processor.

Table 6.1 shows the different codes and numbers you can specify for your system. You can specify either the code or the corresponding number, not both. The default A20 handler is the standard IBM AT handler.

It may be difficult to determine whether your system needs to have the A20 handler specified. If HIMEM.SYS cannot correctly access the A20 handler, you may see an error message while the system is booting, or your system may be prone to crashing when DOS is loaded into the high memory area.

Table 6.1 Values for the /MACHINE:xxxx Option		
System	Code	Number
Acer 1100	ACER1100	6
AT&T 6300 Plus	ATT6300PLUS	5
Bull Micral 60	BULLMICRAL	16
CSS Labs	CSS	12
Dell XBIOS	DELL	17
HP Vectra	FASTHP	14
HP Vectra (A & A+)	HPVECTRA	4
IBM 7552 Industrial Computer	IBM7552	15
IBM AT or 100% compatible	AT	1
IBM PC/AT (alternative delay)	AT1	11
IBM PC/AT (alternative delay)	AT2	12
IBM PC/AT (alternative delay)	AT3	13
IBM PS/2	PS2	2
Philips	PHILIPS	13
Phoenix Cascade BIOS	PTLCASCADE	3
Toshiba 1600 & 1200XE	TOSHIBA	7
Tulip SX	TULIP	9
Wyse 12.5 MHz 286	WYSE	8
Zenith ZBIOS	ZENITH	10

You should probably assume that if your system is specifically listed in Table 6.1, specifying the A20 handler is required. If your system is not listed in Table 6.1, but you see an error message from HIMEM.SYS, or your system becomes unstable when DOS is loaded high, try the AT1, AT2, or AT3 settings, or select a setting for a system similar to your PC.

Why You Might Need the /SHADOWRAM Option

The /SHADOWRAM:*on|off* option specifies whether HIMEM.SYS should attempt to switch off *shadow RAM*—the process of copying the system's ROM BIOS into RAM for faster execution. HIMEM.SYS cannot always control whether shadow RAM is enabled, so this option may not accomplish anything on some systems.

Your system uses the ROM BIOS to hold basic system operating instructions. These very basic instructions are executed frequently, so PC manufacturers often copy them from ROM, which has quite slow access, to RAM, which can be accessed much faster. This allows for a small performance boost; however, access to additional memory is usually more important than the small increase in performance achieved through the use of shadow RAM.

It's usually a good idea to trade a little speed for the extra memory that may be made available by using the **/SHADOWRAM:off** switch. Keep in mind, however, that since HIMEM.SYS cannot always control shadow RAM, this switch may have no effect on your system.

Why You Might Need the /VERBOSE Option

The /VERBOSE option, which you can abbreviate as /V, instructs HIMEM.SYS to display status and error messages while loading. By default, HIMEM does not display any messages unless it encounters an error. You can also display HIMEM.SYS status by pressing and holding the Alt key while HIMEM.SYS loads.

Using the /VERBOSE option can be quite helpful, especially when you are configuring your system. The messages HIMEM.SYS displays can tell you quite a bit of information about HIMEM.SYS's status. You may want to use the F8 key to execute CONFIG.SYS one line at a time so you can examine HIMEM.SYS's messages before they have a chance to scroll off the screen.

Why You Might Need the /TESTMEM Option

The /TESTMEM:*on|off* option determines whether HIMEM.SYS performs a memory test when your computer starts. This option is not available in the version of HIMEM.SYS supplied with MS-DOS 6, but is included in the MS-DOS 6.2 version of HIMEM.SYS.

Your system performs a simple memory test when the power is first turned on or when the reset button is used to perform a "cold boot." Most systems do not perform a memory test when the Ctrl-Alt-Del key combination is used to perform a "warm boot." The extended memory test performed by HIMEM.SYS when the /TESTMEM option is set on (the default) is more extensive than the normal memory test your system performs.

Because the extended memory test performed by HIMEM.SYS results in longer boot times, you may want to disable the memory test while you are experimenting with system configurations. This will allow your system to restart more quickly during your experiments. It's a good idea, however, to enable the memory test once you have determined an optimum configuration. The small additional delay during the boot process could save you from lost data in case any of your PC's memory chips fail.

Understanding EMM386.EXE's Options

EMM386.EXE is the MS-DOS 6 EMS memory manager and upper memory block provider. EMM386.EXE requires access to XMS memory, and therefore must be loaded after HIMEM.SYS. You cannot use EMM386.EXE without also loading HIMEM.SYS (or another XMS memory manager).

Because EMM386.EXE requires an 80386 or higher processor, you cannot use it to provide either EMS memory or upper memory blocks on a system with an 80286 or lower processor. HIMEM.SYS can be used on an 80286 system to provide XMS memory, but MS-DOS 6 does not include a comparable EMS memory manager and upper memory block provider for these types of systems.

You can use EMM386.EXE to provide either EMS memory or upper memory blocks individually, or to provide access to both types of memory at the same time. The MS-DOS 6 version of EMM386.EXE is very much improved over the MS-DOS 5 version. For example, the newer version can automatically share extended memory as XMS or EMS memory as necessary, changing the allocation to suit the needs of your programs. EMM386.EXE also provides some additional memory management functions, which are controlled through the use of its optional switches.

Why You Might Need the /P Option

The /P*xxxx* option specifies the starting address for the 64K EMS page frame. You can specify segment addresses in the range 8000h to 9000h, and C000h through E000h, using 400h increments. For example, you can specify /**P8000** or /**P8400**, but you cannot specify /**P8200**.

> **Note**
>
> Don't confuse the /**P**xxxx option with the P*n*=xxxx option. /**P**xxxx specifies the beginning of a contiguous 64K page frame, while P*n*=xxxx specifies the beginning of a specific page.

Specifying the starting address of the page frame provides control over the size of upper memory blocks. Usually, you'll want to create the largest possible upper memory blocks, so you'll want to place the page frame in a location that does not break an upper memory block into two noncontiguous pieces.

Why You Might Need the A Option

The A=*n* option specifies how many fast alternate register sets to allocate to EMM386.EXE. Fast alternate register sets are used for multitasking, which is running more than one program on your system at the same time. You can specify values between 0 and 254; by default, 7 fast alternate register sets are allocated to EMM386.EXE.

Each fast alternate register set allocated to EMM386.EXE uses about 200 bytes of memory, so don't increase the number allocated to EMM386.EXE unless you are specifically directed to do so by a program's documentation. If memory is very tight on your system, you can experiment with reducing the size of memory used by EMM386.EXE by specifying a smaller number of fast alternate register sets. Normally, however, you'll have little need to use this switch.

Why You Might Need the ALTBOOT Option

The ALTBOOT option specifies that EMM386.EXE should use an alternate method to restart your computer when you press Ctrl-Alt-Del. In most cases, it is unnecessary to use the ALTBOOT option, but if you are unable to reboot your system after loading EMM386.EXE, you may need to use this option.

Unfortunately, it can be very difficult to determine exactly why a system is acting strangely. This is especially true when you are experimenting with system configuration options. The ALTBOOT option should be considered only if you find you cannot perform a "warm boot" using the Ctrl-Alt-Del key combination.

Why You Might Need the B Option

The B=*xxxx* option specifies the lowest segment address available for swapping EMS memory pages. You can specify any value between 1000h and 4000h.

EMS memory pages are made available to programs by making them appear to be located in conventional memory. Normally, pages are swapped above the 256K address, but this switch can permit the swapping to occur at a lower address. Unless you are specifically directed to do so by a program's documentation, you won't need to use this switch.

Why You Might Need the D Option

The D=*nnn* option specifies how much memory, in K, to reserve for buffered direct memory access (DMA). You can specify values between 16 and 256. The default is 32 in MS-DOS 6 (it was 16 in MS-DOS 5).

DMA transfers are used by some types of adapters, such as SCSI adapters. This is especially true if you have a CD-ROM drive installed in your system. Many CD-ROM drives require at least 64K for DMA.

If you don't have enough memory reserved for DMA transfers, your system will probably lock up at some point and display a message similar to the following:

```
EMM386 DMA buffer is too small.
Add D=nn parameter and reboot.
```

If you see this message, you'll have to increase the amount of DMA memory by specifying a larger number with the D=*nnn* option. If you see this error message while you're starting your system, you may need to use the F8 key to bypass the loading of EMM386.EXE. You can then edit CONFIG.SYS to correct the problem. In rare cases, it may be impossible to correct the problem unless you can boot from another disk. This possibility should be enough to convince you to keep an emergency boot diskette handy, especially if you add new hardware to your system.

Why You Might Need the FRAME Option

The FRAME=*xxxx* option specifies the base address for the 64K EMS page frame. You can specify segment addresses in the range 8000h to 9000h, and C000h through E000h, using 400h increments. For example, you can specify **FRAME=8000** or **FRAME=8400**, but you cannot specify **FRAME=8200**.

Specifying the starting address of the page frame provides control over the size of upper memory blocks. Usually, you'll want to create the largest possible upper memory blocks, so you'll want to place the page frame in a location that does not break an upper memory block into two noncontiguous pieces.

The FRAME=*xxxx* option and /P*xxxx* option serve the same purpose; you can use either option if you want to specify the EMS page frame address.

Note

In theory, it is possible to specify **FRAME=NONE** to provide expanded memory but disable the page frame. Unfortunately, although the EMS 4.0 specification lists this as an acceptable option, no programs that require EMS memory can actually function without wasting 64K of upper memory by requiring a page frame.

Why You Might Need the H Option

The H=*nn* option specifies how many handles EMM386.EXE can use. You can specify a number between 2 and 255. The default is 64.

Unless specifically directed to change this value by a program's documentation, there's really no reason to use the H=*nn* option.

Why You Might Need the HIGHSCAN Option

The HIGHSCAN option instructs EMM386.EXE to use an additional check to determine the availability of more upper memory. The HIGHSCAN option causes EMM386.EXE to search upper memory more aggressively, and may result in a larger overall amount of upper memory space. This may allow you to place additional device drivers and TSRs into upper memory, increasing available conventional memory.

On some systems, the HIGHSCAN option may cause EMM386.EXE to use upper memory addresses that are not really available. For example, memory addresses used by network adapter cards may not be recognized when the HIGHSCAN option is used. If so, your system may lock up when you attempt to use the network. See Chapter 4 for more information on identifying available upper memory addresses.

Why You Might Need the I Option

The I=*mmmm-nnnn* option specifies a range of segment addresses in the range A000h to FFFFh to use for upper memory blocks or the EMS page frame. Values are rounded down to the nearest 4K boundary.

The I=*mmmm-nnnn* option is one of the most useful of EMM386.EXE's options. Normally, EMM386.EXE is quite conservative in selecting areas of upper memory for upper memory blocks and the EMS page frame. As you learned in Chapter 4, there are often additional sections of upper memory that can be used for these purposes. For example, to include the monochrome display page memory, you would use the following syntax:

```
I=B000-B7FF
```

You can include more than one section of upper memory by placing more than one I=*mmmm-nnnn* switch in the EMM386.EXE command line.

Generally, it is best to create the largest contiguous upper memory blocks possible. Since some device drivers and TSRs require more memory to load than their memory image size, it's desirable to have upper memory blocks large enough to allow loading such device drivers and TSRs; otherwise, they will be loaded into conventional memory.

Note

If you include the B000–B7FF range in upper memory, you may encounter problems running Windows in 386 enhanced mode. If you are unable to load Windows after including this range of addresses, add the line DEVICE=MONOUMB.386 to the [386enh] section of SYSTEM.INI (in the WINDOWS\SYSTEM directory), and restart Windows.

If you attempt to include upper memory as upper memory blocks or as the EMS page frame, and that memory is already in use, your system may crash. You can use the F8 key during the boot process to allow you to bypass the loading of EMM386.EXE so you can edit CONFIG.SYS. You should also have an emergency boot diskette available when you experiment with including extra upper memory.

It's also possible to include the first section of upper memory as an extension to conventional memory, if you have an EGA or VGA adapter but don't use any graphics modes. The switch **I=A000-AFFF** will increase conventional memory to 704K, but your system will lock up as soon as it attempts to enter a graphics mode. Purely text mode programs, however, can usually function correctly with this memory added to the top of conventional memory.

Two areas of upper memory are usually safe to include even if you use programs that use graphics modes. In addition to the B000–B7FF range mentioned above, the E000–EFFF range is usually safe to use on most systems. If these two ranges are not already being used by EMM386.EXE, explicitly including them can add up to 96K of additional upper memory for upper memory blocks and the EMS page frame.

Why You Might Need the L Option

The L=*nnn* option specifies the amount of XMS memory, in K, that must remain available after EMM386.EXE is loaded. By default, EMM386.EXE uses as much memory as is necessary to provide the amount of EMS memory you request.

If you use programs that require XMS memory, you can use the L=*nnn* option to ensure that those programs have access to a specified minimum amount of XMS memory.

Because the MS-DOS 6 version of EMM386.EXE automatically creates a shared memory pool from which it allocates both EMS and XMS memory as necessary, you should not use the L=*nnn* option unless absolutely necessary. Memory allocated as XMS memory by using the L=*nnn* option does not become part of the shared memory pool, and therefore may not be used in the most efficient manner.

Why You Might Need the M Option

The M*x* option specifies the location of the EMS page frame. Table 6.2 shows the values of *x* to use to specify the address.

The M*x* option is similar to the FRAME=*xxxx* and /P*xxxx* options, but may be a better choice, because you are less likely to enter an incorrect address

Table 6.2	Page Frame Address Values for the Mx Option
Address	**X**
C000	1
C400	2
C800	3
CC00	4
D000	5
D400	6
D800	7
DC00	8
E000	9
8000	10*
8400	11*
8800	12*
8C00	13*
9000	14*

*Do not use values 10–14 on systems with 640K of memory. These values should be used only on systems with 512K of memory.

when using the M*x* option. Usually, you'll want to specify the starting address of the page frame so that you create the largest possible upper memory blocks. Place the page frame in a location that does not break an upper memory block into two noncontiguous pieces.

Why You Might Need the Memory Option

The *memory* option specifies the maximum amount of XMS memory, in K, to allocate as EMS or VCPI memory. You can specify a value between 64 and 32768. The default is all available extended memory, unless you also specify the NOEMS option, which changes the default to zero. Any value you specify is rounded down to the nearest 16K.

Because the MS-DOS 6 version of EMM386.EXE creates a shared memory pool from which EMS and XMS memory are allocated as necessary, you should probably not specify an amount of memory using the *memory* option. Using this option to specify the amount of memory to allocate as EMS/VCPI memory limits the flexibility of the shared memory pool, and prevents the memory you allocate in this manner from being used as XMS memory if needed.

If you have upgraded your system from MS-DOS 5, you may already have a *memory* argument specified in the EMM386.EXE line in CONFIG.SYS. If so, you should remove this argument and allow the newer version of EMM386.EXE to allocate memory as needed. Otherwise, you'll be missing out on one of the major memory management improvements included in MS-DOS 6—the shared memory pool.

EMS memory presents an interesting challenge, because you could be wasting memory by providing EMS memory. Suppose, for example, that one of your device drivers uses EMS memory for its buffers. By watching the screen messages when the driver loads, you can see that the driver uses only 32K of EMS memory for its buffers. If no other programs need EMS memory, the device driver's buffers are using at least 64K of upper memory to hold only 32K of buffers. In addition, XMS memory is also being used.

Rather than wasting both upper memory and XMS memory for the device driver's buffers, you may want to try some alternatives. Consider not providing EMS memory to the device driver so it places its buffers in conventional memory instead of in EMS memory. This might allow you to do away with the EMS page frame, and have an extra 64K of upper memory for loading device drivers and TSRs. You might find that you can move enough device drivers and TSRs into upper memory blocks to more than offset the extra conventional memory used by the offending device driver's buffers. You may also want to call the manufacturer's customer support line, especially if it's an 800 number, and complain about the device driver's use of obsolete EMS memory instead of the more reasonable XMS memory.

Why You Might Need the MIN Option

The MIN=*xxx* option specifies the minimum amount of EMS/VCPI memory (in K) that EMM386.EXE should provide. You can specify any value between 0 and the amount specified by the memory option (or the total amount of XMS memory, if the memory option is not specified). The default is 256K, unless you also specify the NOEMS option, which changes the default to zero. If the memory option specifies a larger amount than you specify using the MIN=*xxx* option, EMM386.EXE may provide an amount of EMS/VCPI memory between the two figures.

Use the MIN=*xxx* option if you use a device driver, TSR, or application program that absolutely requires EMS (or VCPI) memory, but that may be loaded after another device driver or TSR that requests all available XMS memory. Usually, it's better to allow EMM386.EXE simply to provide memory as necessary from the shared memory pool. Dynamic memory allocation from the shared memory pool is generally more efficient, because your system can use all of its memory productively, rather than reserving some for use as EMS/VCPI memory.

Why You Might Need the NOEMS Option

The NOEMS option tells EMM386.EXE to provide upper memory block support, but not to provide EMS (or Virtual Control Program Interface—VCPI) memory. You must still use the CONFIG.SYS directive DOS=UMB (or DOS=HIGH,UMB) to activate upper memory blocks.

EMS memory is becoming far less important as software manufacturers upgrade their software to use XMS memory. If you don't need to provide

EMS memory to any of your programs, use the NOEMS option to prevent EMM386.EXE from using 64K of upper memory for the EMS page frame. If there is no page frame, more upper memory will be available for upper memory blocks. You'll have more room to load device drivers and TSRs, and may end up with more free conventional memory.

Using the NOEMS option may be even more effective than you may think. The EMS page frame is usually taken out of the largest upper memory block. If there is no EMS page frame, the largest upper memory block may grow by 64K, making it possible to load into upper memory device drivers or TSRs that require more than their memory image size to load.

Keep in mind that Windows and Windows programs do not use EMS memory. If you use primarily Windows programs, there may be no reason to provide EMS memory.

Why You Might Need the NOHI Option

The NOHI option prevents EMM386.EXE from loading a portion of its code into the upper memory area, and instead places all of EMM386.EXE into conventional memory. This results in a slight reduction in the size of available conventional memory, and a slight increase in the upper memory area.

Usually, it is better to allow EMM386.EXE to load some of its code into upper memory, but this will reduce the size of upper memory by around 3K. If you are unable to load a large device driver or TSR into upper memory because the largest available upper memory block is just a little too small, it may be worth experimenting with the NOHI option. You may find that by loading all of EMM386.EXE into conventional memory, upper memory grows by just enough to accommodate the device driver or TSR. The result may be an increase in available conventional memory because upper memory is being used more efficiently.

Note

If you try the NOHI option but still can't load the device driver or TSR into upper memory, don't forget to remove the NOHI option from the EMM386.EXE command line in CONFIG.SYS.

Why You Might Need the NOMOVEXBDA Option

The NOMOVEXBDA option prevents EMM386.EXE from moving the extended BIOS data area from conventional memory to upper memory. This is a 1K block of memory that stores system information. Usually, the block of memory is located at the top of conventional memory (at the 639K memory address), but EMM386.EXE moves the block so that memory is not fragmented. Normally, this move does not cause any problems, but some older programs may have difficulty if they expect the extended BIOS data area to be located in its conventional location.

You should not use the NOMOVEXBDA option unless you encounter problems running old programs when EMM386.EXE is loaded. Even in those cases, you should try only the NOMOVEXBDA option without making any other changes to see whether moving the extended BIOS data area is really the problem.

Why You Might Need the NOVCPI Option

The NOVCPI option disables EMM386.EXE's support for VCPI applications, and must be used with the NOEMS option. (Otherwise, the NOVCPI option is ignored.)

VCPI memory support usually isn't needed by current program versions, so using the NOVCPI option may provide additional XMS memory. Of course, if your programs require EMS memory, you will be unable to disable VCPI memory support. If none of your programs require EMS memory, however, you may want to use both the NOEMS and NOVCPI options.

Why You Might Need the ON, OFF, or AUTO Options

The ON, OFF, and AUTO options are related and mutually exclusive options. They specify whether EMS memory support is initially set to on or to off, or is only available when requested by a program. You can use these same options at the DOS command line or in a batch file to switch the state of EMS support.

By default, EMS support is set to on. Some programs, however, are unable to function correctly when EMS support is enabled. You can use these options to supply EMS support only as needed. For example, if you use only one program that requires EMS memory, you can set EMS off initially. You can then start the program using a batch file that includes the line **EMM386 ON** before the command that starts the program, and **EMM386 OFF** after the program exits.

Why You Might Need the Pn Option

The *Pn=xxxx* option specifies the base segment address of an EMS page. *N* specifies the page, which can be 0 to 255, and *xxxx* specifies the segment address, which can be in the ranges 8000h to 9C00h or C000h to EC00h, in 400h increments. If you specify values for pages 0 through 3, they must be contiguous.

Most programs use only the first four contiguous EMS pages. It's possible, however, to use up to 256 EMS pages, each of which is 16K in length. Generally, though, the *Pn=xxxx* option is of little use to the average PC user. If you need to use this option, you can be certain that your program documentation will advise you about the values you must use.

Why You Might Need the RAM Option

The RAM=*mmmm-nnnn* option provides access to both EMS memory and the upper memory area. If you include a range of upper memory segment addresses, EMM386.EXE will use the specified range for upper memory. If you do not include a range of upper memory segment addresses, EMM386.EXE will use the entire available area above 640K and below 1M.

You must still include the CONFIG.SYS directive DOS=UMB (or DOS= HIGH,UMB) to activate upper memory block support. You must use either the RAM or the NOEMS option to provide access to upper memory.

When you specify the RAM option, EMM386.EXE allocates a 64K contiguous block of upper memory as the EMS page frame. This reduces the amount of upper memory that is available for upper memory blocks.

If your programs require either EMS or Virtual Control Program Interface (VCPI) memory, you must use the RAM option to enable this support. If you include this option but EMM386.EXE cannot allocate a 64K contiguous block of upper memory as the EMS page frame, you'll see an error message when you start your system, and no EMS memory will be made available.

If you don't need EMS memory, use the NOEMS option instead of the RAM option. Using the NOEMS option will provide 64K more upper memory space than will using the RAM option.

Why You Might Need the ROM Option

The ROM=*mmmm-nnnn* option specifies a range of segment addresses to use for shadow RAM. You can specify segment address values for *mmmm* and *nnnn* in the range A000 through FFFF, and they will be rounded down to the nearest 4K segment boundary.

Read-only memory (ROM) is slower than RAM, so copying system ROMs into faster RAM may improve system performance slightly. Usually, however, the performance improvement isn't worth the amount of upper memory you'll need to use to hold all of the ROM. If you load few device drivers and TSRs, and you need every last bit of system performance, you may want to try the ROM=*mmmm-nnnn* option. In most cases, however, you would have to perform very careful testing before and after using this option to gauge any performance benefit.

Why You Might Need the VERBOSE Option

The VERBOSE option (which you can abbreviate as V) causes EMM386.EXE to display detailed status and error messages while it is loading. You can also hold down the Alt key while EMM386.EXE is loading to see these detailed messages.

The detailed status and error messages displayed by the VERBOSE option are very useful while you're experimenting with system configurations. By examining these messages, you can determine exactly what EMM386.EXE is doing, and therefore see how well your selected options work together.

You may have a difficult time seeing EMM386.EXE's messages unless you use the F8 key to execute CONFIG.SYS one line at a time. Then you can examine EMM386.EXE's messages before they have a chance to scroll off the screen.

Why You Might Need the W Option

The W=*on|off* option enables or disables support for the Weitek math coprocessor. The default is off.

The Weitek math coprocessor is a special, high-performance math coprocessor sometimes used to speed up complex calculations. This math coprocessor is very uncommon. You should not confuse it with a math coprocessor like the 80287 or 80387, neither of which needs this option turned on.

Note

Only the Weitek math coprocessor needs this option turned on. All other brands of math coprocessors, including Intel and Cyrix, do not use this switch.

Why You Might Need the WIN Option

The WIN=*mmmm-nnnn* option reserves a specified range of segment addresses for use by Windows instead of by EMM386.EXE. You can specify values for *mmmm* and *nnnn* in the range A000 through FFFF, and they are rounded down to the nearest 4K boundary. Addresses excluded using the X=*mmmm-nnnn* option cannot be used by Windows, but the WIN=*mmmm-nnnn* option takes precedence over the RAM, ROM, and I options if their ranges overlap.

Windows uses either upper memory or conventional memory for some system structures called *translation buffers* when you run DOS programs under Windows. If EMM386.EXE has used all upper memory, the translation buffers are placed in each DOS program's conventional memory space, reducing the amount of conventional memory available to the program. You can use the WIN=*mmmm-nnnn* option to tell EMM386.EXE to leave a specified range available for Windows to use for its translation buffers, thus increasing the amount of conventional memory available to DOS programs running under Windows.

Generally, the WIN=*mmmm-nnnn* option isn't needed if you run only Windows programs, or if you don't run extremely memory-intensive DOS programs under Windows. It's usually better to allow EMM386.EXE to use all available upper memory for upper memory blocks, so more device drivers and TSRs can be loaded into upper memory instead of into conventional memory.

Why You Might Need the X Option

The X=*mmmm-nnnn* option specifies a range of upper memory segment addresses that EMM386.EXE should not use for upper memory blocks or the EMS page frame. You can specify addresses in the range A000 to FFFF, and they are rounded down to the nearest 4K boundary. If you specify both X=*mmmm-nnnn* and I=*mmmm-nnnn*, the X=*mmmm-nnnn* takes precedence if you specify overlapping ranges.

Sometimes EMM386.EXE is unable to determine that a range of addresses cannot be used safely, and includes that range in upper memory. This can happen for several reasons. One of the most common is an adapter card, such as a network card, that doesn't initialize its memory space until the card is activated. Since EMM386.EXE loads before the card is used, the card remains invisible during the process of allocating upper memory.

Generally, it's fairly easy to find out the beginning address used by an adapter card, but it may be more difficult to determine how large a space to reserve for the card. The beginning address is usually listed as the *base address*. Network adapter cards often use a base address like D800 (which you may also see as D8000). Chapter 4 showed you how to use tools such as MSD and DEBUG to search through memory, but even those tools sometimes have difficulty showing how much memory space to reserve for an adapter card. So how do you determine exactly how much space to reserve for such an adapter card?

It's important to remember that both the X=*mmmm-nnnn* and I=*mmmm-nnnn* options round down to the nearest 4K boundary. In effect, this means that you can include or exclude memory space in 4K sections. This fact makes determining how much space to exclude for an adapter card much easier, because there are a limited number of 4K blocks in upper memory. Suppose, for example, that you've determined that your network adapter card has a base address of D800. Starting from this address, the next three successive 4K boundaries are located at D900, DA00, and DB00. The end of each 4K block is at D8FF, D9FF, DAFF, and DBFF.

It's safest to start by allocating at least 16K to an adapter board. Therefore, you should start by excluding the range from D800 through DBFF, using the command **X=D800-DBFF**. Once you've included this option in the EMM386.EXE device driver line, you can save CONFIG.SYS, and then reboot your system. (Don't forget to reboot every time you try a changed setting—otherwise, you won't really be using the new setting.) Once the system has restarted, make certain everything is working correctly and no error messages are displayed. Be sure you test the network adapter card by logging onto the network and making certain it works, too.

If excluding the range from D800 through DBFF works correctly, you can either accept the current setup as adequate, or you can experiment to see whether reserving less space for the adapter card works. You may have to spend quite a bit of time adjusting the settings, saving your work, rebooting, and checking the results, but doing so may give you additional upper memory that otherwise wouldn't be available. If you do decide to experiment further, remember to change the ranges in 4K increments. To reserve 12K instead of 16K, use **X=D800-DAFF**.

EMM386.EXE's options give you a great amount of control over upper memory. By using these options carefully, you can increase the amount of upper memory block space, reducing the amount of conventional memory needed for device drivers and TSRs. In the rest of this section we'll examine more of the commands you can use in CONFIG.SYS to further enhance your system's configuration.

Using the ? Command

The ? command is used to pause the execution of CONFIG.SYS and request confirmation before the current command is executed. There is no time-out, so your system waits indefinitely for your response.

You can use the ? command most effectively when you are experimenting with system configurations. In order to ensure that you will be able to see and read any error or status messages that are displayed, however, you'll probably want to include the ? command on at least two lines in CONFIG.SYS—the line containing the device driver command line you want to examine, and the following command line (to pause CONFIG.SYS so you can see what messages were displayed when the device driver loaded).

You can also use the F8 key to control execution of each command line (unless CONFIG.SYS contains the command **SWITCHES /N**).

To use the ? command, place the question mark immediately after the command you want to prompt for. Don't leave any intervening spaces, and place the question mark before any equals sign (=).

Although you could use the ? command to allow you to select different system configurations, this command really isn't ideal for this use. When you use this command, you must confirm each line containing the command, and you must do so every time you boot your system. Your system cannot automatically start with a default configuration if you don't respond, and it simply waits forever for you to enter your choice. For this reason, you're better off using the ? for testing purposes, and using the multiple configuration commands—INCLUDE, MENUCOLOR, MENUDEFAULT, MENUITEM, and SUBMENU—if you sometimes need to boot using a different system configuration.

Using the BREAK Command

The BREAK=*on|off* command specifies whether your system should do extended testing for the Ctrl-C (or Ctrl-Break) key combination. By default, BREAK is off, which means that your PC looks for Ctrl-C only when it normally reads from the keyboard, or when writing to the screen or your printer.

The setting of the BREAK command doesn't have any memory management effects, but it can have a system performance effect. If BREAK is set to on, your system must spend more time looking for the Ctrl-C key combination, so normal operations may be a little slower than usual.

The main reason for setting BREAK to on is to enable you to interrupt a program that isn't responding. You may want to include the command **BREAK=ON** in CONFIG.SYS while you're testing system configuration options, and later remove the command for slightly improved performance.

Using the BUFFERS Command

The BUFFERS=*n,m* command specifies the number of primary and secondary disk buffers your system should reserve. Primary buffers, *n*, can be between 1 and 99. Secondary buffers, *m*, can be between 0 and 8.

Disk buffers are a DOS system structure used to improve disk performance by storing data in memory. If the same data is needed a second time and is still in a buffer, the system does not have to read the data from disk, and considerable time is saved.

Buffers are far less important to system performance when disk caching software, such as SmartDrive, is being used. Although disk caching software performs a similar function to disk buffers, disk caching software is much more efficient, and provides a much larger improvement in system performance.

Each buffer uses approximately 532 bytes of memory. The default buffer setting, which is 15 on a 640K system, uses nearly 8K of conventional memory. The maximum setting of 99 primary and 8 secondary buffers would eat up nearly 56K of conventional memory. Fortunately, you don't need to use such a large number of buffers, and it's possible to reduce the conventional memory used by buffers to a very small amount.

If HIMEM.SYS is loaded and the command DOS=HIGH is included in CONFIG.SYS, the DOS kernel is placed into the high memory area. The DOS kernel doesn't use the entire high memory area, but the unused space doesn't have to go to waste. Even though only one program at a time can use the high memory area, the unused space in the high memory area can be used to hold the disk buffers if you don't allocate too many buffers. The reason this works is that buffers are a DOS system structure, and therefore are considered part of DOS itself.

Generally, there's room for about 24 buffers along with the DOS kernel in the high memory area. The exact number of buffers you allocate usually isn't too critical, so allocating an amount that will fit into the high memory area makes good sense from a memory management perspective. This is especially true if you use disk caching software, because the disk buffers you allocate really won't add very much performance.

Note

If you use the high memory area for purposes other than loading the DOS kernel, the disk buffers will use conventional memory. If you also use disk caching software, reduce the number of buffers to about 3 to minimize the amount of conventional memory used by the buffers.

Usually it's unnecessary to change the secondary buffers from the default of 0. To set the primary buffers to 24, use the command **BUFFERS=24**.

Using the COUNTRY Command

The COUNTRY command configures your system to recognize international date, time, currency, case, and decimal separator conventions. Your MS-DOS manual includes complete information on using this command.

The COUNTRY command has one memory management implication—it increases the size of DOS in memory. If you use this command, available conventional memory will probably be reduced because of this larger size for DOS. Therefore, unless you really need to use the international conventions on your system, it's better to forego using the COUNTRY command, at least from a memory management standpoint.

Using the DEVICE Command

The DEVICE command loads a device driver into conventional memory. Device drivers are special programs that provide capabilities not built into DOS itself. These include management of memory outside the 640K conventional memory space such as upper memory, extended memory, and expanded memory. Other device drivers may provide the ability to access hardware such as SCSI adapters, sound boards, network adapters, and so on.

Because the DEVICE command loads device drivers into conventional memory, it's usually preferable to use the DEVICEHIGH command instead of the DEVICE command. Some device drivers, however, cannot be placed outside of conventional memory. The two MS-DOS 6 memory managers, HIMEM.SYS and EMM386.EXE, are examples of device drivers that must be loaded into conventional memory. In the case of these two device drivers, there's really no other choice, because before the two of them are loaded, your system cannot access any memory other than conventional memory.

Occasionally, you'll find other device drivers that cannot be loaded into upper memory. Usually, the program documentation supplied with the device driver will inform you if the device driver must be loaded into conventional memory. For these types of device drivers, you must use the DEVICE command to load the device driver.

Using the DEVICEHIGH Command

The DEVICEHIGH command loads a device driver into upper memory if possible; otherwise, it loads the device driver into conventional memory. By loading device drivers into upper memory, you can conserve conventional memory for other uses. This makes the DEVICEHIGH command one of the most important CONFIG.SYS commands for memory management.

One of the most important memory management improvements in MS-DOS 6, compared to MS-DOS 5, is the new ability to specify which upper memory region to use for loading device drivers. To do this, you use the /L:*region#* argument following the DEVICEHIGH command. The reason this ability is so important is directly related to the default method of loading device drivers into upper memory. If you don't specify which region to use, each device driver loads into the largest upper memory block that is available when the device driver is loaded.

For example, if two upper memory blocks have 45K and 20K free, by default the 45K block is used first, regardless of the size of the device driver being loaded. This can cause the upper memory blocks to be used in a less than optimum manner. Suppose, though, that you have two device drivers, DRV1.SYS that takes a 16K memory block, and DRV2.SYS that takes a 42K memory block and must be loaded after DRV1.SYS. If the MEM /F command shows the two available upper memory blocks as region 1 for the 45K block and region 2 for the 20K block, you could use the following two commands to load both device drivers into upper memory:

```
DEVICEHIGH=/L:2 DRV1.SYS
DEVICEHIGH=/L:1 DRV2.SYS
```

You can optionally include an argument that specifies how much memory a device driver requires. If the specified upper memory block does not contain at least the specified amount of free memory, the device driver will be loaded into conventional memory instead of upper memory. This optional argument is of the most value for device drivers that expand after they're loaded into memory. Very few device drivers do this, but the *minsize* argument is available if it becomes necessary. If you use this argument, you must place it after the /L:*region#* argument, separated by a comma.

For example, to specify that the device driver C:\UTILITY\MYDRV.SYS be loaded in region 2 of upper memory only if 16K of contiguous upper memory is available in the specified region, you would use the following command line:

```
DEVICEHIGH /L:2,16384 C:\UTILITY\MYDRV.SYS
```

A few device drivers can use more than one region of upper memory. To specify that a device driver can use additional upper memory blocks, use a semicolon following the first region number (and optional memory size) to separate the second region number from the first. You can also specify a minimum memory size for this region, or for any subsequent regions if necessary.

The section "Performing the Load Order Juggling Act," later in this chapter, suggests additional methods of working around the problem of making the most effective use of system memory.

Occasionally, you'll encounter device drivers that cannot be loaded into upper memory:

- Some device drivers cannot be loaded into upper memory because they don't work correctly unless they're loaded in conventional memory. If these types of device drivers are loaded into upper memory, you may lock up your system, or you may experience intermittent crashes.
- Some device drivers cannot be loaded into upper memory because they require more memory to load than their memory image size. In some cases, it's possible to load such device drivers into upper memory if you can free a large enough block of contiguous memory, but sometimes it's just not possible to create a large enough upper memory block.
- Some device drivers cannot be loaded into upper memory because upper memory simply isn't available when they're loaded. HIMEM.SYS and EMM386.EXE are two such device drivers, but device drivers that must be loaded before any memory managers are loaded also fall into this category.

It's important to remember that the DEVICEHIGH command does not fail to load a device driver if upper memory isn't available. Instead, the DEVICE-HIGH command is treated as though you issued the DEVICE command, and the device driver is loaded into conventional memory. As a result, it's not safe to assume that just because you used the DEVICEHIGH command, the device driver actually loaded into upper memory. Use the MEM /C command to determine exactly where each device driver and TSR has been loaded.

Using the DOS Command

The DOS command performs two functions. Used with the UMB parameter, the DOS command enables the use of upper memory—if an upper memory block provider like EMM386.EXE is loaded. Used with the HIGH parameter, the DOS command loads the DOS kernel into the high memory area—if the high memory area is available.

You can combine the HIGH and UMB parameters in the same command, as in

```
DOS=HIGH,UMB
```

Placing the DOS kernel in the high memory area increases the amount of conventional memory available to applications by reducing the amount of conventional memory used by DOS. Not only does the DOS=HIGH command move the DOS kernel into the high memory area, but it also moves the DOS disk buffers into the high memory area if the buffers will fit in the high memory area. (Usually, there's room for about 24 buffers in the high memory area.)

Enabling access to upper memory allows device drivers and TSRs to be loaded into upper memory blocks. This too, increases the amount of conventional memory available to applications.

Before you can use either the HIGH or UMB parameters, you must first load HIMEM.SYS. In addition, the UMB parameter requires that EMM386.EXE be loaded before you use the DOS command.

Loading the DOS kernel into the high memory area and enabling upper memory block access are two very important steps in advanced memory management. These steps ensure that more conventional memory can be made available for applications.

> **Note**
>
> If you're on a network, you may find that your network software requires access to the high memory area. If so, you will not be able to use the HIGH parameter with the DOS command, because only one program can use the high memory area at a time. You can still use the UMB parameter to enable access to upper memory, however.

Using the DRIVPARM Command

The DRIVPARM command defines the standard configuration of a disk drive that is not automatically recognized correctly by DOS. You can also use this command to define the parameters for other types of block devices, such as tape drives that are accessed using a drive letter.

A common use for the DRIVPARM command is to help a system recognize types of disk drives not originally available on the system. For example, if you add 3.5-inch diskette drives on some systems, the PC will assume that the drive is a 360K, 5.25-inch diskette drive. The DRIVPARM command tells the system how to access the drive correctly.

The DRIVPARM command is not a memory management command, but using this command slightly increases the size of DOS in memory, so you should avoid using the DRIVPARM command if possible. One way to test whether the DRIVPARM command is needed is to insert a new, unformatted, high-density diskette in the drive, and then format the diskette without specifying the diskette size, and without having DRIVPARM loaded. If the diskette is formatted to its full capacity, you don't need to use the DRIVPARM command. If the diskette is formatted at a lower capacity, use the DRIVPARM command to specify the drive's specifications.

Using the FCBS Command

The FCBS command specifies the number of file control blocks that can be open at one time. You can specify a value between 1 and 255; the default is 4.

File control blocks are an obsolete method of accessing files. Programmers have been discouraged from using this method of file access since MS-DOS

2.x, so there's really no excuse for a modern program to require the use of file control blocks.

Each additional file control block uses conventional memory. You can save a small amount of memory by including the following command in CONFIG.SYS:

```
FCBS=1
```

Using the FILES Command

The FILES command specifies the number of files that can be open at one time. You can use values between 8 and 255. The default is 8.

Each additional file you specify with the FILES command uses some conventional memory, so you might assume you would want to save memory by specifying the smallest possible value. In reality, however, you must specify a large enough value to accommodate the needs of every program that may be running simultaneously. Unfortunately, it can be difficult to determine how many files each program may attempt to open. One method of determining how many files you must specify is to start with a very low value, such as 8, and try running all of your applications. If you receive an error message telling you that the program is unable to open enough files, you'll know you must increase the number of files that can be open at one time.

This trial and error approach to specifying the number of files that can be open at one time may work, but it may also create difficult problems. Suppose, for example, that you try a low value for the files, and everything seems to be working. A few weeks later, after working for several hours, you try to update a data file, only to be greeted with an error message telling you the data can't be saved because too many files are open. The few bytes of memory you saved by specifying a minimum number of files won't seem quite so important at that point, will they?

A good compromise is possible without applying the trial and error approach. In most cases, 20 files would be adequate for users who run only DOS programs. If you use Windows, or some other environment that allows several programs to run at the same time, you'll need a setting of at least 40. In either case, the 1K to 2K of memory used by the FILES command is good insurance against the problem of being unable to open files when necessary.

Note

Some programs have even higher requirements. Be sure to check the program documentation when you install new software to see whether the FILES setting should be increased.

MS-DOS 6 always places the structures for open files in conventional memory. This is true even when the DOS kernel is loaded into the high memory area.

Using the INCLUDE Command

The INCLUDE=*blockname* command executes the commands contained within a specified, named configuration block. This command is one of the new multiple configuration commands in MS-DOS 6. These commands enable you to create a menu of optional system configurations within CONFIG.SYS so that you don't need multiple copies of CONFIG.SYS for different purposes.

Often, different system configurations differ only slightly from each other. It's usually possible to use a configuration block called [COMMON] to hold the commands that are common to all configurations, but this isn't always possible, nor may it always be the best method of executing common configuration commands. Sometimes, for example, certain device drivers must be loaded before others. If the device drivers that differ between your optional configurations require certain device drivers to be loaded before they are loaded, the INCLUDE=*blockname* command provides a good method of controlling the order in which the device drivers are loaded.

The following example shows a sample CONFIG.SYS file that uses the MS-DOS 6 multiple configuration commands to display a menu that allows the user to load the Interlink driver for transferring files between laptop and desktop systems. The blocks named [INTERLINK] and [NO_DRIVERS] use the INCLUDE command to execute the configuration commands contained in the block named [NORMAL]. The block named [COMMON] is automatically executed after either the [INTERLINK] or [NO_DRIVERS] block has been completed.

```
[MENU]
MENUCOLOR=14,1
```

```
MENUITEM=INTERLINK,    Load Interlink driver
MENUITEM=NO_DRIVERS,   Don't load drivers
MENUDEFAULT=NO_DRIVERS,10

[NORMAL]
Several DEVICE= and DEVICEHIGH= commands may be included here.

[INTERLINK]
INCLUDE NORMAL
DEVICE=C:\DOS\INTERLNK.EXE /DRIVES:10 /AUTO /COM

[NO_DRIVERS]
INCLUDE NORMAL

[COMMON]
DEVICE=C:\WINDOWS\IFSHLP.SYS
BUFFERS=10,0
```

See the sections on the MENUCOLOR, MENUDEFAULT, MENUITEM, and SUBMENU commands later in this chapter for more information on these additional multiple configuration commands.

Using the INSTALL Command

The INSTALL command loads TSR programs into conventional memory. Generally, INSTALL is used to load TSRs that should be loaded only once per DOS session. For example, if you use the FASTOPEN program, the program can be loaded only once each time you boot your system.

Although you could load TSR programs using commands in AUTOEXEC.BAT or at the DOS command prompt, loading them using the INSTALL command in CONFIG.SYS uses slightly less memory. This is because INSTALL does not create an environment for the TSR. Thus, TSRs loaded using the INSTALL command cannot use environment variables. They also cannot use shortcut keys or require COMMAND.COM for handling critical errors. Some TSRs do not function properly if you load them using the INSTALL command.

TSRs that are loaded at the DOS command prompt, or in a batch file such as AUTOEXEC.BAT, receive a copy of the DOS environment. By default, MS-

DOS 6 reserves 256 bytes for the environment. If you use the default environment size, loading four TSRs using the INSTALL command in CONFIG.SYS would save 1K of conventional memory, compared to loading those same TSRs in AUTOEXEC.BAT or at the DOS command prompt.

All DEVICE and DEVICEHIGH commands are processed and executed before any INSTALL commands are processed and executed. You cannot load a TSR before a device driver by placing an INSTALL ahead of the DEVICE and DEVICEHIGH commands.

Using the INSTALLHIGH Command

The INSTALLHIGH command loads TSR programs into upper memory if it is available; otherwise, it loads them into conventional memory. The INSTALLHIGH command is used for exactly the same purposes as the INSTALL command.

The INSTALLHIGH command is not shown in the documentation provided with MS-DOS 6, but you can use the command just as you would the INSTALL command. The same restrictions that apply to the INSTALL command also apply to the INSTALLHIGH command. Like the INSTALL command, the INSTALLHIGH command is processed after all DEVICE and DEVICEHIGH commands.

If your TSR programs can function correctly without a copy of the DOS environment, without shortcut keys, and without using COMMAND.COM as a critical error handler, loading them using the INSTALLHIGH command is a good way to save memory. Since TSRs loaded with the INSTALLHIGH command don't receive a copy of the DOS environment, they can fit into a slightly smaller upper memory block than is possible if you load them in AUTOEXEC.BAT or at the DOS command prompt. This especially important if you increase the environment size, because each TSR loaded using the INSTALLHIGH command saves an amount of memory equal to the environment size.

The INSTALLHIGH command is an important part of your advanced memory management toolkit. Sometimes, even a very small amount of additional space in upper memory blocks makes the difference between being able to load everything you want into upper memory, and loading some items into conventional memory.

Using the LASTDRIVE Command

The LASTDRIVE command specifies the maximum number of disk drives you can access. You can specify any drive letter between A and Z. By default, DOS allocates structures for one drive following the last physical drive in your system.

You must specify drive letters at least as high as the last drive letter you want to access as a substituted drive or on a network. For example, if you create three substituted drives on a PC that has two diskette drives and a hard disk, you must specify a LASTDRIVE of at least F.

Networks often use drive M: as a network drive, especially if email is in use on the network. You must specify a LASTDRIVE high enough to allow access to the last network drive letter you intend to map.

MS-DOS creates data structures in conventional memory for each drive letter you specify. Allocating too many drive letters simply wastes memory. For example, setting LASTDRIVE to Z uses slightly over 2K of conventional memory, while providing no extra benefits over a more appropriate setting. Unless you are connected to a network or use substituted drives, it's usually best to allow DOS to allocate the default number of drive letters.

Using the MENUCOLOR Command

The MENUCOLOR=x,y command sets the color of the text and the background for the startup menu used to select multiple configurations. This color combination is then used to display all subsequent text until another command changes screen colors or screen modes. Table 6.3 shows the values to use for the text (x) and the background (y). Note, however, that colors 8 through 15 may cause your screen to blink.

If you don't specify a background color, the text will be displayed on the default black background.

Although the MENUCOLOR command isn't necessary from a memory management standpoint, it does show that the ANSI.SYS device driver does not really need to be loaded simply to change screen colors. It's too bad MS-DOS 6 doesn't remember the colors you set with the MENUCOLOR command, or include another command for setting the screen colors from the

Table 6.3	Color Values for the MENUCOLOR Command
Color	**Number**
Black	0
Blue	1
Green	2
Cyan	3
Red	4
Magenta	5
Brown	6
White	7
Gray	8
Bright blue	9
Bright green	10
Bright cyan	11
Bright red	12
Bright magenta	13
Yellow	14
Bright white	15

DOS prompt. That way, you wouldn't be tempted to waste memory loading ANSI.SYS just because you want your DOS screens to be a little more colorful.

Using the MENUDEFAULT Command

The MENUDEFAULT=*blockname,timeout* command specifies the default configuration block that will be selected from a startup menu if the user does not make a selection. Optionally, the command also specifies a length of time, from 0 to 90 seconds, after which the default selection is automatically executed. The specified option is also the option that is highlighted when the menu is displayed.

This command is one of the multiple configuration commands that were new to MS-DOS 6. These commands enable you to create a single CONFIG.SYS file containing several different system configurations, and to select from those configuration options at system startup.

You use the MENUDEFAULT=*blockname,timeout* command to automatically process your standard configuration options when you boot your PC. This ensures that your system will normally be configured correctly for most purposes, and will use a nonstandard configuration only when you specifically make the alternate selection as your system boots.

It's a good idea to specify a *time-out* value short enough to prevent undue delays during the boot process, but long enough to allow you to make an alternate selection if necessary. If you're setting up a system for an inexperienced user, you'll want to include a longer delay so the user can read and understand the options before the default selection is automatically executed. If no *time-out* value is specified, the system waits indefinitely until the Enter key is pressed.

Using the MENUITEM Command

The MENUITEM=*blockname,menu_text* command specifies an item on a startup menu. If you specify the optional *menu_text*, the text you specify will be displayed instead of the *blockname*.

The MENUITEM=*blockname,menu_text* command is one of the multiple configuration commands new to MS-DOS 6. These commands enable you to create a single CONFIG.SYS file containing several different system configurations, and to select from those configuration options at system startup.

The startup menu must have the block name [MENU] as its first line, with no other commands on the line. If you wish, you can then use the MENUCOLOR command to specify screen colors for the startup menu. Following this, you can use up to nine MENUITEM commands. (Each menu can have up to nine items, but you can use the SUBMENU command to create additional menus if you need additional choices.) Finally, the MENUDEFAULT command specifies the default selection and the time-out. The following is a typical startup menu:

```
[MENU]
MENUCOLOR=14,1
MENUITEM=INTERLINK,          Load Interlink driver
MENUITEM=NO_DRIVERS,         Don't load drivers
MENUDEFAULT=NO_DRIVERS,10
```

In this example, the first line includes the block name [MENU] to define the startup menu. The second line sets the screen colors to display yellow text on a blue background. The third line defines the first item displayed on the menu. In this case, the text "Load Interlink driver" driver is displayed, and if this item is selected, the configuration block named INTERLINK is executed. The fourth line defines the next menu item, and the fifth line specifies the default selection and time-out.

You have considerable flexibility in creating configuration block names. The only real rules are these:

- Configuration block names must be enclosed in square brackets [].
- Configuration block names must be unique, but can contain up to 70 characters.
- Spaces, backslashes, forward slashes, commas, semicolons, equals signs, and square brackets are not allowed in configuration block names.
- If a MENUITEM command specifies an invalid or missing configuration block name, the item is not displayed in the startup menu.

The multiple configuration commands are very important MS-DOS 6 memory management tools, because they allow you the flexibility to create optimized system configurations for special purposes. By keeping all optional configurations within a single CONFIG.SYS file, these commands help ensure that as you upgrade your system or your software, the correct versions of device drivers will be included in all configurations.

Using the NUMLOCK Command

The NUMLOCK=*on|off* command specifies whether the Num Lock key is set to on or off when the system starts. This command really serves little purpose, and has no memory management function. Using this command is simply a matter of personal preference.

Using the REM Command

The REM command, which you can abbreviate with a semicolon, places comments in your CONFIG.SYS file. This command has two primary purposes, both important as you experiment with advanced memory management.

The most obvious purpose of the REM command is to place notes in CONFIG.SYS explaining how other command lines function. You may, for example, want to note special settings you're trying with a device driver such as EMM386.EXE. If a conflict arises, you'll easily be able to see why, for instance, you excluded a particular memory segment range.

The second purpose of the REM command is to disable CONFIG.SYS command lines temporarily by turning them into comments. This is especially useful when you're trying a series of different settings, because you can retain a record of the exact settings you've already tried. You may even want to add comment lines detailing the success of the various combinations. Once you've decided on the optimal configuration you may want to remove the extra lines, because even though comment lines aren't executed, they still may slow the boot process slightly.

CONFIG.SYS lines that start with REM aren't displayed when CONFIG.SYS is processed unless you add the command **ECHO ON** to an earlier line in the file. Use **ECHO OFF** to turn off echoing of command lines you've disabled with REM—otherwise, it's easy to become confused about which lines are actually being executed, and which are simply comment lines.

Using the SET Command

The SET *variable=string* command places a value in a DOS environment variable. You can later use the value of this environment variable to control program flow in a batch file, or to pass system information to some application programs.

MS-DOS 6 automatically sets the value of an environment variable called CONFIG. If you create a startup menu, this variable is set to the block name of the selected configuration block. Later in this chapter, you'll see how you can use this variable in AUTOEXEC.BAT.

Setting values for environment variables can, however, have a negative effect on memory management. Although device drivers and TSRs loaded in CONFIG.SYS don't receive a copy of the DOS environment, all TSRs and application programs loaded by batch files or at the command prompt do receive a copy of the DOS environment. Depending on how large the DOS environment is, this can use considerable memory. In the next section you'll learn how to minimize this effect.

Tip

One very common environment variable is the PATH variable that is used by MS-DOS to find executable program files. It is quite common for application programs to require that their directories be placed in the PATH variable. Unfortunately, commands typed at the command prompt, such as the PATH command, are limited to 127 characters. Since the command must be followed by a space, this normally limits the length of the PATH environment variable to 122 characters, which is often far too short to include all of the program directories you might want to include.

CONFIG.SYS command lines aren't limited to 127 characters, however, so you can use the SET PATH command in CONFIG.SYS (in MS-DOS 6) to set a much longer program search path. If you set the PATH variable in CONFIG.SYS, be sure to remember to remove any PATH command from AUTOEXEC.BAT. A few programs may have difficulty with a PATH variable longer than 122 characters, but most programs should function just fine with the longer PATH set in CONFIG.SYS.

Using the SHELL Command

The SHELL command specifies the name and location of the command interpreter, which is usually COMMAND.COM. Used in combination with COMMAND, the SHELL command can also be used to specify the DOS environment size. For example, the following command specifies C:\DOS as the location of COMMAND.COM, the command interpreter, and increases the environment size to 384 bytes (the /E:*nnn* sets the environment size):

```
SHELL=C:\DOS\COMMAND.COM C:\DOS\ /E:384 /P
```

Increasing the environment size has serious implications for memory management. Each TSR and program loaded at the command prompt, or in a batch file such as AUTOEXEC.BAT, inherits a copy of the DOS environment. If you increase the environment size, the amount of memory used by each of these TSRs and programs increases by the amount of the increase in the environment size. If the environment size is 256 bytes too large, each TSR and program uses 256 bytes more memory than necessary.

It's important, therefore, to make certain you don't increase the environment size any more than necessary. To determine how large the environment should be, enter the following commands at the DOS prompt:

```
SET > SETSIZE.TXT
DIR SETSIZE.TXT
```

The size displayed for SETSIZE.TXT indicates the amount of memory used by the DOS environment variables currently allocated. To minimize the amount of memory wasted by setting the environment size too large, set your environment slightly larger than the size of SETSIZE.TXT. The environment size should be set to a multiple of 16 bytes. To determine the minimum size for your environment, divide the size of SETSIZE.TXT by 16, round the result up to the next integer value, and multiply that value by 16.

For example, if SETSIZE.TXT is listed as 344 bytes, divide 344 by 16 to obtain the value of 21.5. Round this up to 22, and multiply by 16 to obtain the correct value of 352 bytes for the environment size.

Note

Setting a minimal size for the DOS environment allows very little room for additional environment variables. Sometimes batch files or other programs create temporary environment variables that may not be visible using the technique noted above. If you receive the message "Out of environment space" when you run a batch file or an application program, increase the size of the DOS environment slightly. Remember to increase the environment size in 16-byte increments.

Using the STACKS Command

The STACKS=n,s command specifies the number of data stacks your system should allocate for programs to handle hardware interrupts. You can specify 0 or 8 through 64 for n (the number of stacks), and 0 or 32 through 512 for s (the size of the stacks in bytes). Except for 8088-based systems, the default is STACKS=9,128.

A common setting for STACKS is 9,256, which allocates 9 stacks of 256 bytes each, using almost 3K of conventional memory. You may be able to specify STACKS=0,0 to save the memory otherwise allocated for this system structure.

It's difficult to determine whether the 0,0 setting is working correctly, because the standard description states that the "computer becomes unstable" when the values are set too low. Unless you are prepared to do extensive testing after making this single change, it's nearly impossible to know whether STACKS=0,0 will work correctly on your PC. This is one case where you're truly on your own, so good luck!

Using the SUBMENU Command

The SUBMENU=*blockname,menu_text* command specifies an item on the startup menu that will display an additional menu if selected. This command is one of the multiple configuration commands new in MS-DOS 6.

The SUBMENU command is very similar to the MENUITEM command discussed earlier. Both commands can appear only in a menu block in CONFIG.SYS.

You can use the SUBMENU command if you have very complex system setup requirements that demand additional selections beyond an initial choice. Usually, though, you'll find it's more convenient to limit the number of choices a user must make when starting the system. Requiring a user to make too many selections increases the risk of errors.

Using the SWITCHES Command

The SWITCHES command specifies certain special options during the boot process. Table 6.4 summarizes these options.

Note

In MS-DOS 6.2, you can press Ctrl-F5 or Ctrl-F8 to bypass loading of DBLSPACE.BIN. To prevent a user from doing this, and therefore being unable to access compressed drives, add SWITCHES /N to the DBLSPACE.INI file.

Table 6.4	Options for the SWITCHES Command
Option	Description
/F	Eliminates the 2-second delay during startup after the "Starting MS-DOS ..." message is displayed.
/K	Forces an enhanced keyboard to behave like a conventional keyboard.
/N	Prevents use of the F5 or F8 key to bypass CONFIG.SYS and AUTOEXEC.BAT.
/W	Specifies that the WINA20.386 file has been moved to a directory other than the root directory.

The SWITCHES /W setting is necessary only if you are using Windows 3.0 in 386 enhanced mode and have moved the WINA20.386 file away from the root directory. If you have upgraded to Windows 3.1 or Windows for Workgroups, you do not need to use this setting, and can save some disk space by deleting the WINA20.386 file.

Be absolutely certain your system is functioning correctly before you add SWITCHES /F or SWITCHES /N to your CONFIG.SYS file. These settings could make it very difficult to start your system if there is an error in CONFIG.SYS or AUTOEXEC.BAT, unless you have an emergency boot diskette.

Many of the CONFIG.SYS options have memory management implications that go far beyond what you might normally expect. Even small changes are often multiplied as they spread their effects across the broad range of device drivers and TSRs you load each time you start your system. Next we'll look at how your AUTOEXEC.BAT file further affects your system.

Using AUTOEXEC.BAT Options

After CONFIG.SYS, AUTOEXEC.BAT is the second special user-created configuration file your system reads each time you start your PC. Once the commands in CONFIG.SYS have been executed, those in AUTOEXEC.BAT are processed. Both files can contain commands that configure your system, but only CONFIG.SYS can be used to load device drivers. Both files can contain commands that load TSRs, but only AUTOEXEC.BAT can be used to load TSRs that need a copy of the DOS environment.

Note

Strictly speaking, MS-DOS 6 has a third special configuration file, DBLSPACE.INI, that is processed when your system boots (if you have installed DoubleSpace disk compression). This file is not usually modified by the PC user, and really has little effect on memory management. DBLSPACE.INI options are therefore not discussed in this book.

From a memory management perspective, there are relatively few changes you can make in AUTOEXEC.BAT that affect the amount of available memory. You may be able to adjust the parameters passed to some TSRs you load in AUTOEXEC.BAT, but in most cases, these changes will have little effect on memory usage. Let's have a look at what you can do in AUTOEXEC.BAT to enhance your memory utilization.

Using the CHOICE Command

The CHOICE command is used to create a menu of selections in a batch file, usually in AUTOEXEC.BAT, and to allow the user to make a selection from the displayed choices. Use the following syntax with the CHOICE command:

```
CHOICE /C:keys /N /S /T:c,nn text
```

/C:keys specifies the set of keys the user can press in response to the prompt. CHOICE indicates which key was pressed by returning a value in ERRORLEVEL, with the first key in the list as ERRORLEVEL 1, the second as ERRORLEVEL 2, and so on.

/N specifies that no prompt should be displayed.

/S specifies that CHOICE will be case sensitive, forcing the user to press the correct upper- or lowercase character.

/T:c,nn specifies the default selection, *c*, and the time-out in seconds, *nn*. The time-out can be 0 to 99 seconds.

text specifies any text you want to be displayed before the prompt. If you include a forward slash (/), you must enclose *text* in quotation marks.

You can use the CHOICE command to create a menu similar to the startup menu you create in CONFIG.SYS. Usually, ECHO commands are placed on preceding lines to display the menu selections, and the CHOICE command displays a prompt and waits for the user's selection. You then test for the value of ERRORLEVEL to determine how the batch file should respond to the user's selection.

Note

When checking the value of ERRORLEVEL, always check for the highest values first. If ERRORLEVEL has a value of 2, tests for both ERRORLEVEL 2 and ERRORLEVEL 1 will succeed. A test for ERRORLEVEL 3 however, would, fail in this instance.

Although you can use the CHOICE command to create an additional startup menu, you may want to consider using the CONFIG.SYS startup menu to make all selections, and then use the CONFIG environment variable to control which selections are made in AUTOEXEC.BAT. This method will reduce the number of selections a user must make to start your system, and therefore reduce the possibility of errors. Let's have a look at the CONFIG environment variable next.

Using the CONFIG Variable

The CONFIG variable is an MS-DOS 6 environment variable automatically set each time you boot your PC. This environment variable is set to the name of the configuration block (less the square brackets []) selected in the CONFIG.SYS startup menu. If no CONFIG.SYS startup menu exists, the CONFIG variable is blank.

You can test the value of the CONFIG variable in AUTOEXEC.BAT (or in other batch files as necessary) to determine which selection the user made from the startup menu. Use the results of this test to branch to different sections of AUTOEXEC.BAT, depending on your needs. This can eliminate the need for the user to make a second selection in AUTOEXEC.BAT.

For example, suppose your CONFIG.SYS startup menu looks like this:

```
[MENU]
MENUCOLOR=14,1
```

```
MENUITEM=GAMES,   Load Game Configuration
MENUITEM=NORMAL,  Don't Load Game Drivers
MENUDEFAULT=NORMAL,10
```

If the user accepts the default selection, the CONFIG variable will have the value NORMAL. If the alternate selection is chosen, the CONFIG variable will have the value GAMES. You might use this value by adding the following to the end of AUTOEXEC.BAT:

```
IF %CONFIG%==NORMAL GOTO END
REM    Automatically load game program if GAMES
REM    was the selection in the start up menu
MYGAME
:END
```

If the user selects GAMES from the startup menu, any special configuration commands necessary to run the MYGAME program will be executed, and AUTOEXEC.BAT will automatically load the program. This is an especially good method to use if you're setting up a system for someone who has difficulty making selections, or who is prone to keying errors.

Using the LOADHIGH Command

The LOADHIGH command, which you can abbreviate as LH, is a MS-DOS 6 memory management command you can use at the DOS prompt, or in a batch file such as AUTOEXEC.BAT. This command loads a TSR into upper memory if possible; otherwise, the TSR is loaded into conventional memory.

One of the most important memory management improvements in MS-DOS 6, compared to MS-DOS 5, is the new ability to specify which upper memory region to use for loading device drivers and TSRs. To do this, use the /L:region# argument following the DEVICEHIGH command in CONFIG.SYS, or following the LOADHIGH command. If you don't specify which region to use, each device driver or TSR loads into the largest upper memory block which is available when the device driver or TSR is loaded, so the ability to control where device drivers or TSRs are loaded makes memory management much easier.

To use the LOADHIGH command, you can simply add the command to the beginning of a line in AUTOEXEC.BAT that loads a TSR program. If a large enough contiguous upper memory block is available, the TSR is loaded into upper memory. The LOADHIGH command does not fail if no upper memory block is large enough to load the TSR; instead, the TSR program is simply loaded into conventional memory—no error message is displayed.

If you want to specify which region is to be used, you use the optional /L:*region1,minsize1;region2,minsize2;...* argument to specify one or more regions, and the amount of memory the TSR requires. If the specified upper memory block does not contain at least the specified amount of free memory, the TSR will be loaded into conventional memory instead of upper memory. This optional argument is of the most value for TSRs that expand after they're loaded into memory. Very few TSRs do this, but the *minsize* argument is available if it becomes necessary. If you use this argument, you must place it after the /L:*region#* argument, separated by a comma.

For example, to specify that the TSR C:\UTILITY\MYTSR.COM be loaded in region 2 of upper memory only if 16K of contiguous upper memory is available in the specified region, you would use the following command line:

```
LOADHIGH /L:2,16384 C:\UTILITY\MYTSR
```

A few TSRs can use more than one region of upper memory. To specify that a TSR can use additional upper memory blocks, use a semicolon following the first region number (and optional memory size) to separate the second region number from the first. You can also specify a minimum memory size for this region, or for any subsequent regions if necessary.

The section "Performing the Load Order Juggling Act," later in this chapter, suggests additional methods of working around the problem of making the most effective use of system memory.

Occasionally, you'll encounter TSRs that cannot be loaded into upper memory:

- Some TSRs cannot be loaded into upper memory because they don't work correctly unless they're loaded in conventional memory. If these types of TSRs are loaded into upper memory, you may lock up your system, or you may experience intermittent crashes.

- Some TSRs cannot be loaded into upper memory because they require more memory to load than their memory image size. In some cases, it's possible to load such TSRs into upper memory if you can free a large enough block of contiguous memory, but sometimes it's just not possible to create a large enough upper memory block.

It's important to remember that the LOADHIGH command does not fail to load a TSR if upper memory isn't available. Instead, the LOADHIGH command is ignored, and the TSR is loaded into conventional memory. As a result, it's not safe to assume that just because you used the LOADHIGH command, the TSR actually loaded into upper memory. Use the MEM /C command to determine exactly where each device driver and TSR has been loaded.

Each TSR program you can load into upper memory instead of conventional memory increases the amount of free conventional memory. Most TSRs can function correctly in upper memory, so you should load as many TSRs using the LOADHIGH command as possible.

Before you can use the LOADHIGH command successfully, three commands must be executed in CONFIG.SYS:

1. The HIMEM.SYS device driver must be loaded.
2. The EMM386.EXE device driver must be loaded.
3. The DOS=UMB (or DOS=HIGH,UMB) command must be executed.

Consider the INSTALLHIGH Option

Instead of loading TSRs into upper memory using the AUTOEXEC.BAT command LOADHIGH, you may want to consider loading them using the CONFIG.SYS command INSTALLHIGH. Although the two commands serve a similar purpose, TSRs loaded using the INSTALLHIGH command may use slightly less memory because they don't receive their own copy of the DOS environment, as they do when loaded using LOADHIGH.

TSRs that require a copy of the DOS environment, that use shortcut keys, or that depend upon COMMAND.COM to handle critical errors cannot be loaded using the INSTALLHIGH command, so LOADHIGH is the only way to load these TSRs into upper memory. See the earlier section on CONFIG.SYS options for more information on the INSTALLHIGH command.

In MS-DOS 6, the LOADHIGH command has one major advantage over the INSTALLHIGH command: the ability to specify which upper memory region to use for loading the TSR. If you use the INSTALLHIGH command, the TSR will be loaded into the largest available upper memory block, which may not be the most efficient use of upper memory.

Using MemMaker

Although MS-DOS 5 provided basic memory management tools, those tools weren't very easy to use. If you wanted to take advantage of the memory management options, your only choice was to make changes to CONFIG.SYS and AUTOEXEC.BAT manually. The prospect of making such fundamental modifications to the very files that could totally lock up your system if you made a simple mistake kept a large number of PC users from taking advantage of MS-DOS 5's memory management options.

MS-DOS 6 offers enhanced versions of MS-DOS 5's memory management tools, but it also includes a new, automatic memory management tool. That tool, MemMaker, can perform memory optimization tasks so well that only the most advanced MS-DOS experts can do much better. Frankly, even the experts usually let MemMaker do its best before they try any additional fine-tuning. After all, why do everything the hard way?

In this section, we'll take a short look at how to use MemMaker. Using this program is quite simple, and even using the custom mode only requires you to answer a few extra questions.

MemMaker has two operating modes. You can select express mode and allow the program to use its default selections, or you can use custom mode for a little more control. Regardless of the mode you want to use, begin by entering the command **MEMMAKER** at the DOS prompt. Once the program loads, you'll see a screen similar to Figure 6.1.

Using Express Mode

MemMaker's default operating mode is express mode. When you press Enter to continue from the screen shown in Figure 6.1, you're given the option to select express or custom mode (see Figure 6.2). To use express mode, press Enter again.

If your system has an 80386 or higher processor and extended memory, MemMaker then begins by looking for unused areas of upper memory.

```
Welcome to MemMaker.

MemMaker makes more conventional memory available by moving memory-
resident programs and device drivers into the upper memory area.

While running MemMaker, you will be able to make some choices.
MemMaker displays options in highlighted text. (For example, you can
change the "Continue" option below.) To accept the highlighted
option, press ENTER.  To choose a different option, press the
SPACEBAR until the option you want appears, and then press ENTER.

For help while you are running MemMaker, press F1, or see Chapter
X, "Making More Memory Available," in the MS-DOS User's Guide.

          Continue or Exit? Continue




ENTER=Accept Selection   SPACEBAR=Change Selection   F1=Help   F3=Exit
```

Figure 6.1   Run MemMaker for automatic memory optimization.

```
There are two ways to run MemMaker.

Use Express Setup if you want MemMaker to optimize your computer's
memory automatically.

Use Custom Setup if you are an experienced user who wants to
control the changes that MemMaker makes to your system files.

          Use Express or Custom Setup? Express Setup






ENTER=Accept Selection   SPACEBAR=Change Selection   F1=Help   F3=Exit
```

Figure 6.2   Select Express mode to accept the default options.

Usually, there are one or more regions of unused memory address space that can be used for upper memory blocks.

After determining how much upper memory is available, MemMaker examines your device drivers and TSRs to see how much memory each needs to load and to run. Once this information has been gathered, MemMaker begins its real task—determining the best combination of device driver and TSR memory loading position for optimal memory use.

MemMaker then prepares to test its new copies of CONFIG.SYS and AUTOEXEC.BAT by displaying a message telling you it has found a recommended configuration. Press Enter to allow MemMaker to reboot your PC.

Be sure to watch for error messages as your system reboots. If none appear, and your PC seems to run correctly, MemMaker will inform you of whether it was able to improve upon the existing configuration. You'll probably be pleasantly surprised by the results.

If your system locks up or doesn't finish booting, press **Ctrl-Alt-Del** to reboot. MemMaker will restart, and the screen instructions will step you through the process of either trying again or returning to your old system configuration.

If MemMaker is unable to optimize your memory configuration properly, you can use the command **MEMMAKER /UNDO** to return CONFIG.SYS and AUTOEXEC.BAT to their original settings.

Using Custom Mode

MemMaker's express mode uses fairly conservative default settings. Often, MemMaker can find a better system configuration with just a little help on your part.

To try the MemMaker custom optimization mode, select Custom Optimization from the MemMaker screen shown in Figure 6.2. To select Custom Optimization, press the Spacebar and then press Enter. The screen shown in Figure 6.3 will appear.

You can then select the options you wish to change. The options are:

- "Specify which drivers and TSRs to include during optimization?" Select this option if you know certain device drivers or TSRs must not be

```
                        Advanced Options

Specify which drivers and TSRs to include during optimization?   No
Set aside upper memory for EMS page frame?                       Yes
Scan the upper memory area aggressively?                         Yes
Optimize upper memory for use with Windows?                      Yes
Create upper memory in the monochrome region (B000-B7FF)?        No
Keep current EMM386 memory exclusions and inclusions?            Yes
Move Extended BIOS Data Area from conventional to upper memory?  Yes



To move to a different option, press the UP ARROW or DOWN ARROW key.
To accept all the settings and continue, press ENTER.




ENTER=Accept All   SPACEBAR=Change Selection   F1=Help   F3=Exit
```

Figure 6.3   Use custom optimization mode for more control over
MemMaker's operation.

loaded into upper memory. Usually, MemMaker knows which device drivers and TSRs cannot be loaded into upper memory, so the default setting of No does not have to be changed unless your system locks up after MemMaker reboots.

- "Scan the upper memory area aggressively?" Select this option to specify whether EMM386.EXE should look in memory segments C600 through F7FF (Yes) or limit the range to C600 through EFFF (No) when it looks for available upper memory addresses. This option can result in an extra 32K of upper memory if Yes is selected, but may also cause some systems to lock up.

- "Optimize upper memory for use with Windows?" This option specifies whether EMM386.EXE should set aside upper memory block space for the Windows translation buffers, which are system structures used by non-Windows programs running under Windows. It's usually best to set this option to No, since this will leave more upper memory available. In spite of the title of this option, setting this to Yes does not benefit Windows programs.

- "Create upper memory in the monochrome region (B000–B7FF)?" This option specifies whether EMM386.EXE includes the 32K monochrome display adapter page in upper memory. It's usually safe to change this option to Yes, although if you have a super VGA adapter, you may have to add DEVICE=MONOUMB.386 to the [386enh] section of SYSTEM.INI to be able to run Windows correctly.

- "Keep current EMM386 memory exclusions and inclusions?" This option specifies whether EMM386.EXE will continue to keep your current I= and X= settings. It's usually best to change this option to No, because this may result in additional upper memory space being discovered. If you have an adapter that requires an X= setting because it is invisible to EMM386.EXE at boot time, modify your CONFIG.SYS to remove all of the I= and X= settings except the one you know you really need. Then run MemMaker again and set this option to Yes.

- "Move Extended BIOS Data Area from conventional to upper memory?" This option specifies whether the Extended BIOS Data Area (EBDA) moves from the end of conventional memory to upper memory, freeing an additional 1K of conventional memory. Leave this option set to Yes unless you encounter problems that seem to have no other solution. In that case, try setting this to No to see if the problem disappears.

Using the MEMMAKER.STS Report

MemMaker generates a report as it is working that stores information Mem-Maker uses as it optimizes memory. This report is stored in a file called MEMMAKER.STS, and fortunately, MemMaker does not delete this report when the program completes its task. You can use portions of the MEMMAKER.STS report to help you optimize memory manually.

The MEMMAKER.STS report contains information you'd otherwise have difficulty obtaining. The most useful information tells you how device drivers and TSRs use memory. This is especially useful for device drivers and TSRs that take different amounts of memory to load than they do once they're settled into a memory block. For example, the following excerpt from a MEMMAKER.STS file shows how two sample device drivers and TSRs use memory:

```
Command=C:\FAX\SATISFAX.SYS
Line=35
```

```
FinalSize=4016
MaxSize=29328
FinalUpperSizes=0
MaxUpperSizes=0
ProgramType=DEVICE

Command=C:\DOS\MOUSE
Line=15
FinalSize=17088
MaxSize=56928
FinalUpperSizes=0
MaxUpperSizes=0
ProgramType=PROGRAM
```

If you simply looked at the MEM /C report, you probably wouldn't be able to determine why you have trouble loading these two items into upper memory. Looking at the MEMMAKER.STS report, however, makes it quite clear that both of these require quite a bit more memory to load than they use once they're actually in memory. This also explains why memory management experts almost always start by running MemMaker before they even try manual optimization—you have to run MemMaker if you want to generate the MEMMAKER.STS report.

In the sample MEMMAKER.STS report, you can see that the mouse driver requires a free, contiguous memory block of 56,928 bytes to load. Once loaded, the memory requirement shrinks to 17,088 bytes—one third the size needed for loading. This discrepancy is the cause of most of the problems you'll encounter when attempting to load your device drivers and TSRs into upper memory. In the next section we'll examine some techniques you can use in working around such problems.

Performing the Load Order Juggling Act

Once you've applied all the memory management tricks you've learned so far, you probably have more conventional memory available than you ever had before. But now that you have a feel for advanced memory management, you're probably also a little frustrated because you haven't been able to accomplish quite as much as you'd like. You probably still have one or two device drivers or TSRs in conventional memory that you'd like to load into upper memory. It's time to bring out the last "big gun" of MS-DOS 6 advanced memory management techniques, the load order juggling act.

Reordering Device Drivers and TSRs

The *load order juggling act* is the term I use to describe the process of making better use of memory resources by changing the order in which device drivers and TSRs are actually loaded into memory. You may wonder how changing the order in which device drivers and TSRs are loaded into memory can affect memory usage. After all, simply changing the order in which device drivers and TSRs are loaded doesn't change the amount of memory they use, does it?

It's true that device drivers and TSRs will still use the same amount of memory no matter what order they're loaded in. What changes along with load order, though, is how the device drivers and TSRs fit together in memory. To understand how changing the load order can have this effect, think of the pieces of a jigsaw puzzle. If you line up the puzzle pieces in a row, the row will be longer if the pieces are arranged at random than it will if the pieces are arranged so they fit together.

Of course, device drivers and TSRs don't fit together like jigsaw puzzle pieces, but the order in which they're loaded can result in a similar effect. There are several reasons for this:

- Some device drivers and TSRs require more memory to load than their memory image size. If a device driver or TSR cannot find an upper memory block large enough for its load size, the device driver or TSR will load into conventional memory.
- TSR programs loaded using the INSTALLHIGH command in CONFIG.SYS use slightly less memory than if the same TSR program is loaded using the LOADHIGH command in AUTOEXEC.BAT. Sometimes this small difference can be enough to leave just the extra amount of memory that allows another TSR to load into upper memory instead of into conventional memory.

Let's consider some examples that show how these factors affect your memory management scheme.

First, suppose you load a device driver, DRVA.SYS, that takes 55K of memory to load, but has a memory image size of 18K. In addition, you load another device driver, DRVB.SYS, that requires 37K of memory, both during and after loading. If you have an upper memory block that's 57K in size, you can load the two device drivers into the upper memory block only if you load DRVA.SYS before you load DRVB.SYS. You have to consider, though, whether the two device drivers are truly independent of each other. If DRVA.SYS must be loaded before DRVB.SYS, consider the memory image size of each to determine which makes better use of upper memory. Load the device driver with the smallest memory image size into conventional memory.

Next, suppose you load several TSR programs that don't require a copy of the DOS environment, shortcut keys, or COMMAND.COM's critical error handler. In addition, you use the SHELL= command in CONFIG.SYS to increase the DOS environment size to 1024 bytes. By using the INSTALL-HIGH command in CONFIG.SYS, you'll save 1K of upper memory for each TSR. This small saving may be just enough to allow an additional TSR to fit into an upper memory block, compared to loading the same TSRs using LOADHIGH in AUTOEXEC.BAT. By moving the loading of these TSRs from AUTOEXEC.BAT to CONFIG.SYS, you've saved the conventional memory that would normally be used by one of the TSRs.

Of course, MS-DOS 6 allows you to specify which upper memory block region to use for loading specific device drivers and TSRs, so it isn't always as important to load device drivers and TSRs in a particular order. Even so, when you consider how some device drivers and TSRs change their size after loading, the order of loading can make a real difference.

Limitations to Reordering

There are some limitations to what you can accomplish through reordering the loading sequence of your device drivers and TSRs. These limitations can sometimes prevent you from accomplishing your goal of placing all device drivers and TSRs into upper memory, leaving the maximum possible free conventional memory.

- Device drivers are always loaded before TSR programs. You cannot change this by placing INSTALLHIGH commands before DEVICEHIGH commands in CONFIG.SYS.

- Some device drivers and TSRs require a certain load order. In some cases, a device driver or TSR depends on another device driver or TSR that must be loaded first. In other cases, device drivers or TSRs cannot function correctly if certain other device drivers or TSRs have already been loaded.

- A few device drivers cannot be loaded once a memory manager has been loaded. One example is certain SCSI adapter device drivers that must be placed first in CONFIG.SYS.

As you experiment with changing the load order of device drivers and TSRs, use the MEM command options you learned in Chapter 4 to track your success. Printed copies of each version of CONFIG.SYS and AUTOEXEC.BAT, along with printed copies of the MEM reports, will provide good documentation of your progress. Don't forget to write the current date and time on each set of printouts.

Bypassing CONFIG.SYS and AUTOEXEC.BAT

It's always possible to make typing errors, or to use a command in CONFIG.SYS or AUTOEXEC.BAT that isn't compatible with your PC. These types of problems make it very important for the memory management experimenter to have a tested, emergency boot diskette. This is true even in MS-DOS 6, which allows you to bypass CONFIG.SYS and AUTOEXEC.BAT by pressing the correct keys as you boot. Remember, the SWITCHES command can be added to CONFIG.SYS to effectively eliminate this safety feature.

Be sure you create and test your emergency boot diskette before you begin your experiments. You don't want to wait until there actually is an emergency to find out that your diskette doesn't work!

Table 6.5 summarizes the emergency keys you can use during the boot process to stop MS-DOS 6 from executing configuration commands.

Summary

Memory management became much easier in MS-DOS 6 than it had been in MS-DOS 5. The tools included in MS-DOS 6 were both more powerful and

Table 6.5	Emergency Configuration Bypass Keys
Key	**Purpose**
F5	Bypasses CONFIG.SYS and AUTOEXEC.BAT.
F8	Allows you to selectively execute CONFIG.SYS commands. In MS-DOS 6, allows you to bypass AUTOEXEC.BAT. In MS-DOS 6.2, allows you to selectively execute AUTOEXEC.BAT commands.
Ctrl-F5	In MS-DOS 6.2, bypasses loading of DBLSPACE.BIN, CONFIG.SYS, and AUTOEXEC.BAT.
Ctrl-F8	In MS-DOS 6.2, bypasses loading of DBLSPACE.BIN, and allows you to selectively execute CONFIG.SYS and AUTOEXEC.BAT commands.

more flexible. In addition, MemMaker brought some much needed automation to the process.

In this chapter you learned that MS-DOS 6's powerful memory management tools really do allow you to improve the way your system operates. Whether you use the strictly hands-on approach, the fully automatic MemMaker approach, or a combination of the two, you now have more control over one of the most important areas of your PC.

Chapter 7

Managing Your Memory with Novell DOS 7

Novell DOS 7 is an important new player in the PC operating system arena. Its ancestors were the versions of DR-DOS from Digital Research, which recently became a part of Novell, a company better known for networking products than for stand-alone operating systems.

As a new entry, Novell DOS 7 offers some unique options not found in any competing operating system. These include built-in networking, security options, multitasking, and an effective method of expanding the amount of conventional memory available to application programs. Novell DOS 7 also offers many configuration options that will seem quite familiar to anyone who moves from one of the MS-DOS versions. But even these seemingly familiar options often include Novell's own special enhancements and important differences from their MS-DOS counterparts.

As with MS-DOS, taking advantage of all of Novell DOS 7's new features requires at least an 80386 processor in your system. Novell DOS 7 offers full support of upper memory, the high memory area, and the XMS memory standard for extended memory on modern PCs. It also offers a new memory standard, DPMS, which I'll discuss later in this chapter.

Novell DOS 7's memory management tools are similar to those in MS-DOS 5, but they also include options that go far beyond the capabilities of MS-DOS 6. Just as in the MS-DOS versions, however, taking full advantage of Novell DOS 7's memory management options requires a little hands-on work. Novell DOS 7 has a very good setup program that can do much of the basics, but to get the most out of your system, you'll have to spend a little time doing some fine-tuning.

Advanced memory management in Novell DOS 7 starts with understanding and modifying the two primary system configuration files, CONFIG.SYS and AUTOEXEC.BAT. Although quite similar to their MS-DOS counterparts, the commands used in these two files contain some surprises, especially for someone upgrading from MS-DOS. You can't assume you'll be able to simply install Novell DOS 7 and expect everything to work as you expect. Let's have a look at the Novell DOS 7 memory management options, starting with CONFIG.SYS.

In this chapter I'll show you how to take advantage of the advanced memory management possibilities built into Novell DOS 7. I'll also explain why you might want to use some of the more obscure options, and what effect they'll have on your PC.

Memory management in Novell DOS 7 can be broken down into three areas:

- The first area consists of the commands and directives you'll use in CONFIG.SYS. This file presents the first system configuration opportunity on any PC, because this is the first user file processed when you start your system.

- The second area consists of the commands you'll use in AUTOEXEC.BAT. This is the second user file processed during startup.

- The third area is something I call the *load order juggling act*. Often, this is the most difficult area to understand, but one that can produce quite impressive results.

Note

Advanced memory management techniques require an understanding of the subjects presented in the earlier chapters of this book. If you aren't comfortable with some of the topics covered earlier, please take the time to review any matter that doesn't seem clear before you begin experimenting with your system's configuration.

Using CONFIG.SYS Options

CONFIG.SYS is very important in configuring your system. If CONFIG.SYS exists in the root directory of the boot disk, any commands or directives it contains are read and executed as part of the system startup process. Many of the system configuration options can be used only when placed in CONFIG.SYS; you cannot exercise these options any other way.

Note

Novell DOS 7 can use an alternate system configuration file, which you specify using the CHAIN command (discussed later in this section). Since this alternate system configuration file must be called from CONFIG.SYS, however, you can consider it simply an extension, not a replacement for CONFIG.SYS.

Because most of the CONFIG.SYS system configuration options cannot be executed at the command line, it's often difficult to see exactly what happens as they are processed. Error or information messages displayed during the processing of CONFIG.SYS usually scroll by so quickly that you might miss important details. If you're not watching your screen closely, and if you're not a speed reader, you might never realize that something is wrong. This makes it even more important to make certain that your CONFIG.SYS file is correctly structured, and that every line it contains is absolutely correct.

Fortunately, an important modification to one of the system files, IBM-BIO.COM, was incorporated in Novell DOS 7. If you press the F8 key when you see the message "Starting DOS..." while your system is booting, you will be prompted before each line in CONFIG.SYS and AUTOEXEC.BAT is executed. This makes it much easier to see any error or information messages that may be displayed.

In Novell DOS 7, you can also bypass CONFIG.SYS and AUTOEXEC.BAT entirely by pressing the F5 key when the message "Starting DOS..." is displayed.

Even though the F5 and F8 key methods of controlling the processing of CONFIG.SYS and AUTOEXEC.BAT commands make experimenting with system configuration options much safer in Novell DOS 7, it's always best to play it safe. Always try your proposed changes on a boot diskette first, and copy them to your hard disk only after you've verified that a new configuration works correctly.

For Novell DOS 7 memory management purposes, a device driver, EMM386.EXE, is one of the most important items that appear in CONFIG.SYS. If you've upgraded from MS-DOS, many of the options for this device driver will seem familiar, but there are some very important differences in the Novell DOS 7 version of this device driver. It's very important to understand how to use this device driver, especially if you've upgraded from an earlier DOS version. Otherwise, you won't be able to apply any of the other Novell DOS 7 advanced memory management techniques. Because of this importance, I'll start the discussion of CONFIG.SYS options by looking at this device driver in detail.

Why You Don't Need HIMEM.SYS

If you've moved to Novell DOS 7 from MS-DOS, you may wonder why I'm not discussing HIMEM.SYS. After all, Novell DOS 7 does include a version of HIMEM.SYS, and in MS-DOS, HIMEM.SYS must be installed before EMM386.EXE.

The reason I'm not going to discuss Novell DOS 7's HIMEM.SYS is simple. As I mentioned earlier, there are some very important differences between MS-DOS and Novell DOS 7. The memory managers represent one of these areas of major difference. Unlike MS-DOS's EMM386.EXE, Novell DOS 7's EMM386.EXE is a complete memory manager. In Novell DOS 7, EMM386.EXE doesn't need an additional XMS memory manager—that function is built into EMM386.EXE itself. The HIMEM.SYS file included in Novell DOS 7 is an XMS memory manager, but is used only on PCs with 80286 processors. There's no need to use HIMEM.SYS on systems with an 80386 or higher processor.

> ### Note
>
> If you've moved to Novell DOS 7 from a previous version of MS-DOS, be certain you don't include a command in CONFIG.SYS to load HIMEM.SYS. You'll waste memory, and probably encounter conflicts between the two memory managers as well.

Understanding EMM386.EXE's Options

EMM386.EXE is the Novell DOS 7 XMS memory manager, EMS memory manager, and upper memory block provider. Do not load HIMEM.SYS or another XMS memory manager in addition to EMM386.EXE.

Because EMM386.EXE requires an 80386 or higher processor, you cannot use it to provide XMS memory, EMS memory, or upper memory blocks on a system with an 80286 or lower processor. HIMEM.SYS can be used on an 80286 system to provide XMS memory, but Novell DOS 7 does not include a comparable EMS memory manager and upper memory block provider for these types of systems.

You can use EMM386.EXE to provide XMS memory, EMS memory, or upper memory blocks individually, or to provide access to all three types of memory at the same time. EMM386.EXE also provides some additional memory management functions, which are controlled through the use of its optional switches.

Note

The slash preceding each of EMM386.EXE's options is optional; you can specify the options with or without the slash.

Why You Might Need the /AUTO, /OFF, and /ON Options

The /AUTO option specifies that EMM386.EXE should supply EMS and XMS memory support automatically when requested by a program. This is the default setting for EMM386.EXE. The /OFF option specifies that EMM386.EXE should not supply EMS or XMS memory, and that the system should remain in real mode rather than protected mode or virtual 8086 mode. The /ON option specifies that EMM386.EXE should supply EMS or XMS memory.

The ON, OFF, and AUTO options are related and mutually exclusive options. You can use these same options at the DOS command line or in a batch file to switch the state of EMS and XMS support.

Some programs are unable to function correctly when EMM386.EXE is enabled. You can use these options to control EMM386.EXE as needed. For example, if you use one program that requires real mode, you can set EMM386.EXE on automatic initially. You can then start the program using a batch file that includes the line **EMM386 OFF** before the command that starts the program, and **EMM386 ON** after the program exits. Unfortunately, this technique may not work if EMM386.EXE is supplying upper or EMS memory.

Normally, it's best to allow EMM386.EXE to be loaded and function automatically. That way the program's services will be available as needed.

Why You Might Need the /COMPAQ Option

The /COMPAQ=*on|off* option specifies whether EMM386.EXE can use special methods to supply an additional 256K of memory on a Compaq PC. The default is on, which enables this extra memory. This option has no effect on PCs made by manufacturers other than Compaq.

Most Compaq 80386 or higher PCs can function correctly when EMM386.EXE is supplying the extra 256K of memory, but it is possible to encounter conflicts if you add third-party adapter boards or use programs that use DOS extenders. It can be difficult to determine if the additional memory support is causing any problems, however, so you may have to experiment to see if setting this option to off eliminates the conflicts. If you see no difference when this option is set to off, be sure to change the setting back to on so you'll have access to the maximum amount of memory.

Why You Might Need the /DPMI Option

The /DPMI option enables DOS Protected Mode Interface (DPMI) memory support. DPMI is one common method of accessing extended memory, and is used by some non-Windows programs such as Lotus 1-2-3 Release 3.4.

You do not need to use the /DPMI option to run Windows programs, nor to run standard DOS programs that don't use DOS extenders. If your programs do not require DPMI support, do not include this option on the EMM386.EXE command line.

You do need to use the /DPMI option if you use the Novell DOS 7 Task Manager in multitasking mode.

Why You Might Need the /EXCLUDE Option

The /EXCLUDE=*mmmm-nnnn* option specifies a range of upper memory segment addresses that EMM386.EXE should not use for upper memory blocks or the EMS page frame. You can specify addresses in the range A000 to FFFF. If you specify both /EXCLUDE=*mmmm-nnnn* and /INCLUDE=*mmmm-nnnn*, the /EXCLUDE=*mmmm-nnnn* takes precedence if you specify overlapping ranges.

Sometimes EMM386.EXE is unable to determine that a range of addresses cannot be used safely, and includes that range in upper memory. This can happen for several reasons. One of the most common is an adapter card, such as a network card, that doesn't initialize its memory space until the card is activated. Since EMM386.EXE loads before the card is used, the card remains invisible during the process of allocating upper memory.

Generally, it's fairly easy to find out the beginning address used by an adapter card, but it may be more difficult to determine how large a space to reserve for the card. The beginning address is usually listed as the *base address*. Network adapter cards often use a base address like D800 (which you may also see as D8000). Chapter 4 showed you how to use tools such as MSD and DEBUG to search through memory, but even those tools sometimes have difficulty showing how much memory space to reserve for an adapter card. So how do you determine exactly how much space to reserve for such an adapter card?

Usually, it's best to allocate upper memory in 4K blocks. This size block is small enough that you won't waste much memory if a device driver or TSR doesn't use the entire block, and it is large enough so you won't waste too much time.

Following this strategy, you can include or exclude memory space in 4K sections. This makes determining how much space to exclude for an adapter card much easier, because there are a limited number of 4K blocks in upper memory. Suppose, for example, that you've determined that your network adapter card has a base address of D800. Starting from this address, the next three successive 4K boundaries are located at D900, DA00, and DB00. The end of each 4K block is at D8FF, D9FF, DAFF, and DBFF.

It's safest to start by allocating at least 16K to an adapter board. Therefore, you should start by excluding the range from D800 through DBFF, using the command /EXCLUDE=**D800-DBFF**. Once you've included this option in the

EMM386.EXE device driver line, you can save CONFIG.SYS, and then reboot your system. (Don't forget to reboot every time you try a changed setting— otherwise, you won't really be using the new setting.) Once the system has restarted, make certain everything is working correctly and no error messages are displayed. Be sure you test the network adapter card by logging onto the network and making certain it works, too.

If excluding the range from D800 through DBFF works correctly, you can either accept the current setup as adequate, or you can experiment to see whether reserving less space for the adapter card works. You may have to spend quite a bit of time adjusting the settings, saving your work, rebooting, and checking the results, but doing so may give you additional upper memory that otherwise wouldn't be available. If you do decide to experiment further, remember to change the ranges in 4K increments. To reserve 12K instead of 16K, use **/EXCLUDE=D800-DAFF**.

Why You Might Need the /FRAME Option

The /FRAME=*auto|none|address* option enables you to specify whether to supply EMS memory, and, optionally, where to place the 64K EMS page frame. The default setting is auto, which allows EMM386.EXE to place the page frame in any unused 64K block between segment addresses C000 and FFFF.

If you specify /FRAME=none, EMM386.EXE does not create the EMS page frame, and support for EMS memory is disabled. If your device drivers, TSRs, and application programs do not require EMS memory, specify /FRAME=none to create the maximum available upper memory. Because EMM386.EXE does not create the EMS page frame if you specify /FRAME=none, this option provides at least 64K more upper memory.

The /FRAME=address option specifies an exact segment address for the base address of the 64K EMS page frame. Specifying the starting address of the page frame provides control over the size of upper memory blocks. Usually, you'll want to create the largest possible upper memory blocks, so you'll want to place the page frame in a location that does not break an upper memory block into two noncontiguous pieces.

The /FRAME=none option for the Novell DOS 7 EMM386.EXE memory manager differs from the similar option in the MS-DOS EMM386.EXE memory manager. Although both commands disable the EMS page frame, the MS-DOS version of this command attempts to provide EMS memory without using the page frame. In reality, though, both versions of the command have the same effect, because no programs that require EMS memory can actually function without wasting 64K of upper memory by requiring a page frame.

Why You Might Need the /GATEA20 Option

The /GATEA20=*type* option specifies the type of computer you're using so EMM386.EXE can properly access extended memory. Usually, EMM386.EXE can work correctly without having this option specified, but in some cases, specifying the type of system is necessary, or may improve performance.

EMM386.EXE uses something called an *A20 handler* to access extended memory. *A20* refers to the twenty-first memory address line, the first memory address line that accesses memory above the 1M address. The first 20 memory address lines, A0–A19, are present on all PCs, regardless of their processors. The A20 line is available only on systems with an 80286 or higher processor.

Table 7.1 shows the different codes you can specify for your system. The default A20 handler is the standard IBM AT handler.

It may be difficult to determine whether your system needs to have the A20 handler specified. If EMM386.EXE cannot correctly access the A20 handler, you may see an error message while the system is booting, or your system may be prone to crashing when DOS is loaded into the high memory area.

You should probably assume that if your system is specifically listed in Table 7.1, specifying the A20 handler is required. If your system is not listed

Table 7.1 Values for the /GATEA20=*type* Option	
System	**Type**
HP Vectra	HP
IBM AT or 100% compatible	AT
IBM PS/2	PS2
XMS	XMS

in Table 7.1, but you see an error message from EMM386.EXE, or your system becomes unstable when DOS is loaded high, select a setting for a system similar to your PC.

Why You Might Need the /INCLUDE Option

The /INCLUDE=*mmmm-nnnn* option specifies a range of segment addresses in the range A000h to FFFFh to use for upper memory blocks or the EMS page frame.

The /INCLUDE=*mmmm-nnnn* option is one of the most useful of EMM386.EXE's options. Normally, EMM386.EXE is quite conservative in selecting areas of upper memory for upper memory blocks and the EMS page frame. As you learned in Chapter 4, there are often additional sections of upper memory that can be used for these purposes.

You can include more than one section of upper memory by placing more than one /INCLUDE=*mmmm-nnnn* switch in the EMM386.EXE command line.

Note

If you include the B000–B7FF range in upper memory, you may encounter problems running Windows in 386 enhanced mode. If you are unable to load Windows after including this range of addresses, try adding the line **device=MONOUMB.386** to the [386enh] section of SYSTEM.INI (in the WINDOWS\SYSTEM directory), and restart Windows. If this does not solve the problem, you can chose to run Windows in standard mode or remove the B000–B7FF range from the /INCLUDE option.

Generally, it is best to create the largest contiguous upper memory blocks possible. Since some device drivers and TSRs require more memory to load than their memory image size, it's desirable to have upper memory blocks large enough to allow loading such device drivers and TSRs; otherwise, they will be loaded into conventional memory.

If you attempt to include upper memory as upper memory blocks or as the EMS page frame, and that memory is already in use, your system may crash. You can use the F8 key during the boot process to allow you to bypass the loading of EMM386.EXE so you can edit CONFIG.SYS. You should also have an emergency boot diskette available when you experiment with including extra upper memory.

It's also possible to include the first section of upper memory as an extension to conventional memory, if you have an EGA or VGA adapter but don't use any graphics modes. The /VIDEO option discussed later in this section is designed for this purpose.

Two areas of upper memory are usually safe to include even if you use programs that use graphics modes. In addition to the B000–B7FF range mentioned above, the E000–EFFF range is usually safe to use on most systems. If these two ranges are not already being used by EMM386.EXE, explicitly including them can add up to 96K of additional upper memory for upper memory blocks and the EMS page frame.

Why You Might Need the /INT15 Option

The /INT15=*nnnn* option specifies how much extended memory, in K, is reserved for access through the interrupt 15h interface method. You can specify a value between 64 and 65,535. The default is zero.

Older programs that use their own DOS extenders usually cannot use XMS memory, but instead often use a method of allocating extended memory through a DOS service called the *interrupt 15h interface*. If you use these types of programs, you must use the /INT15=*nnnn* option to enable them to access extended memory.

Any extended memory allocated through the interrupt 15h interface cannot also be used as XMS memory. This conflict between methods of accessing extended memory can usually be eliminated by upgrading to newer versions of your application programs, since most programs that use extended memory now recognize the XMS standard.

If you are unable or unwilling to upgrade to an XMS-aware program, you may want to consider one of the multiple configuration options discussed in Chapter 3. When you need to use the old DOS extended program, boot using a special configuration that supplies extended memory through the interrupt 15h interface. When you aren't using the DOS extended program, boot your system using a configuration that supplies all extended memory through the XMS standard. This will allow you to run Windows and other modern XMS-aware programs.

Why You Might Need the /MULTI Option

The /MULTI option provides DPMI support for the Novell DOS 7 Task Manager, allowing multitasking to function correctly. If you use the Novell DOS 7 SETUP program to select multitasking, this option is automatically added to your EMM386.EXE command line. This option is not added if you select task swapping instead of multitasking.

When you use the Novell DOS 7 Task Manager, it's possible to have several applications running on your PC at the same time. Each application must have access to its own memory, which is not shared with other applications. Although the Task Manager can use your hard disk to create "virtual" memory, performance considerations dictate that you have enough physical memory in your system to provide every running application with as much memory as it needs. Because multitasking means that the applications continue running when they are placed in the background, only actual physical memory can provide the level of performance you expect from your applications.

The Task Manager uses the DPMI specification to access all extended memory installed in your system. This allows the Task Manager to fool your programs into thinking they are using standard conventional memory, when they may actually be executing in protected mode extended memory.

Why You Might Need the /ROM Option

The /ROM=*start-end*|*auto*|*none* option specifies whether the system's read-only memory (ROM) is copied to RAM for faster execution.

The /ROM=*start-end* option specifies a range of segment addresses to use for shadow RAM. You can specify segment address values for *mmmm* and *nnnn* in the range A000 through FFFF. The /ROM=*auto* option specifies that all of ROM is copied to RAM, and uses memory addresses determined by EMM386.EXE. The /ROM=*none* option specifies that ROM is not copied to RAM.

Read-only memory (ROM) is slower than RAM, so copying system ROMs into faster RAM may improve system performance slightly. Usually, however, the performance improvement isn't worth the amount of upper memory you'll need to use to hold all of the ROM. If you load few device drivers and TSRs, and you need every last bit of system performance, you may want to try the ROM=*start-end* option. In most cases, however, you would have to perform very careful testing before and after using this option to gauge any performance benefit.

Why You Might Need the /USE Option

The /USE=*start-end* option forces EMM386.EXE to use a specified range of upper memory addresses as upper memory blocks or for the EMS page frame. The /USE=*start-end* option is similar to the /INCLUDE=*start-end* option, except that /USE forces the use of a memory area, while /INCLUDE only suggests the use of the specified area.

Normally, EMM386.EXE is able to discover most available upper memory regions without assistance. If you want to use an additional upper memory region that EMM386.EXE is unable to discover without assistance, it's much safer to use the /INCLUDE option rather than the /USE option. If you make a mistake specifying an address range with the /USE option, it's quite possible to lock your system, or to overwrite programs or corrupt data. None of these possibilities will improve your day!

In rare instances, you may be absolutely certain that it's safe to use an upper memory region. Even so, EMM386.EXE may refuse to use the specified range, regardless of whether you specify the range with the /INCLUDE option. In such cases, the only method open to you is to use the /USE option. Be very careful, though, and always make certain you have an emergency boot diskette handy.

Why You Might Need the /VIDEO Option

The /VIDEO=*start-end* option includes the first section of upper memory as an extension to conventional memory, if you have an EGA or VGA adapter but don't use any graphics modes.

The switch **/VIDEO=A000-AFFF** will allow conventional memory to be increased to 704K, but only for programs that don't use graphics modes. Purely text mode programs, however, can usually function correctly with this memory added to the top of conventional memory.

This option is similar to the /INCLUDE option, but the /VIDEO option can be enabled and disabled from the DOS command line using the MEMMAX command. This allows you to use the extra memory for application programs when possible, and to return the memory to the video adapter when necessary.

After you have used the /VIDEO option to enable the use of the additional memory, you must use the command **MEMMAX +V** to actually begin using the extra memory. You can use this command in a batch file or at the command prompt. You must then use the command **MEMMAX -V** to return the memory addresses to the graphics adapter before you attempt to use any programs that switch your system into a graphics mode. Otherwise, your system will lock up as soon as it attempts to enter a graphics mode.

One good method of using this additional memory is to include the command **MEMMAX -V** at the beginning of any batch file that starts programs that use graphics modes, and **MEMMAX +V** at the end of the batch file. If you use this method, you should also add **MEMMAX +V** to AUTOEXEC.BAT. If you normally start programs without using batch files, you may simply want to leave video memory available for graphics mode programs by default, and switch the memory using **MEMMAX +V** at the beginning of any batch file that starts programs that use only text modes, and **MEMMAX -V** at the end of the batch file.

You may be surprised to find that many programs don't use graphics modes, even though they display boxes and menus on the screen. It's quite possible to change screen colors, draw lines and boxes, and create quite complex-looking screens using only text modes. Most DOS utilities, for example, use text modes, even in their full-screen versions. Some of these utilities, such as DISKOPT, can use the extra memory for better performance, or to increase the number of files they can process.

Why You Might Need the /VXD Option

The /VXD=*path* option specifies the location of the EMM386.EXE VxD (virtual device driver) for Windows in 386 enhanced mode. The default is the location of EMM386.EXE.

VxDs are 32-bit programs that are the foundation of Windows in 386 enhanced mode. They simulate devices, a necessary function in the Windows 386 enhanced mode multitasking environment.

It's unlikely that you'll need to use the /VXD option, unless you receive an updated Windows memory manager that replaces the functions provided by EMM386.EXE. Most VxD files have the extension 386, such as the MONOUMB.386 file used to allow Windows to run in 386 enhanced mode when the monochrome display adapter page is used for upper memory blocks.

Why You Might Need the /WEITEK Option

The /WEITEK=*on|off* option enables or disables support for the Weitek math coprocessor. The default is off.

The Weitek math coprocessor is a special, high-performance math coprocessor sometimes used to speed up complex calculations. This very uncommon math coprocessor should not be confused with a math coprocessor like the 80287 or 80387, neither of which needs this option turned on.

Note

Only the Weitek math coprocessor needs this option turned on. All other brands of math coprocessors, including Intel and Cyrix, do not use this switch.

Why You Might Need the /WINSTD Option

The /WINSTD option provides support for Windows 3.0 in Standard mode by disabling upper memory. This option is not required for Windows 3.1 or for Windows for Workgroups.

By disabling upper memory support, you cannot use upper memory blocks for loading device drivers and TSRs. This will reduce the amount of conventional memory available to applications.

You should never use this option. Either upgrade to Windows 3.1, or run Windows 3.0 in 386 enhanced mode. Windows 3.1 is a much improved version of Windows—it is more stable and has many more standard features.

There's no reason anyone should still be using Windows 3.0, and even less reason to give up upper memory support to do so.

Why You Might Need the /XBDA Option

The /XBDA option prevents EMM386.EXE from moving the extended BIOS data from conventional memory to upper memory. This is a 1K block of memory that stores system information. Usually, the block of memory is located at the top of conventional memory (at the 639K memory address), but EMM386.EXE moves the block so that memory is not fragmented. Normally, this move does not cause any problems, but some older programs may have difficulty if they expect the extended BIOS data area to be located in its conventional location.

You should not use the /XBDA option unless you encounter problems running old programs when EMM386.EXE is loaded. Even in those cases, you should try only the /XBDA option without making any other changes to see whether moving the extended BIOS data area is really the problem.

EMM386.EXE's options give you a great amount of control over upper memory. By using these options carefully, you can increase the amount of upper memory block space, reducing the amount of conventional memory needed for device drivers and TSRs. In the rest of this section, we'll examine more of the commands you can use in CONFIG.SYS to further enhance your system's configuration.

Understanding DPMS.EXE

One of the biggest problems you'll encounter as you upgrade your PC is a severe lack of available memory. Of course, expanded memory, upper memory, and extended memory have all been created as solutions to this problem, but each of these has its limitations.

It seems like every new piece you add to your system comes with its own device driver or TSR program that must be loaded before the new equipment can function. Generally, there are only two possible locations for the device drivers and TSRs—conventional or upper memory. Of course, one of the primary goals of advanced memory management is usually to maximize available conventional memory, so upper memory is generally the preferred location for all of these device drivers and TSRs. Unfortunately, even upper memory begins to look quite small once you start loading device drivers, TSRs, disk caching software, disk compression software, network drivers, and so on.

Novell DOS 7 breaks new ground in memory management by providing DPMS—DOS Protected Mode Services, a method of allowing specially designed device drivers and TSRs to run in extended memory. Device drivers and TSRs that use DPMS can free both conventional and upper memory for other device drivers and TSRs, making your memory management tasks much more successful.

How Do I Load DPMS?

Loading DPMS is quite simple. DPMS.EXE is a device driver that provides DPMS memory. To load DPMS.EXE, add the following command to CONFIG.SYS:

```
DEVICE=C:\NWDOS\DPMS.EXE
```

Note

Be sure to place the DPMS.EXE device driver command after the CONFIG.SYS line that installs EMM386.EXE.

The DPMS.EXE device driver does not use any arguments.

What Uses DPMS?

Device drivers and TSRs must be specially written to take advantage of DPMS memory. As a result, there aren't too many DPMS-aware device drivers and TSRs available yet. In fact, the only DPMS-aware device drivers and TSRs currently available are included with Novell DOS 7.

The version of the Stacker disk compression software included in Novell DOS 7 uses DPMS memory if it is available. Other Novell DOS 7 device drivers and TSRs that use DPMS memory include the disk caching program, NWCACHE.EXE; the

CD-ROM extensions, NWCDEX.EXE; the deleted files tracking program, DEL-WATCH.EXE; and the network desktop server, SERVER.EXE.

You don't have to tell device drivers or TSRs to use DPMS memory. If device drivers or TSRs are DPMS-aware and DPMS memory is available, they automatically use the DPMS memory. You only have to load the DPMS.EXE device driver prior to loading DPMS-aware device drivers or TSRs.

> ### Note
>
> Because DPMS-aware device drivers and TSRs use DPMS memory automatically if it is available, no error occurs if DPMS memory is not available when they are loaded. Instead, the device drivers or TSRs are simply loaded into conventional or upper memory.

DPMS is a DOS version independent memory management specification. It does not depend on any Novell DOS 7 specific services, and is compatible with most DOS versions.

Using the ? Command

The ? command is used to pause the execution of CONFIG.SYS and request confirmation before the current command is executed. The default operation of this command is no time-out, so your system waits indefinitely for your response. You can use the TIMEOUT command, discussed later in this section, to cause the command to be bypassed if the user does not respond.

You can use the ? command quite effectively when you are experimenting with system configurations. In order to ensure that you will be able to see and read any error or status messages that are displayed, however, you'll probably want to include the ? command on at least two lines in CONFIG.SYS—the line containing the device driver command line you want to examine, and the following command line (to pause CONFIG.SYS so you can see what messages were displayed when the device driver loaded).

You can also use the F8 key to control execution of each command line.

To use the ? command, place the question mark at the beginning of the line containing the command you want to prompt for. You can optionally include a prompt you want displayed by placing the prompt in quotes between the question mark and the command you want to prompt for.

Although you could use the ? command to allow you to select different system configurations, it really isn't ideal for this use. When you use this command, you must confirm each line containing the ? command, and you must do so every time you boot your system. You're better off using the ? for testing purposes, and using the SWITCH command if you sometimes need to boot using a different system configuration.

Using the BREAK Command

The BREAK=*on|off* command specifies whether your system should do extended testing for the Ctrl-C (or Ctrl-Break) key combination. By default, BREAK is off, which means that your PC looks for Ctrl-C only when it normally reads from the keyboard, or when writing to the screen or your printer.

The setting of the BREAK command doesn't have any memory management effects, but it can have a system performance effect. If BREAK is set to on, your system must spend more time looking for the Ctrl-C key combination, so normal operations may be a little slower than usual.

The main reason for setting BREAK to on is to enable you to interrupt a program that isn't responding. You may want to include the command **BREAK=ON** in CONFIG.SYS while you're testing system configuration options, and later remove the command for slightly improved performance.

Using the BUFFERS Command

The BUFFERS=*nn* command specifies the number of disk buffers your system should reserve. Buffers can be between 3 and 99. The default is 15.

Disk buffers are a DOS system structure used to improve disk performance by storing data in memory. If the same data is needed a second time and is still in a buffer, the system does not have to read the data from disk, and considerable time is saved.

Buffers are far less important to system performance when disk caching software, such as NWCACHE, is being used. Although disk caching software performs a similar function to disk buffers, disk caching software is much more efficient, and provides a much larger improvement in system performance.

Each buffer uses some memory. Fortunately, you don't need to use a large number of buffers, and it's possible to reduce the conventional memory used by buffers to a very small amount.

If EMM386.EXE is loaded, the DOS kernel is placed into the high memory area. The DOS kernel doesn't use the entire high memory area, but the unused space doesn't have to go to waste. Even though only one program at a time can use the high memory area, the unused space in the high memory area can be used to hold the disk buffers if you don't allocate too many buffers. The reason this works is that buffers are a DOS system structure, and therefore are considered part of DOS itself.

The exact number of buffers you allocate usually isn't too critical, so allocating a number that will fit into the high memory area makes good sense from a memory management perspective. This is especially true if you use disk caching software, because the disk buffers you allocate really won't add very much performance. You can use the **MEM /F** command to determine how the high memory area is being used.

Note

If you use the high memory area for purposes other than loading the DOS kernel, the disk buffers will use conventional memory. If you also use disk caching software, reduce the number of buffers to about 3 to minimize the amount of conventional memory used by the buffers.

Using the CHAIN Command

The CHAIN=*filespec* command transfers control to another configuration file other than CONFIG.SYS. If the named file exists, control is transferred as soon as the CHAIN command is executed, and the balance of the commands in CONFIG.SYS are ignored. If the named file does not exist, control returns to CONFIG.SYS and the rest of its commands are executed.

The CHAIN command can be a very important memory management tool, especially if you often install new software written by today's crop of extremely inconsiderate programmers. Many installation programs make changes to CONFIG.SYS and AUTOEXEC.BAT, sometimes without asking for permission or even without telling you what changes they've made. This can be very frustrating, because you may have spent many hours devising the perfect system configuration, only to have your work destroyed by an arrogant programmer's modifications.

If you place a CHAIN command as the first line of CONFIG.SYS, your "real" configuration file will be untouched by installation programs. You can even go one step farther and use the SHELL command, discussed later in this section, to execute a batch file other than AUTOEXEC.BAT.

Of course, the CHAIN command has other uses in addition to protecting yourself from unauthorized changes to your configuration files. If you use multiple, very complex configurations, you may be able to reduce the amount of time required to boot your system by placing each separate configuration in its own configuration file. Use the SWITCH command to execute the appropriate CHAIN commands for each of your special configurations.

Using the CLS Command

The CLS command clears the screen. Although you wouldn't normally think of clearing the screen as a memory management function, there are instances when the ability to clear the screen can help. For example, if you are having difficulties with a specific device driver, you can clear the screen before loading the device driver so you'll be able to see the device driver's messages more clearly.

You will also find the CLS command useful if you create multiple configuration menus with the SWITCH command. Clear the screen before displaying your menu so the PC user will have an easier time reading your menu.

Using the COUNTRY Command

The COUNTRY command configures your system to recognize international date, time, currency, case, and decimal separator conventions. Your Novell DOS 7 manual includes complete information on using this command.

The COUNTRY command has one memory management implication—it increases the size of DOS in memory. If you use this command, available conventional memory will probably be reduced because of this larger size for DOS. Therefore, unless you really need to use the international conventions on your system, it's better to forego using the COUNTRY command, at least from a memory management standpoint.

Using the CPOS Command

The CPOS *rr,cc* command positions the cursor at a specific row (*rr*) and column (*cc*) on your screen. Valid numbers are 1 to 25 for row and 1 to 80 for column.

You can use the CPOS command to help you create your multiple configuration menus. This command provides enhanced ability to make your menus appear more professional and easy to read.

Using the DEVICE Command

The DEVICE command loads a device driver into conventional memory. Device drivers are special programs that provide capabilities not built into DOS itself. These include management of memory outside the 640K conventional memory space, such as upper memory, extended memory, and expanded memory. Other device drivers may provide the ability to access hardware such as SCSI adapters, sound boards, network adapters, and so on.

Because the DEVICE command loads device drivers into conventional memory, it's usually preferable to use the DEVICEHIGH command instead of the DEVICE command. Some device drivers, however, cannot be placed outside of conventional memory. The Novell DOS 7 memory manager, EMM386.EXE, is an example of a device driver that must be loaded into conventional memory. In the case of this device driver, there's really no other choice, because before it is loaded, your system cannot access any memory other than conventional memory.

Occasionally, you'll find other device drivers that cannot be loaded into upper memory. Usually, the program documentation supplied with the device driver will inform you if the device driver must be loaded into conventional memory. For these types of device drivers, you must use the DEVICE command to load the device driver.

Using the DEVICEHIGH Command

The DEVICEHIGH command loads a device driver into upper memory if possible; otherwise, it loads the device driver into conventional memory. When you load device drivers into upper memory, conventional memory is conserved for other uses. This makes the DEVICEHIGH command one of the most important CONFIG.SYS commands for memory management.

Note

You can also specify this command as HIDEVICE, but DEVICEHIGH is preferable for compatibility with MS-DOS.

You can optionally include an argument that specifies how much memory a device driver requires. If no upper memory block contains at least the specified amount of free memory, the device driver will be loaded into conventional memory instead of upper memory. This optional argument is of the most value for device drivers that expand after they're loaded into memory. Very few device drivers do this, but the SIZE=*xxxx* argument is available if it becomes necessary. If you use this argument, you must place it between the DEVICE-HIGH command and the name of the device driver, and you must specify the memory size in hexadecimal format. For example, to specify that the device driver C:\UTILITY\MYDRV.SYS be loaded in upper memory only if 16K of contiguous upper memory is available, you would use the following command line:

```
DEVICEHIGH SIZE=4000 C:\UTILITY\MYDRV.SYS
```

If more than one upper memory block is available, the DEVICEHIGH command will load each device driver into the upper memory block which has the largest free block. For example, if two upper memory blocks have 45K and 20K free, the 45K block is used first, regardless of the size of the device driver being loaded. This can cause the upper memory blocks to be used in a less than optimum manner. The section "Performing the Load Order Juggling Act," later in this chapter, suggests methods of working around this problem.

Occasionally, you'll encounter device drivers that cannot be loaded into upper memory:

- Some device drivers cannot be loaded into upper memory because they don't work correctly unless they're loaded in conventional memory. If these types of device drivers are loaded into upper memory, you may lock up your system, or you may experience intermittent crashes.

- Some device drivers cannot be loaded into upper memory because they require more memory to load than their memory image size. In some cases it's possible to load such device drivers into upper memory if you can free a large enough block of contiguous memory, but sometimes it's just not possible to create a large enough upper memory block.

- Some device drivers cannot be loaded into upper memory because upper memory simply isn't available when they're loaded. EMM386.EXE is one such device driver, but device drivers that must be loaded before any memory managers are loaded also fall into this category.

It's important to remember that the DEVICEHIGH command does not fail to load a device driver if upper memory isn't available. Instead, the DEVICE-HIGH command is treated as though you issued the DEVICE command, and the device driver is loaded into conventional memory. As a result, it's not safe to assume that just because you used the DEVICEHIGH command, that device driver actually loaded into upper memory.

Using the DOS Command

The DOS=*high|umb|low* command specifies the position of the DOS kernel in memory. The three arguments specify the high memory area, upper memory, and conventional memory, respectively.

Placing the DOS kernel in the high memory area increases the amount of conventional memory available to applications by reducing the amount of conventional memory used by DOS. Not only does the DOS=HIGH command move the DOS kernel into the high memory area, but it also moves several DOS system structures (such as buffers and files) into the high memory area if they will fit in the high memory area.

Before you can use either the HIGH or UMB parameters, you must first load EMM386. Loading the DOS kernel into the high memory area is an important step in advanced memory management, and one that ensures that more conventional memory can be made available for applications.

> ### Note
>
> There's a very important difference between the Novell DOS 7 and MS-DOS versions of this command. If you move to Novell DOS 7 from MS-DOS, be aware that the Novell DOS 7 version only specifies the location of the DOS kernel—it does not enable upper memory block support. If your CONFIG.SYS file includes the command DOS=UMB, the DOS kernel is loaded into upper memory, not the high memory area.

Using the DRIVPARM Command

The DRIVPARM command defines the standard configuration of a disk drive that is not automatically recognized correctly by DOS. You can also use this command to define the parameters for other types of block devices, such as tape drives that are accessed using a drive letter.

A common use for the DRIVPARM command is to help a system recognize types of disk drives not originally available on the system. For example, if you add 3.5-inch diskette drives on some systems, the PC will assume that the drive is a 360K, 5.25-inch diskette drive. The DRIVPARM command tells the system how to access the drive correctly.

The DRIVPARM command is not a memory management command, but using this command slightly increases the size of DOS in memory, so you should avoid using the DRIVPARM command if possible. One way to test whether the DRIVPARM command is needed is to insert a new, unformatted, high-density diskette in the drive, and then format the diskette without specifying the diskette size, and without having DRIVPARM loaded. If the diskette if formatted to its full capacity, you don't need to use the DRIVPARM command. If the diskette is formatted at a lower capacity, use the DRIVPARM command to specify the drive's specifications.

Using the ECHO Command

The ECHO=*text* command displays messages on your screen. The ECHO command is one of the commands you use to create multiple configuration menus. This enables you to create a single CONFIG.SYS file containing several different system configurations, and to select from those configuration options at system startup.

Multiple configurations are very important memory management tools, because they allow you the flexibility to create optimized system configurations for special purposes. By keeping all optional configurations within a single CONFIG.SYS file, these commands help ensure that as you upgrade your system or your software, the correct versions of device drivers will be included in all configurations.

Usually, ECHO commands are followed by a SWITCH command to input and act upon the user's response. You may also want to use the TIMEOUT command to select a default configuration if the user does not respond.

Using the EXIT Command

The EXIT command ends the execution of CONFIG.SYS commands. You can use this command in conjunction with multiple configurations, exiting from CONFIG.SYS when the proper set of configuration commands has been executed.

Using the FASTOPEN Command

The FASTOPEN=*nn* command specifies that a record of files be retained in memory so those same files can later be reopened more quickly. You can specify a value between 128 and 32768. The default is 512.

Although the FASTOPEN command slightly improves disk performance, each position in the filename table uses 2 bytes of memory. If you were to specify the maximum value of 32,768 files, FASTOPEN would use 64K of memory. The default of 512 entries uses 1K of memory, and probably should not be increased. If every byte of memory is crucial, you may want to use the minimum setting of 128 files.

Using the FCBS Command

The FCBS=*m,n* command specifies the number of file control blocks that can be open at one time. *M* specifies the number that can be open at one time, *n* specifies the number that are protected from being closed automatically by DOS. You can specify values between 1 and 255.

File control blocks are an obsolete method of accessing files. Programmers have been discouraged from using this method of file access since MS-DOS 2.x, so there's really no excuse for a modern program to require the use of file control blocks.

Each additional file control block uses some memory, although if the DOS kernel is in the upper memory area, the file control block structure is also placed in upper memory if possible. You can save a small amount of memory by including the following command in CONFIG.SYS:

```
FCBS=1,1
```

Using the FILES Command

The FILES=*nn* command specifies the number of files that can be open at one time. You can use values between 20 and 255. The default is 20.

Each additional file you specify with the FILES command uses some memory, so you might assume that you would want to save memory by specifying the smallest possible value. In reality, however, you must specify a large enough value to accommodate the needs of every program that may be running simultaneously. Unfortunately, it can be difficult to determine how many files each program may attempt to open. One method of determining how many files you must specify is to start with a very low value, such as 20, and try running all of your applications. If you receive an error message telling you that the program is unable to open enough files, you'll know you must increase the number of files that can be open at one time.

This trial and error approach to specifying the number of files that can be open at one time may work, but it may also create difficult problems. Suppose, for example, that you try a low value for the files, and everything seems to be working. A few weeks later, after working for several hours, you try to update a data file, only to be greeted with an error message telling you that the data can't be saved because too many files are open. The few bytes of memory you saved by specifying a minimum number of files won't seem quite so important at that point, will they?

A good compromise is possible without applying the trial and error approach. In most cases, 20 files would be adequate for users who only run DOS programs. If you use Windows, the Task Manager, or some other environment that allows several programs to run at the same time, you'll need a setting of at least 40. In either case, the 1K to 2K of memory used by the FILES command is good insurance against the problem of being unable to open files when necessary.

Note

Some programs have even higher requirements. Be sure to check the program documentation when you install new software to see if the FILES setting should be increased.

Novell DOS 7 places the structures for open files in the high memory area if the DOS kernel is loaded into the high memory area, and there is enough room for the open file structures.

Using the GOSUB Command

The GOSUB command causes a change in the order of execution of CONFIG.SYS commands. When a GOSUB command is encountered, execution transfers to a block of commands that start with a labeled statement (specified as an argument in the GOSUB command). The labeled set of commands is executed until a RETURN command is encountered, and then command execution returns to the statement following the GOSUB command.

The GOSUB command executes something that programmers commonly term "calling a subroutine." This method of executing a series of instructions offers the advantage of being able to call the same set of commands from several different statements, and then return to the proper place after the commands are executed. If you create multiple configurations within a single CONFIG.SYS file, you can use the GOSUB command to execute a common series of commands without duplicating those commands in each separate configuration block.

This command is very useful for advanced memory management, because it provides a very good method of using blocks of configuration commands as needed, while at the same time allowing you to make certain each command you use is the most current version. To use this command, make certain each configuration block has a unique label as its first line, and the RETURN command as its last line.

Using the GOTO Command

The GOTO command, like the GOSUB command, causes a change in the order of execution of CONFIG.SYS commands. When a GOTO command is encountered, execution branches unconditionally to a block of commands that start with a labeled statement (specified as an argument in the GOTO command). Unlike the GOSUB command, however, command execution does not return to the statement following the GOTO command when the specified series of commands ends.

The GOTO command executes something that programmers commonly term "branching." This method of executing a series of instructions is one often favored by inexperienced programmers, and often results in "spaghetti code," programs that are so convoluted that not even the original programmer can follow program flow.

Why is there such a difference between the GOSUB and GOTO commands? Why is one so useful, while the other is such a problem? The difference results from the discipline necessary to use each of these commands properly. While using GOSUB requires you to think about modularity—the ability to break down a task such as system configuration into small, easily understood modules—using GOTO allows you to forget about the big picture and create a real mess.

If you create multiple configurations within a single CONFIG.SYS file, you can use the GOSUB command to execute a common series of commands without duplicating those commands in each separate configuration block. If you use GOTO, you can only use a common series of commands in a very limited way, and you can't easily return to the original command block to execute additional commands.

Use the GOTO command with extreme care. There are instances where GOTO is the appropriate choice, but usually the GOSUB command is the better option.

Using the HIDEVICE Command

The HIDEVICE command loads device drivers into upper memory. This command is the equivalent of the DEVICEHIGH command. Please see the earlier section on the DEVICEHIGH command for more information.

Using the HIINSTALL Command

The HIINSTALL command loads TSRs into upper memory. This command is the equivalent of the INSTALLHIGH command. Please see the INSTALLHIGH command later in this section for more information.

Using the HISTORY Command

The HISTORY=*on[,nnnn[,on|off]]|off* command controls whether the extended command line editing feature will be available. Specify *on* to make extended command line editing available, or *off* to disable extended command line editing. *Nnnn* specifies the size of the memory buffer that stores the command history, and you can specify 128 to 4096 bytes. The default is 512 bytes. The *on|off* argument following the buffer size specifies whether command editing will be in insert mode (*on*) or overwrite mode (*off*).

The extended command line editing feature is very handy, but the command buffer does use some memory. Usually, the default buffer size of 512 bytes is a good compromise, because this buffer size can hold up to approximately 10 commands, but doesn't really use much memory. Keep in mind, however, that command lines can contain up to 127 characters, so if you use very long commands, a larger buffer may be needed if you want to recall previous commands.

Unless you're very short on available memory, the benefits offered by the HISTORY command are probably worth the amount of memory used by this command.

Note

If you're used to MS-DOS, keep in mind that the Novell DOS 7 HISTORY command performs the extended command line editing function of the MS-DOS DOSKEY command.

Using the INSTALL Command

The INSTALL command loads TSR programs into conventional memory. Generally, INSTALL is used to load TSRs that should be loaded only once per DOS session. For example, if you use the CURSOR program, the program can be loaded only once each time you boot your system.

Although you could load TSR programs using commands in AUTOEXEC.BAT or at the DOS command prompt, loading them using the INSTALL command in CONFIG.SYS uses slightly less memory. This is because INSTALL does not create an environment for the TSR. Thus TSRs loaded using the INSTALL command cannot use environment variables. They also cannot use shortcut keys, or require COMMAND.COM for handling critical errors. Some TSRs do not function properly if you load them using the INSTALL command.

TSRs that are loaded at the DOS command prompt, or in a batch file such as AUTOEXEC.BAT, receive a copy of the DOS environment. By default, DOS reserves 256 bytes for the environment. If you use the default environment size, loading four TSRs using the INSTALL command in CONFIG.SYS would save 1K of conventional memory, compared to loading those same TSRs in AUTOEXEC.BAT or at the DOS command prompt.

All DEVICE and DEVICEHIGH commands are processed and executed before any INSTALL commands are processed and executed. You cannot load a TSR before a device driver by placing an INSTALL ahead of the DEVICE and DEVICEHIGH commands.

Using the INSTALLHIGH Command

The INSTALLHIGH command loads TSR programs into upper memory if it is available; otherwise, it loads them into conventional memory. The INSTALL-HIGH command is used for exactly the same purposes as the INSTALL command. The HIINSTALL command is an alternate form of the INSTALLHIGH command.

You can use the INSTALLHIGH command just as you would the INSTALL command. The same restrictions which apply to the INSTALL command also apply to the INSTALLHIGH command. Like the INSTALL command, the INSTALLHIGH command is processed after all DEVICE and DEVICEHIGH commands.

If your TSR programs can function correctly without a copy of the DOS environment, without shortcut keys, and without using COMMAND.COM as a critical error handler, loading them using the INSTALLHIGH command is a good way to save memory. Since TSRs loaded with the INSTALLHIGH command don't receive a copy of the DOS environment, they can fit into a slightly smaller upper memory block than is possible if you load them in AUTOEXEC.BAT or at the DOS command prompt. This especially important if you increase the environment size, because each TSR loaded using the INSTALLHIGH command saves an amount of memory equal to the environment size.

The INSTALLHIGH command is an important part of your advanced memory management toolkit. Sometimes even a very small amount of additional space in upper memory blocks makes the difference between being able to load everything you want into upper memory, and loading some items into conventional memory.

Using the LASTDRIVE Command

The LASTDRIVE command specifies the maximum number of disk drives you can access. You can specify any drive letter between A and Z. By default, DOS allocates structures for each physical drive and each logical drive in your system.

You must specify drive letters at least as high as the last drive letter you want to access as a substituted drive or on a network. For example, if you create three substituted drives on a PC that has two diskette drives and a hard disk, you must specify a LASTDRIVE of at least F.

Networks often use drive M: as a network drive, especially if email is in use on the network. You must specify a LASTDRIVE high enough to allow access to the last network drive letter you intend to map.

Novell DOS 7 creates data structures in memory for each drive letter you specify. Allocating too many drive letters simply wastes memory. For example, setting LASTDRIVE to Z uses slightly over 2K of conventional memory, while providing no extra benefits over a more appropriate setting. Unless you are connected to a network or use substituted drives, it's usually best to allow DOS to allocate the default number of drive letters.

Note

Novell DOS 7 allocates drive structures in a slightly different manner than MS-DOS. If you move to Novell DOS 7 from MS-DOS, remember that MS-DOS automatically allocates data structures for one additional drive, but Novell DOS 7 does not automatically allocate data structures for any extra drives.

Using the REM Command

The REM command, which you can abbreviate with a semicolon, places comments in your CONFIG.SYS file. This command has two primary purposes, both important as you experiment with advanced memory management.

The most obvious purpose of the REM command is to place notes in CONFIG.SYS explaining how other command lines function. You may, for example, want to note special settings you're trying with a device driver such as EMM386.EXE. If a conflict arises, you'll easily be able to see why, for instance, you excluded a particular memory segment range.

The second purpose of the REM command is to temporarily disable CONFIG.SYS command lines by turning them into comments. This is especially useful when you're trying a series of different settings, because you can retain a record of the exact settings you've already tried. You may even want to add comment lines detailing the success of the various combinations. Once you've decided on the optimal configuration you may want to remove the extra lines, because even though comment lines aren't executed, they still may slow the boot process slightly.

Using the RETURN Command

The RETURN command specifies the end of a configuration block, and causes CONFIG.SYS execution to return to the statement following the GOSUB or SWITCH command that called the block.

Each configuration block called by a GOSUB or SWITCH command must end with a RETURN command. Such configuration blocks are sometimes called *subroutines*, and are modular blocks of commands that can be called from a number of different locations.

Using the SET Command

The SET *variable=string* command places a value in a DOS environment variable. You can later use the value of this environment variable to control program flow in a batch file, or to pass system information to some application programs.

Novell DOS 7 automatically sets the values of several environment variables. See "Using Environment Variables" later in this chapter for more information on using these environment variables.

If you create a startup menu, you may want to set an environment variable, such as CONFIG, to the block name of the selected configuration block. Later in this chapter, you'll see how you can use this variable in AUTOEXEC.BAT.

Setting values for environment variables can, however, have a negative effect on memory management. Although device drivers and TSRs loaded in CONFIG.SYS don't receive a copy of the DOS environment, all TSRs and application programs loaded by batch files or at the command prompt do receive a copy of the DOS environment. Depending on how large the DOS environment is, this can use considerable memory. In the next section you'll learn how to minimize this effect.

Using the SHELL Command

The SHELL command specifies the name and location of the command interpreter, which is usually COMMAND.COM. Used in combination with COMMAND, the SHELL command can be used to specify the DOS environment size, and to specify whether the command processor is loaded into the high memory area, upper memory, or conventional memory. For example, the following command specifies C:\NWDOS as the location of COMMAND.COM, the command interpreter, and increases the environment size to 384 bytes (the /E:*nnn* sets the environment size):

```
SHELL=C:\NWDOS\COMMAND.COM C:\NWDOS\ /E:384 /P
```

Increasing the environment size has serious implications for memory management. Each TSR and program loaded at the command prompt or in a batch file such as AUTOEXEC.BAT inherits a copy of the DOS environment. If you increase the environment size, the amount of memory used by each of these TSRs and programs increases by the amount of the increase in the environment size. If the environment size is 256 bytes too large, each TSR and program uses 256 bytes more memory than necessary.

It's important, therefore, to make certain you don't increase the environment size any more than necessary. To determine how large the environment should be, enter the following commands at the DOS prompt:

```
SET > SETSIZE.TXT
DIR SETSIZE.TXT
```

Note

Setting a minimal size for the DOS environment allows very little room for additional environment variables. Sometimes batch files or other programs create temporary environment variables that may not be visible using the technique noted above. If you receive the message "Out of environment space" when you run a batch file or an application program, increase the size of the DOS environment slightly.

The size displayed for SETSIZE.TXT indicates the amount of memory used by the DOS environment variables currently allocated. To minimize the amount of memory wasted by setting the environment size too large, set your environment slightly larger than the size of SETSIZE.TXT.

For example, if SETSIZE.TXT is listed as 344 bytes, you might want to use 350 to 360 bytes for the environment size.

Using the STACKS Command

The STACKS=*n,s* command specifies the number of data stacks your system should allocate for programs to handle hardware interrupts. You can specify 0 or 8 through 64 for *n* (the number of stacks), and 0 or 32 through 512 for *s* (the size of the stacks in bytes). Except for 8088-based systems, the default is STACKS=9,128.

A common setting for STACKS is 9,256, which allocates 9 stacks of 256 bytes each, using almost 3K of conventional memory. You may be able to specify STACKS=0,0 to save the memory otherwise allocated for this system structure.

It's difficult to determine whether the 0,0 setting is working correctly, because the standard description states that the "computer becomes unstable" when the values are set too low. Unless you are prepared to do extensive testing after making this single change, it's nearly impossible to know whether STACKS=0,0 will work correctly on your PC. This is one case where you're truly on your own, so good luck!

Using the SWITCH Command

The SWITCH *label1, label2, ..., labeln* command waits for a user response and then executes named configuration blocks based on that response. Each SWITCH command can switch between up to 9 configuration blocks. The first named configuration block is executed if the user enters 1, the second if the user enters 2, and so on. Unless the TIMEOUT command (discussed next) is used to specify a time-out value, the SWITCH command waits indefinitely for the user response. If a time-out value is specified, the first item in the list of named configuration blocks is selected when the time-out expires.

The SWITCH command is a very important memory management tool. You can use this command, along with the ECHO command, to create and display a startup menu enabling you to chose configuration options when you boot your PC.

Each named configuration block called by the SWITCH command must begin with a unique label and end with a RETURN command. Execution of CONFIG.SYS commands returns to the line following the SWITCH command after the named configuration block has been executed. Make certain you set up your CONFIG.SYS file in a manner that accounts for this return in execution; otherwise, you may execute commands you did not intend to process.

Using the TIMEOUT Command

The TIMEOUT=*n* command specifies the number of seconds each ? or SWITCH command should wait before making a default selection. The default is 0, which causes the system to wait indefinitely for the user response.

It's usually a good idea to specify a time-out value long enough to allow the user to make a proper selection, but short enough to minimize the delay if no response in entered. Ten seconds should be long enough for most users, but you may want to allow additional time for users who have a difficult time entering a response or reading the screen prompts.

Many of the CONFIG.SYS options have memory management implications that go far beyond what you might normally expect. Even small changes are often multiplied as they spread their effects across the broad range of device drivers and TSRs you load each time you start your system. Next we'll look at how your AUTOEXEC.BAT file further affects your system.

Using AUTOEXEC.BAT Options

After CONFIG.SYS, AUTOEXEC.BAT is the second special user-created configuration file your system reads each time you start your PC. Once the commands in CONFIG.SYS have been executed, those in AUTOEXEC.BAT are processed. Both files can contain commands that configure your system, but only CONFIG.SYS can be used to load device drivers. Both files can contain commands that load TSRs, but only AUTOEXEC.BAT can be used to load TSRs that need a copy of the DOS environment.

Note

Strictly speaking, Novell DOS 7 has a third special configuration file, STACKER.INI, that is processed when your system boots (if you have installed Stacker disk compression). This file is not usually modified by the PC user, and really has little effect on memory management. STACKER.INI options are therefore not discussed in this book.

From a memory management perspective, there are relatively few changes you can make in AUTOEXEC.BAT that affect the amount of available memory. You may be able to adjust the parameters passed to some TSRs you load in AUTOEXEC.BAT, but in most cases these changes will have little effect on memory usage. Let's have a look at what you can do in AUTOEXEC.BAT to enhance your memory utilization.

Using the CHOICE Command

The CHOICE command is used to create a menu of selections in a batch file, usually in AUTOEXEC.BAT, and to allow the user to make a selection from the displayed choices. Use the following syntax with the CHOICE command:

```
CHOICE /C:keys /N /S /T:c,nn text
```

/C:keys specifies the set of keys the user can press in response to the prompt. CHOICE indicates which key was pressed by returning a value in ERRORLEVEL, with the first key in the list as ERRORLEVEL 1, the second as ERRORLEVEL 2, and so on. The set of keys cannot include a forward slash, tab, or space.

/N specifies that no prompt should be displayed.

/S specifies that CHOICE will be case sensitive, forcing the user to press the correct upper- or lowercase character.

/T:c,nn specifies the default selection, *c*, and the time-out in seconds, *nn*. The time-out can be 0 to 99 seconds.

text specifies any text you want to be displayed before the prompt. The text cannot include a forward slash.

You can use the CHOICE command to create a menu similar to the startup menu you create in CONFIG.SYS. Usually, ECHO commands are placed on preceding lines to display the menu selections, and the CHOICE command displays a prompt and waits for the user's selection. You then test for the value of ERRORLEVEL to determine how the batch file should respond to the user's selection.

Note

When checking the value of ERRORLEVEL, always check for the highest values first. If ERRORLEVEL has a value of 2, tests for both ERRORLEVEL 2 and ERRORLEVEL 1 will succeed. A test for ERRORLEVEL 3 however, would, fail in this instance.

Although you can use the CHOICE command to create an additional startup menu, you may want to consider using the CONFIG.SYS startup menu to make all selections, and then use an environment variable, such as CONFIG, to control which selections are made in AUTOEXEC.BAT. This method will reduce the number of selections a user must make to start your system, and therefore reduce the possibility of errors. Let's have a look at environment variables next.

Using Environment Variables

Environment variables are a method of storing information about your system that can then be used by batch files or other programs. They are often used in batch files to control the execution of batch file commands.

Novell DOS 7 has several special environment variables, in addition to the more common ones such as PATH and PROMPT. Table 7.2 summarizes the Novell DOS 7 environment variables.

You can use environment variables in many ways. For example, you could create a batch file that executes a specified series of commands each Monday morning. You can also create environment variables of your own in CONFIG.SYS, perhaps to indicate which selection the user made in the startup menu, and then control additional configuration options in AUTOEXEC.BAT by examining the value of those variables. The next section shows you one way to do this.

Table 7.2 Novell DOS 7 Environment Variables

Variable	Description
AM_PM	Period of the day—AM or PM
APPEND	The current APPEND search path
COMSPEC	The location of the command interpreter
DAY	Numeric day of month—01 to 31
DAY_OF_WEEK	Text day of week—Monday, Tuesday, etc.
ERRORLEVEL	Error return code
FULL_NAME	User's full name
GREETING_TIME	Morning, afternoon, or evening
HOUR	Clock hour—1 to 12
HOUR24	24-hour clock hour—00 to 23
LOGIN_NAME	User's login name
MINUTE	Clock minute—00 to 59
MONTH	Numeric month—1 to 12
MONTH_NAME	Text month—May, June, December, etc.
NDAY_OF_WEEK	Numeric day of week—1 to 7, 1=Sunday
NWDOSCFG	The directory containing the system configuration files
OS	The current operating system name, NWDOS
OS_VERSION	Operating system version number
P_STATION	Physical station number
PATH	The current PATH search path
PEXEC	Used to specify a command to run whenever the system PROMPT is displayed
PROMPT	The current system prompt
SECOND	Clock second—00 to 59
SHORT_YEAR	Numeric two-digit year—94, 95, etc.
STATION	Station number
TEMP	The directory used to hold temporary files
VER	The current operating system version
YEAR	Numeric four-digit year—1994, 1995, etc.

Using the CONFIG Variable

If you create a startup menu in CONFIG.SYS, you may want to also create an environment variable called CONFIG, and set this environment variable to the name of the configuration block selected in the CONFIG.SYS startup menu.

You can then test the value of the CONFIG variable in AUTOEXEC.BAT (or in other batch files as necessary) to determine which selection the user made from the startup menu. Use the results of this test to branch to different sections of AUTOEXEC.BAT, depending on your needs. This can eliminate the need for the user to make a second selection in AUTOEXEC.BAT.

For example, suppose your CONFIG.SYS startup menu looks like this:

```
; Start Up Menu
TIMEOUT 10
ECHO   1. Load Game Configuration
ECHO 2. Don't Load Game Drivers
ECHO Please make your selection (1 or 2)
SWITCH LOADGAMES, NOGAMES
EXIT
:LOADGAMES
SET CONFIG=LOADGAMES
Some configuration lines
RETURN
:NOGAMES
SET CONFIG=NOGAMES
Some configuration lines
RETURN
```

If the user accepts the default selection, the CONFIG variable will have the value LOADGAMES. If the alternate selection is chosen, the CONFIG variable will have the value NOGAMES. You might use this value by adding the following to the end of AUTOEXEC.BAT:

```
IF %CONFIG%==NOGAMES GOTO END
REM    Automatically load game program if LOADGAMES
REM    was the selection in the startup menu
MYGAME
:END
```

If the user selects "1. Load Game Configuration" from the startup menu, any special configuration commands necessary to run the MYGAME program would be executed, and AUTOEXEC.BAT would automatically load the program. This is an especially good method to use if you're setting up a system for someone who has difficulty making selections, or who is prone to keying errors.

Using the LOADHIGH Command

The LOADHIGH command, which you can abbreviate as LH or HILOAD, is the one Novell DOS 7 memory management command you can use at the DOS prompt, or in a batch file such as AUTOEXEC.BAT. This command loads a TSR into upper memory if possible; otherwise, the TSR is loaded into conventional memory.

To use the LOADHIGH command, simply add the command to the beginning of a line in AUTOEXEC.BAT that loads a TSR program. If a large enough contiguous upper memory block is available, the TSR is loaded into upper memory. The LOADHIGH command does not fail if no upper memory block is large enough to load the TSR; instead, the TSR program is simply loaded into conventional memory—no error message is displayed.

Each TSR program you can load into upper memory instead of conventional memory increases the amount of free conventional memory. Most TSRs can function correctly in upper memory, so you should load as many TSRs using the LOADHIGH command as possible.

Before you can use the LOADHIGH command successfully, the EMM386.EXE device driver must be loaded in CONFIG.SYS.

Consider the INSTALLHIGH Option

Instead of loading TSRs into upper memory using the AUTOEXEC.BAT command LOADHIGH, you may want to consider loading them using the CONFIG.SYS command INSTALLHIGH. Although the two commands serve a similar purpose, TSRs loaded using the INSTALLHIGH command may use slightly less memory because they don't receive their own copy of the DOS environment, as they do when loaded using LOADHIGH.

TSRs that require a copy of the DOS environment, that use shortcut keys, or that depend upon COMMAND.COM to handle critical errors cannot be loaded using the INSTALLHIGH command, so LOADHIGH is the only way to load these TSRs into upper memory. See the earlier section on CONFIG.SYS options for more information in the INSTALLHIGH command.

Regardless of whether you use the INSTALLHIGH command or the LOAD-HIGH command, the TSR will be loaded into the largest available upper memory block, which may not be the most efficient use of upper memory. Let's have a look at how you may be able to use memory more efficiently.

Performing the Load Order Juggling Act

Once you've applied all the memory management tricks you've learned so far, you probably have more conventional memory available than you ever had before. But now that you have a feel for advanced memory management, you're probably also a little frustrated because you haven't been able to accomplish quite as much as you'd like. You probably still have one or two device drivers or TSRs in conventional memory that you'd like to load into upper memory. It's time to bring out the last "big gun" of Novell DOS 7 advanced memory management techniques, the load order juggling act.

Reordering Device Drivers and TSRs

The *load order juggling act* is the term I use to describe the process of making better use of memory resources by changing the order in which device drivers and TSRs are actually loaded into memory. You may wonder how changing the order in which device drivers and TSRs are loaded into memory can affect memory usage. After all, simply changing the order in which device drivers and TSRs are loaded doesn't change the amount of memory they use, does it?

It's true that device drivers and TSRs will still use the same amount of memory no matter what order they're loaded in. What changes along with load order, though, is how the device drivers and TSRs fit together in memory. To understand how changing the load order can have this effect, think of the pieces of a jigsaw puzzle. If you line up the puzzle pieces in a row, the row will be longer if the pieces are arranged at random than it will if the pieces are arranged so they fit together.

Of course, device drivers and TSRs don't fit together like jigsaw puzzle pieces, but the order in which they're loaded can result in a similar effect. There are several reasons for this:

- Some device drivers and TSRs require more memory to load than their memory image size. If a device driver or TSR cannot find an upper memory block large enough for its load size, the device driver or TSR will load into conventional memory.

- TSR programs loaded using the INSTALLHIGH command in CONFIG.SYS use slightly less memory than if the same TSR program is loaded using the LOADHIGH command in AUTOEXEC.BAT. Sometimes this small difference can be enough to leave just the extra amount of memory that allows another TSR to load into upper memory instead of into conventional memory.

Let's consider some examples that show how these factors affect your memory management scheme.

First, suppose you load a device driver, DRVA.SYS, that takes 55K of memory to load, but has a memory image size of 18K. In addition, you load another device driver, DRVB.SYS, that requires 37K of memory, both during and after loading. If you have an upper memory block that's 57K in size, you can only load the two device drivers into the upper memory block if you load DRVA.SYS before you load DRVB.SYS. You have to consider, though, whether the two device drivers are truly independent of each other. If DRVA.SYS must be loaded before DRVB.SYS, consider the memory image size of each to determine which makes better use of upper memory. Load the device driver with the smallest memory image size into conventional memory.

Next, suppose you load several TSR programs that don't require a copy of the DOS environment, shortcut keys, or COMMAND.COM's critical error handler. In addition, you use the SHELL= command in CONFIG.SYS to increase the DOS environment size to 1024 bytes. By using the INSTALL-HIGH command in CONFIG.SYS, you'll save 1K of upper memory for each TSR. This small saving may be just enough to allow an additional TSR to fit into an upper memory block, compared to loading the same TSRs using LOADHIGH in AUTOEXEC.BAT. By moving the loading of these TSRs from AUTOEXEC.BAT to CONFIG.SYS, you've saved the conventional memory that would normally be used by one of the TSRs.

Limitations to Reordering

There are some limitations to what you can accomplish through reordering the loading sequence of your device drivers and TSRs. These limitations can sometimes prevent you from accomplishing your goal of placing all device drivers and TSRs into upper memory, leaving the maximum possible free conventional memory.

- Device drivers are always loaded before TSR programs. You cannot change this by placing INSTALLHIGH commands before DEVICEHIGH commands in CONFIG.SYS.

- Some device drivers and TSRs require a certain load order. In some cases, a device driver or TSR depends on another device driver or TSR that must be loaded first. In other cases, device drivers or TSRs cannot function correctly if certain other device drivers or TSRs have already been loaded.

- A few device drivers cannot be loaded once a memory manager has been loaded. One example is certain SCSI adapter device drivers that must be placed first in CONFIG.SYS.

As you experiment with changing the load order of device drivers and TSRs, use the MEM command options you learned in Chapter 4 to track your success. Printed copies of each version of CONFIG.SYS and AUTOEXEC.BAT, along with printed copies of the MEM reports, will provide good documentation of your progress. Don't forget to write the current date and time on each set of printouts.

Bypassing CONFIG.SYS and AUTOEXEC.BAT

It's always possible to make typing errors, or to simply use a command in CONFIG.SYS or AUTOEXEC.BAT that isn't compatible with your PC. These types of problems make it very important for the memory management experimenter to have a tested, emergency boot diskette. This is true even in Novell DOS 7 which allows you to bypass CONFIG.SYS and AUTOEXEC.BAT by pressing the correct keys as you boot.

Be sure you create and test your emergency boot diskette before you begin your experiments. You don't want to wait until there actually is an emergency to find out your diskette doesn't work!

Table 7.3	Emergency Configuration Bypass Keys
Key	**Purpose**
F5	Bypasses CONFIG.SYS and AUTOEXEC.BAT.
F8	Allows you to selectively execute CONFIG.SYS and AUTOEXEC.BAT commands.

Table 7.3 summarizes the emergency keys you can use during the boot process to stop Novell DOS 7 from executing configuration commands.

Summary

Novell DOS 7 includes some powerful memory management tools. Although similar in some ways to the MS-DOS memory management tools, Novell's memory management tools require their own unique approach. In addition, Novell DOS 7 includes some specialty items, such as DPMS memory and DPMS-aware device drivers and TSRs, that you simply won't find in any other operating system.

In this chapter, you learned that Novell DOS 7's powerful memory management tools really do allow you to improve the way your system operates. By taking a hands-on approach, you're able to go far beyond the basic configuration supplied by the setup program, and are able to make much better use of your system's resources.

Appendix A

Troubleshooting

I never forget a face, but I'll make an exception in your case.

—Groucho Marx

When you have problems with your PC, it can seem like there's no hope. Sometimes you can be going along just fine when all of a sudden your system crashes. If you've been using your current configuration for some time, there may be few, if any, clues to what's causing the problem.

Fortunately, memory management problems usually show up soon after you make a system configuration modification. You may see an error message when you restart your system or when you try to run a program. You may even find your system refusing to boot with a new configuration. Such clues provide pretty good evidence that your memory management attempts are at the root of the problem. Let's have a short look at some common problems you may encounter, so you can fix them quickly.

Can't Run Programs

One of the best methods of determining whether your memory management efforts are causing problems is to try running your application programs. Many programs, especially large applications, place huge demands on your system's memory resources. Thus, even when DOS itself has no difficulties dealing with a new system configuration, some of your programs may protest loudly when they can't access the correct type or amount of memory.

If you encounter such problems, your first step should be to review the changes you've made in your system configuration files, CONFIG.SYS and AUTOEXEC.BAT. Examine the changes carefully to make certain you didn't inadvertently mistype an entry. If everything looks correct, temporarily change back to your previous configuration, reboot your system, and retry the application program. If the problem goes away, you've located the configuration change that may be incompatible with the application program. If the problem doesn't go away, you know that the configuration change wasn't the culprit and you'll have to look elsewhere.

If the configuration change seems to be the problem, review the material in Chapter 3 on determining the types of memory you need. Make certain you provide the correct type (EMS or XMS) memory to suit your applications.

Expanded Memory Not Available

If you see this message, one or more of your device drivers, TSRs, or application programs requires EMS memory, but your current configuration isn't providing this type of memory. There are several possible solutions. You can reconfigure EMM386.EXE to provide EMS memory, but this will use a 64K block of upper memory for the EMS page frame. You may be able to reconfigure the device drivers, TSRs, or application programs to use another type of memory, such as conventional or XMS memory. Finally, you can complain loudly to the software manufacturer for burdening you with the EMS memory millstone, and ask when they're going to stop being dinosaurs and start using modern memory management techniques (or would they prefer you upgraded to a competing product?).

Memory Error at xxxx:yyyy

You probably won't be surprised to hear this, but programmers often take the path that's easiest for them, regardless of whether it's best for you. That's one reason you may see a message telling you there's a memory error at 4032:AF10, or some other, equally difficult to understand address.

In Chapter 2, you learned that many different segment:offset addresses could refer to the same memory location. When you see a "memory over-flow" or other similar message that shows you a specific memory address, you can use the techniques you learned in Chapter 2 to determine the actual memory page:offset location of the memory error. Using this information, you can see whether your memory management experiments have caused the conflict. For example, if you include a range of memory addresses, and you later receive memory conflicts in that address range, there's clearly a problem with using some of the addresses. An adapter board may be using some of those addresses, for example. You may need to exclude certain memory addresses from use as upper memory to eliminate the problem.

Memory Parity Errors

Memory parity errors result when your system detects an error in RAM that indicates that data isn't being stored accurately. Such errors usually result from hardware problems, such as memory chips that "forget" what they're supposed to remember.

Memory parity errors aren't usually related to memory management con-flicts directly, but your experiments with memory management may serve to highlight problems you never noticed before. The reason for this is simple: Before you started applying advanced memory management techniques, quite a bit of your system's memory probably wasn't being used. Once you begin using all of your PC's memory, parity errors may show up when the defective memory chips are indeed used.

Not all memory parity errors are cause for concern. If you encounter a sin-gle parity error, and then your system seems to work just fine for many days or weeks, the error was probably just random and nothing to worry about. If you start to receive parity errors quite often, though, you've got a hardware problem to solve. The solution may be as simple as making certain nothing is causing your PC to overheat, or it may require replacing some defective memory.

Packed File Corrupt Message

The message "packed file corrupt" sounds pretty scary, doesn't it? You may see this message when you try to run a program after you've loaded the DOS kernel into the high memory area—but don't worry, it doesn't mean that your system has been invaded by a virus. This message simply tells you that the program can't run in the first memory page, which is now free because the DOS kernel was moved. Yes, I know that the "packed file corrupt" message doesn't quite bring this to mind, but you weren't looking for messages that made sense, were you?

Fixing this problem is easy. Just add the command **LOADFIX** to the beginning of the command line when you load your application. Your application program won't have quite as much conventional memory available (because LOADFIX wastes the first 64K memory page), but it will run correctly.

Screen Suddenly Goes Crazy

If your screen suddenly goes crazy, perhaps displaying information in an unusual manner or not showing anything at all, you've probably created a conflict with video memory by including some video memory addresses in upper memory. In some cases it's okay to use certain video memory addresses, but you have to be careful. For example, if you include the A000–AFFF memory page, you can't use programs that switch into a graphics mode.

For more details on using video memory addresses, refer to the chapter on your system's memory manager.

Stack Overflow Message

A stack overflow message tells you that the STACKS= command in CONFIG.SYS needs to be adjusted to a higher value. You're most likely to see a stack overflow message if you've tried the STACKS=0,0 setting. Try STACKS=9,256 to see if the problem is resolved.

System Halts

If your system simply locks up, you've got the worst kind of problem possible, because finding the cause may be very difficult. There are basically three distinct times your system may halt, each caused by different types of problems:

- System halts during POST (Power On Self Test). This type of problem usually indicates a serious hardware problem. Usually, you'll at least see a message informing you of "POST error #," which identifies the type of problem. You'll need help from your service technician on this one.

- System halts during boot. This type of problem usually indicates a software incompatibilty, such as loading the wrong device driver or attempting to load a device driver in upper memory when the device driver is incompatible with upper memory. This is a system configuration problem, which you can solve by rebooting your system with your emergency boot diskette (or pressing F8 during boot if supported by your DOS version) and editing CONFIG.SYS. You did make that emergency boot diskette, didn't you?

- System halts when running a program. This type of problem is probably caused by memory conflicts. You may need to experiment to find the source of this problem.

Where's My Memory?

If you've added memory to your system, but it doesn't seem to be there according to the various memory reports, you may need to access your PC's setup routines to make the memory available. See your owner's manual for information on accessing the setup routines (often called "CMOS setup").

Windows Won't Start

If you find that Windows won't start after you've optimized your system's memory configuration, you may need to add the command device=MONOUMB.386 to the [386Enh] section of SYSTEM.INI in the Windows directory. Use EDIT (or another text-only editor) to make the change. Save the file, reboot, and try Windows again. If this doesn't solve the problem, you may not be able to include the monochrome display adapter page in upper memory.

Not Enough Memory

You may see several variations on this message. It may be as simple as "Not enough memory," the message may tell you the amount of memory needed, or it may even tell you the type of memory that is needed. Regardless of the actual message, this is your starting point for memory management. Review the program's documentation to determine its memory requirements, and then use the techniques you learned in this book to provide for those requirements. Don't forget to consider the multiple configuration options if your programs have widely varying needs.

Appendix B

Adding Memory

Thanks for the Memory.

—Leo Robin, "Big Broadcast"

No matter how hard you work at memory management, there's only so much you can do with a limited resource. Sooner or later it may be necessary to add more memory modules (chips) to your PC. There are several questions you need to answer before you can go buy additional memory:

- How much more memory will fit in your PC?
- What type of memory module does your PC use (SIMMs, DIPs, etc.)?
- What size of memory modules can you add (1M, 2M, 4M)?
- What speed should the memory modules run at?

Do You Have Room for More Memory?

There are two methods of adding memory to a PC. The first, adding memory modules to the system board (or "motherboard"), is usually the best method—

it's the cheapest and ensures that your computer will run as fast as possible. The second method, adding an entirely new memory board, isn't usually the best choice, but may be your only option in some cases. Memory boards are expensive and run at your PC's expansion bus speed, which may be many times slower than the processor's speed.

Adding memory to the system board is the preferred method for several reasons:

1. System board memory operates at the highest possible speed, usually at the speed of the processor. This type of memory expansion provides the best system performance.

2. Adding memory to the system board is usually the least expensive memory expansion option, because you simply insert the new memory into existing memory sockets.

3. You don't need to use an expansion slot to add memory to the system board.

Caution

The circuits in your PC, including the memory modules, are very sensitive to static. Don't handle any components in your system any more than necessary, and always touch the metal frame in your PC before adding or removing any boards or memory modules.

How can you tell if your system board has room for additional memory? You have to do two things—check your system's documentation, and look inside your PC. Yes, I know the documentation that came with your PC was probably written in a foreign language and then translated by someone who didn't understand either that language or English, but you really do need to know what it says. Besides, even if you can't understand what the owner's manual says, the person selling you additional memory will need the information.

Usually, your owner's manual will tell you how much memory your system board can hold. This may be something like 8M, 16M, 32M, or 64M. You should compare this number to the amount of memory actually in your system. If you don't know how much memory you already have, you can reboot your computer and watch the memory check. (You will see numbers rolling over like a car odometer in the corner of your screen—remember that these numbers are listed in bytes.) You can also verify how much memory you have by opening up your computer and looking.

Next, you'll have to see if any empty space exists in the memory expansion slots on your system board. If you've never looked inside a PC, you may want to ask someone who knows PC hardware to help, but there's really nothing in there that can hurt you once you've unplugged the power. Here's what you need to do:

1. Turn off the power and unplug the power cord. Don't rely on the switch on a power strip—make sure you actually unplug the cord.

2. Carefully place your monitor out of the way. You'll have to disconnect the data cable from your system to the monitor, so make certain you keep track of where it was connected.

3. Remove any other cables, such as the keyboard and mouse cables, also noting where each of them is connected. You might want to make a drawing to help when you reassemble everything.

4. Remove the screws that hold the cover onto the computer. To make certain you don't remove any screws you shouldn't, look in your owner's manual. Be extra careful about this point, because if you remove too many screws you'll have a real mess!

5. Look for the memory slots on your system board. In most modern PCs, this will be contained in eight parallel sockets. If you're lucky, at least four of those sockets will be empty. Again, refer to your owner's manual to make certain you're looking at the correct components.

Now you have two important pieces of information. First, you know the maximum amount of memory that can be installed on your PC's system board, and second, you know whether any of the memory sockets are empty. Next you must determine what type of memory you need to use to expand your system.

Figuring Out What Kind of Memory You Need

Modern PCs use SIMMs (Single Inline Memory Modules) for their system board memory. SIMMs are a special type of computer chip that snaps right onto your PC's system board. Older PCs often used individual memory chips (also called DIPs—Dual Inline Packages), but SIMMs are the most common memory type today.

SIMMs come in several different types, and only certain ones will work in your system. If you buy the wrong ones, they either won't fit or won't work if you install them. Don't make an expensive mistake—make certain you get the correct SIMMs for your PC. A typical SIMM will have a long string of numbers to list exactly what it is. We'll examine these numbers so that you know what kind of memory to order. Typical SIMM names looks like this:

- 256Kx9 -70
- 1MEGx9 70
- 2MEGx9 70ns

SIMMS are rated according to their capacity; some common designations are shown above. The first set of numbers indicates the amount of memory the SIMM has. In the examples above, the first SIMM holds 256K, the second SIMM holds 1Meg, and the third SIMM holds 2Meg.

The second piece of information in a SIMM's name indicates its structure. In all the examples above, x9 indicates that the SIMM has a 9-bit structure. PCs use nine-bit memory, because this allows special circuits to check for parity errors. All PC SIMMs use some multiple of nine bits (usually x9, but occasionally x36). Don't make the mistake of getting SIMMs meant for other computers like the Mac—those have only eight bits and are designated x8. Check your computer's manual to see what type you need.

The third piece of information in a SIMM's name indicates its speed rating. SIMMs come in a variety of speeds, such as 100ns, 80ns, 70ns, or 60ns. Smaller speed rating numbers indicate faster SIMMs. Most often the speed rating is indicated by a dash and a number appended to the part number, such as -7 for 70ns SIMMs, but there are other ways to represent this. All the examples above refer to 70-nanosecond SIMMs. Always make certain any new SIMMs you buy are at least as fast as any already in your system. Faster SIMMs won't speed up your PC, but slower ones will cause problems.

Finally, SIMMs may have 36 or 72 pins. Here, too, you must make certain you get the correct SIMMs. Most PCs require 72 pin SIMMs for proper operation. Again, just check your manual.

Buying Memory

Once you know what type of SIMMs you need, you're ready to buy and install your new memory. One option is to buy the memory from the vendor who sold you your system. Another is to deal with a company that specializes in memory products. This method may be less expensive, although the original vendor may offer the advantage of installing and testing the new memory.

If you prefer to save some money, make certain you have the information noted above (what SIMMs are already in your system, how many open memory sockets there are, and how much total memory you want in your PC) and your owner's manual ready before you place your call. Some memory vendors you may want to consider include:

- Nevada Computer at (800) 982-2926 or (702) 294-0204
- Advanced Computer Products at (800) 366-3227 or (714) 558-8813
- L.A. Trade at (800) 433-3726 or (310) 539-0019

Installing SIMMs

If you have open memory sockets, adding more memory is pretty easy. You just buy the right SIMMs and insert them in the open sockets. Usually inserting SIMMs is a two-step process. First you insert the SIMM at an angle, and second you snap it up into an upright position. Your owner's manual should show how the memory sockets in your system work.

Caution
Most systems can use more than one SIMM capacity, but you'll probably have to set some switches or move some jumpers to tell your PC what you've installed. Also, be advised that you can only install certain combinations of SIMM capacities in your PC. For instance, you probably cannot install a 1M, a 2M, and a 4M all next to each other. Your owner's manual is the only reliable information source on these matters.

If you don't have open memory sockets, life gets a little more complicated. Recall that SIMMs come in several different capacities. Computer manufacturers often use the cheapest SIMMs they can to provide as much memory as you originally ordered with your system. This can mean that all eight SIMM sockets are filled with 256x9 SIMMs (if you have 2M in your system) or 1MEGx9 SIMMs (if you have 8M in your system). If all the sockets are filled, you'll have to remove and discard some existing SIMMs in order to add more memory. Seems like a waste, but sometimes that's your only option. Fortunately, you can usually just remove four (or sometimes two) old SIMMs, and use larger capacity SIMMs in the newly available sockets.

Well, there you have it. Buying and installing additional memory isn't something you're likely to do very often, but it's not too difficult.

Appendix C

History of PCs

All PCs use some variation of the Intel 80x86 processor (such as the 8088, 8086, 80286, 80386, 80486, or Pentium). Whether the chip itself is made by Intel, IBM, Cyrix, AMD, or one of the other clone manufacturers, the same set of basic instructions—*machine level instructions*—is executed by any member of the 80x86 processor chip family. It is this basic set of instructions that is so important in making PCs compatible with the original IBM-PC, and therefore able to use the same application programs.

Note

Actually, there's more to being IBM-PC compatible than the basic set of processor instructions, but for the purposes of this discussion, this is the most important distinction. Certain support chips must also be present in the system, and the computer must respond to software by performing the same, correct set of actions.

While all of the 80x86 processors include an identical set of basic intructions and therefore capabilities, there are also many differences among the family members. As you can imagine, the newer chips include features that were unavailable when the older chips were designed. For example, the 80286 is able to use 16 times as much memory as the 8088 and the 8086—16M instead of 1M. Of course, the newer chips also have other new features, such as a larger internal command set, but all the old commands work, too.

The 80386 and later processors could address even more memory than the 80286, and have an even larger set of internal commands. Even more significant for memory management purposes, however, is their ability to use *logical* addresses to make *physical* memory appear to be in a different location than it is in reality. You might think of logical memory addresses as temporary forwarding addresses, such as you might use if you went on a month-long vacation to a mountain cabin. Although everyone would still send your mail to your normal home address, the post office would forward that mail to your temporary address. No one need know your actual location to send you mail, because mail sent to your home address (your logical address) would be forwarded to your actual location (your physical address).

It's this ability to remap memory that makes the 80386 and later processors far superior at managing memory than the earlier processors. In fact, the advantage these newer processors have over the older ones is so great that totally different memory management schemes are necessary when you drop below the 80386 level. This is most easily seen in the memory management tools that are included in MS-DOS 5, MS-DOS 6, and Novell DOS 7. Only the most basic memory management options are supported for anything less than an 80386, but all three operating systems include very capable memory managers that require at least an 80386.

Why Not the 286 and the 8088?

Millions of older IBM-PCs, XTs, ATs, and their clones are still in daily use all over the world. These systems provide their owners with all the computing power many people will ever require. In fact, many of these systems will probably still be in service for quite a few years to come.

Since there are so many older systems still in use, you may wonder why I'm ignoring the subject of memory management on these fine old PCs. Frankly, the decision to cover only systems with an 80386 or higher processor was fairly easy. The advanced memory management capabilities of these newer systems were the key to allowing developers to produce more complex and powerful applications. The older systems, while still useful, just don't have the power necessary to run the new programs. Since advanced memory management is necessary only if you want to use the newer generation of applications, the older systems have no need for advanced memory management.

What Is Memory Management?

Do you really know what PC memory management involves or why it's so important? Do you understand how our PCs evolved to their current level and how that history affects memory management? Do you somehow feel that memory management is probably too complicated to understand, much less master? Can you really learn enough from one book to make your PC a top performer?

If you're wondering about the answers to any of these questions, the following sections are definitely intended for you. Let's clear up any fuzziness or uneasiness you may be feeling.

A Short History of the PC and DOS for Those Interested

In spite of what you may think, the IBM-PC really wasn't the first small computer. In the mid-1970s, several different brands of noncompatible computer systems existed. Apple had its Apple II, Radio Shack had the TRS-80, Atari had several models, and many other long-forgotten computers were also available. Most of these early systems were purchased by hobbyists, but some of them found their way into small businesses run by very adventurous people. Unfortunately, there weren't very many small computers, and the programs for one brand of system couldn't run on another brand of system. This meant that the few business programs that were available were generally of low quality and quite expensive.

In an attempt to standardize small computer systems so that the same programs could run on computers from different manufacturers, Digital Research developed an operating system called CP/M (Control Program for Micro-computers). CP/M worked only on specific types of computers, of course, but many different manufacturers developed CP/M-based systems. CP/M was a real breakthrough, because it created a much larger market for programs, and therefore resulted in lower-cost, higher-quality programs. Once the application programs became better, cheaper, and more readily available, more businesses became interested in these small computer systems.

IBM, whose fortunes were dependent on selling machines to businesses, soon took note of this interest in small computers. Their response at first was to ignore these "toy" computers, but even IBM couldn't ignore a tidal wave for long. Once CP/M became popular enough to generate a small business market, IBM decided to produce a small computer to meet the demands of that market. Instead of creating everything from scratch, though, IBM decided to use a combination of already available components. In a move they must now surely regret (especially given the 20–20 nature of hindsight), they also decided to buy an operating system for their new system, the IBM-PC.

Two young men named Bill Gates and Paul Allen had a small programming business they called Microsoft. The company's main product was a BASIC interpreter (a programming language) for microcomputers. Their real success, however, was the operating system that became known as MS-DOS.

Why Is Memory Management Important?

Ultimately, the main reason that PC memory management is so important today is linked directly to the backward compatibility in DOS. For MS-DOS 6 to function correctly on the original, 1981 model IBM-PC, it can't use the capabilities of the newest processors found in all modern PCs. It can't use more memory than was available on the original IBM-PC, and it can't depend on processor instructions, which only exist in the newer systems. But without advanced memory management, you can't use the newest programs, which require access to much more memory.

To see just why this backward compatibility presents such a problem, consider what would happen in the automobile industry if all automobiles had to use wheels that were compatible with those on the Ford Model T. No matter how much improvement you might make in other areas, the old wheels would really limit a new car's performance. True, a tire manufacturer might be able to develop a very wide, high-performance tire that fit the old style wheel, but the new tire couldn't be used on the Model T because it wouldn't fit the wheel wells.

In a sense, this example is exactly like the advanced memory management schemes that provide the 80386, 80486, and Pentium systems with extra capabilities while still running DOS. The old style wheel (the basic operating system, or DOS) provides compatibility with the obsolete equipment, while the new style tire (the advanced memory manager) provides some additional performance on the newer systems. Since the advanced memory manager, like the wide performance tire, works only with the newer systems, PCs that use the older generations of processors cannot benefit from their services.

As we've become more sophisticated in our understanding of PCs and their capabilities, we've also become more demanding of the application programs we use. We want more power, more performance, and we want programs that are easier to use. Where we once considered Visicalc to be a powerful application, we now demand that our spreadsheets be able to calculate and graph complex statistical scenarios automatically, hold much more data, and be fully three-dimensional. Modern word processors need more than simple stand-alone spell checkers—users today want grammar checkers, WYSIWYG (What You See Is What You Get) displays, and fancy fonts. Simple text adventure games have been replaced by three-dimensional flight simulators with digitized sound and advanced graphics.

All of these new features in our software programs require ever more power from our PCs. More powerful programs usually demand quite a lot more memory, too. Where early PC programs often required 256K of memory, many of today's programs require at least four to ten times as much memory.

If you don't have your system properly configured, you either won't be able to run these programs, or they may run so slowly you won't want to run them.

Let's look at some examples. My first experience with a spreadsheet program was using Visicalc on a Radio Shack TRS-80 Model 1 with 48K of memory. The program was a real breakthrough, but it sure was crude by today's standards.

Jumping forward to modern times, let's consider one of today's popular spreadsheet favorites. Lotus 1-2-3 Release 2.4 requires at least 384K of memory, but that's without loading the WYSIWYG add-in. If you want WYSIWYG, you'll need at least 512K. Want to use another add-in, too? Then you'll need at least 640K. I suppose, though, that you'd like to do some real work and actually load a big spreadsheet. If so, you'll probably need even more memory, but it has to be the right kind, *expanded memory*.

Imagine, though, that instead of the DOS-based Lotus 1-2-3 Release 2.4, that you wanted to use today's flagship of spreadsheets, Quattro Pro 5.0 for Windows. Now you're talking a minimum of 4M of memory, but this time you must have a different type of memory, *extended memory*. You'll probably want at least 8M once you add a disk cache for performance, and decide you want to play Solitare while you're thinking about your budget report.

Finally, imagine you want to play a game on your PC instead of using the system for business. If you choose one of the most sophisticated of today's PC games, you'll probably be greeted with the message "Not enough memory" before being dumped back to the DOS prompt. This may be true even if you have several megabytes of memory installed, because unless the memory is configured correctly, it may well be the wrong type for the game program. That doesn't mean that you can't run the game, just that you have to learn how to manage your system's memory.

By now, you can see that memory management is really very important. If you want to do anything more sophisticated than using old programs on an obsolete PC, managing your system's memory resources correctly can be the key. Proper memory management techniques can certainly make your system perform better, and may be the only difference between being able to run programs and not running them at all. Proper memory management can also make the difference between a system that is too slow to use and one that flies through its tasks.

Limitations of the Early PCs

When IBM designed the first IBM-PC, most existing small computers used processors that were limited in their ability to address and use memory. Most, in fact, could use a maximum of 64K. While talented programmers often produced some pretty remarkable results within this severe limitation, there's only so much you can do with 64K of memory. Many trade-offs were necessary, and these generally translated into programs that had severe limitations, or that were difficult to use. As you allocated more system resources to a program's computing capabilities, you had fewer resources left over for niceties such as good-looking screens or on-line help systems.

In the late 1970s and early 1980s, small computers were at a crossroads. While some hardy and brave souls made great efforts to use the early systems effectively in their businesses, those efforts were far too often paid back in extreme frustration. The small computers of the era just weren't powerful enough to be good business computers.

I mentioned earlier that IBM basically assembled existing components to create the IBM-PC. One of the components they selected, the 8088 processor from Intel, was quite new, but was directly related to Intel's existing 8080 processor (and its competitor, the Zilog Z80). There was a very interesting difference between the 8088 and the earlier generation of processors, however. The 8088 had four extra memory address lines, and this allowed the chip to use 16 times as much memory—1M instead of 64K.

Note

The Intel 8088 processor was a variation of a slightly more powerful Intel processor called the 8086. The primary difference between the two was in the manner they sent data to memory. The 8086 sent data in 2-byte (or 16-bit) pieces, while the 8088 used 1-byte (8-bit) pieces. Internally, both chips processed data 16 bits at a time, but the 8-bit external data processing of the 8088 meant that IBM could save a little money designing the system board. This extra translation step from 16-bit internal to 8-bit external also meant that the 8088 was slightly slower that the 8086, but the performance difference wasn't enough to make much difference.

Index